James Peill has been the curato
2009. He was brought up in the W
at Edinburgh University. He w
where he was a specialist in t̶h̶e̶ ̶.̶.̶.̶ ̶d̶e̶p̶a̶r̶t̶m̶e̶n̶t̶ and an
auctioneer. The author of *The English Country House* (2013), he has also
co-authored *Irish Furniture* (2007) and *The Irish Country House* (2010)
with the Knight of Glin.

Glorious Goodwood

A Biography of England's Greatest Sporting Estate

James Peill

CONSTABLE

CONSTABLE

First published in Great Britain in 2019 by Constable
This paperback edition published in Great Britain in 2020

A CIP catalogue record for this book is available from the British Library.

ISBN: 978-1-47212-825-6

Typeset in Dante by SX Composing DTP, Rayleigh, Essex
Printed and bound in Great Britain by Clays Ltd, Elcograf S.p.A.

Papers used by Constable are from well-managed forests
and other responsible sources.

MIX
Paper from
responsible sources
FSC® C104740

Constable
An imprint of
Little, Brown Book Group
Carmelite House
50 Victoria Embankment
London EC4Y 0DZ

An Hachette UK Company
www.hachette.co.uk

www.littlebrown.co.uk

For Saskia, Flora, Beatrice, Octavia and Lettice,
my favourite descendants of Charles II

Contents

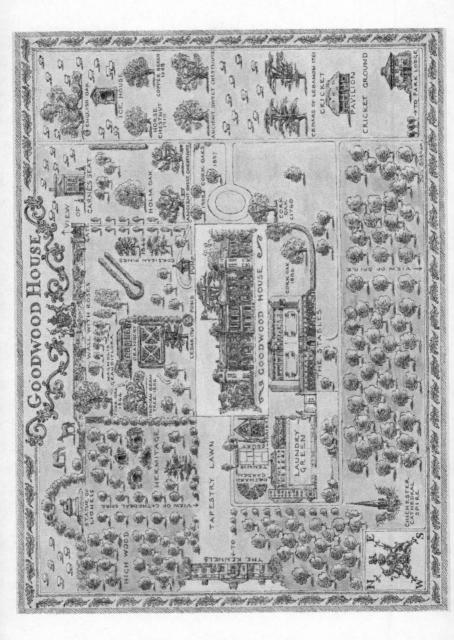

GOODWOOD HOUSE

EN LA ROSE · JE · FLURIE

The Most High Puissant and
Noble Prince CHARLES LENOX,
Duke of Richmond, Lenox & Aubigny
Earl of March and Darnley, and
Baron of Settrington & Methuen.

THE DUKES OF RICHMOND

(Simplified family tree)

King Charles II = Louise Renée de Penancoët de Keroualle, cr. Duchess of Portsmouth & Duchess d'Aubigny
(1630–1685)

CHARLES, 1ST DUKE OF RICHMOND & LENNOX = Anne, dau. of Lord Brudenell
(1672–1723)   (1669–1722)

CHARLES, 2ND DUKE OF RICHMOND, = Sarah, dau. of 1st Earl Cadogan   Louisa = 3rd Earl of Berkeley   Anne = 2nd Earl of Albemarle
LENNOX & AUBIGNY   (1706–1751)
(1701–1750)

CHARLES, 3RD DUKE OF RICHMOND,   George   Caroline   Emily   Louisa   Sarah   Cecilia
LENNOX & AUBIGNY   = Louisa, dau.   = Henry Fox,   = James,   = Thomas Conolly   = (1) Sir
(1735–1806)   of 4th   later 1st Lord   Earl of Kildare,   Charles
= Mary, dau. of 3rd Earl of Elgin &   Marquess of   Holland   later 1st Duke of   Bunbury, Bt
Ailesbury (1740–1796)   Lothian   Leinster   (2) Hon. George
Napier

CHARLES, 4TH DUKE OF RICHMOND,   Maria   Emilia   Georgina
LENNOX & AUBIGNY
(1764–1819)
= Charlotte, dau. of 4th Duke of Gordon
(d. 1842)

CHARLES, 5TH DUKE OF RICHMOND, John George Henry William Frederick Sussex Arthur Mary Sarah Georgiana Jane Louisa Charlotte Sophia
LENNOX & AUBIGNY
(1791–1860)
= Caroline, dau. of 1st Marquess of
Anglesey (1796–1874)

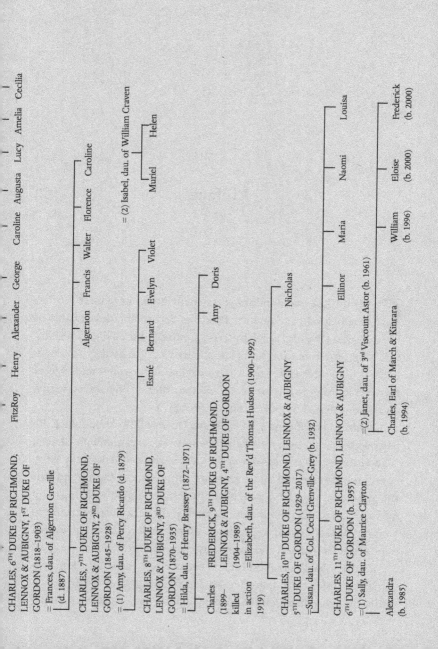

CHARLES, 6TH DUKE OF RICHMOND, LENNOX & AUBIGNY, 1ST DUKE OF GORDON (1818–1903)

= Frances, dau. of Algernon Greville (d. 1887)

FitzRoy   Henry   Alexander   George   Caroline   Augusta   Lucy   Amelia   Cecilia

CHARLES, 7TH DUKE OF RICHMOND, LENNOX & AUBIGNY, 2ND DUKE OF GORDON (1845–1928)

=(1) Amy, dau. of Percy Ricardo (d. 1879)

=(2) Isabel, dau. of William Craven

Algernon   Francis   Walter   Florence   Caroline

Muriel   Helen

CHARLES, 8TH DUKE OF RICHMOND, LENNOX & AUBIGNY, 3RD DUKE OF GORDON (1870–1935)

= Hilda, dau. of Henry Brassey (1872–1971)

Esmé   Bernard   Evelyn   Violet

Charles (1899–killed in action 1919)

FREDERICK, 9TH DUKE OF RICHMOND, LENNOX & AUBIGNY, 4TH DUKE OF GORDON (1904–1989)

=Elizabeth, dau. of the Rev'd Thomas Hudson (1900–1992)

Amy   Doris

CHARLES, 10TH DUKE OF RICHMOND, LENNOX & AUBIGNY 5TH DUKE OF GORDON (1929–2017)

=Susan, dau. of Col. Cecil Grenville-Grey (b. 1932)

Nicholas

CHARLES, 11TH DUKE OF RICHMOND, LENNOX & AUBIGNY 6TH DUKE OF GORDON (b. 1955)

=(1) Sally, dau. of Maurice Clayton

=(2) Janet, dau. of 3rd Viscount Astor (b. 1961)

Ellinor   Maria   Naomi   Louisa

Alexandra (b. 1985)

Charles, Earl of March & Kinrara (b. 1994)

William (b. 1996)   Eloise (b. 2000)   Frederick (b. 2000)

Preface

Over the last two hundred years, many books have been written about Goodwood and the Dukes of Richmond, descendants of King Charles II by his French mistress, Louise de Keroualle. In writing this book, my intention has been simply to tell the story to a new generation. I have interwoven the storyline with scenes and objects that aim to bring to life the house and the different characters, with a continuous thread of sport running through it.

Goodwood has been the home of the Dukes of Richmond since the late seventeenth century, although the story starts earlier with Charles II and Louise, the parents of the first duke. The first half of the book covers the seventeenth and eighteenth centuries and the second half the nineteenth and twentieth centuries; an epilogue brings the narrative up to the present day. Inevitably, the action strays from the confines of Goodwood; separate chapters are devoted to the fourth duke's time in Brussels and the family estates in Scotland.

A duke holds the highest rank in the peerage and a dukedom was usually coupled with considerable landholdings and wealth. As a result, the great ducal families occupied prominent places in national life. The Dukes of Richmond were no exception and, over the centuries, Goodwood became their power base with sport playing the leading role. There is a different tale to tell for each of the Dukes of Richmond and I have only been able to touch upon the huge contribution that many of them made to the nation's history. But in so doing, I hope I have captured their individual characters and that of their duchesses and wider family members. Some have been radical; some have been staunchly traditional. Above all, they have aspired to do their duty as each thought fit, whether it be to king, country, or those under their care. It is not just a story of survival but one of innovation and, at times, surprise, set against the backdrop of British history.

*King Charles II, serial womaniser and father of the first
Duke of Richmond, painted by Samuel Cooper in 1665
(© Trustees of the Goodwood Collection)*

1

Royal Origins

'. . . the Duchess of Portsmouth and her son, the Duke of Richmond, are the persons above all others in the world whom I love the most . . .'

Charles II, 1684

There is something quintessentially English about Goodwood. Even the name is comforting. Lying in the gentle lowlands at the foot of the South Downs, the house is encompassed by a well-wooded park dotted with ancient horse chestnuts, gnarled oaks and majestic cedars of Lebanon. Sussex benefits from a mild climate and, on a clear summer's day, tantalising glimpses of the sea are caught, glinting on the horizon, reminding one that the south coast with its pebbly beaches is only a few miles away. Goodwood is not a huge stately pile dominating the landscape, but it is imposing nevertheless. In many ways, the house is unique in appearance with its copper-domed turrets flanking each of its three symmetrical façades and its flint walls.

The great columned portico with its first-floor balcony is instantly recognisable. It opens into the hall where more columns march across the rear and sporting pictures by Stubbs adorn the walls depicting hunting, shooting and horseracing at Goodwood. Canaletto's famous views of London hang above the fireplaces in the old part of the house, an eighteenth-century peep show of the views from Richmond House. Next door, Gobelins tapestries and rococo furniture suggest the opulence of a French embassy, as do the tiers of Sèvres china gleaming in the cabinets of another room. Ranks of portraits gaze down from the walls and shelves of leather-bound books fill two libraries. Historically significant furniture designed by William Kent jostles for position with Napoleon's campaign chair and crocodile-mounted dining chairs. Every object and picture has a story to tell, with some being linked to critical moments in British history: the 1745 Jacobite Rebellion; Waterloo; and the Great War.

Although Goodwood has had its fair share of guests over the last three centuries, even more have passed by the front of the house on their journey through the park, en route to enjoy one of the sports for which it has become famous. Kings, queens, lords and ladies have all joined the happy throng who feel a special connection with the place. Some people only visit once – more often than not on a balmy summer's day – but many others return again and again; happy memories are formed, and it soon becomes a part of their lives.

There is a rhythm to the year at Goodwood that stretches back over three hundred years to when life in the house revolved around hunting and shooting in the winter months, and cricket in the summer. As new sports were embraced by family members, so they, too, were added to the yearly round, each taking advantage of the natural landscape – horseracing and golf up in the Downs, motorsport and flying in the lowlands.

Part of Goodwood's attraction lies in the bonhomie of its owners. Whether this is an inherited sense of largesse originating with their royal ancestor, Charles II, or whether it stems from living in the place is hard to discern, but it is clear that the Dukes of Richmond have been generous hosts, welcoming not only their friends and family, but also total strangers to share in their love of sport and the beauty of the surroundings. It is a daunting thought that over the course of their tenure, literally millions of people have passed through the gates of the park and continue to do so each year.

To fully understand present-day Goodwood, it is necessary to travel back in time and become acquainted with Louise de Keroualle. As the matriarch of the Dukes of Richmond, whose presence can still be felt at Goodwood today, the story begins in earnest with her.

*   *   *

On a cool autumn evening in October 1671, a lady's silk stocking was flung from a splendid canopied bed at Euston Hall, near Newmarket. This symbolic act marked the loss of innocence for Louise de Keroualle, a pretty young French maiden of aristocratic birth; the man who threw the stocking was none other than the king of England, Charles II. Louise had been perfectly framed in a plot, devised by Charles's willing accomplices and hosts, the Earl and Countess of Arlington, to break her resistance to the king's advances.

The Arlingtons had assembled a glittering house party to enjoy the horseracing at Newmarket and filled their house 'from one end to the other, with Lords, Ladys, & Gallants'.[¹] The king loved horseracing, often riding himself, and had just finished building his own palace in Newmarket. Lord Arlington was Secretary of State and one of Charles's favourites. Together with his wife, the Countess of Sutherland, and Colbert de Croissy, the French ambassador, they had dreamt up the idea of staging a burlesque wedding in which Louise was the bride and the king the bridegroom.

Charles had been pursuing Louise for just over a year, ever since her arrival at court the previous September to take up a position as maid of honour to the queen. As a virtuous Catholic girl, becoming another of the king's many mistresses was not an attractive proposition and Louise allowed dreams to float through her head of one day taking her mistress's place and becoming Queen of England. However, there were others at court who had their own ideas for the young beauty. Lord Arlington, a charming but ruthlessly ambitious courtier, saw in

Louise a means of ousting the Duke of Buckingham, his arch rival and another of the king's favourites. If Louise became the king's mistress and confidante, she could sour the king's relationship with Buckingham and get her revenge on him for deserting her at Dieppe on her journey to England. Lady Arlington only thought of the reward she might get from the French king, Louis XIV, for playing her part in an even bigger conspiracy: a spy in the bedchamber. Louis' plan was that Louise would become mistress to his cousin Charles and act as a French spy, sending reports of the goings-on at court and, more importantly, keeping Charles favourable to French interests. Colbert was given the task of putting the plan into action.

Charles had first set eyes on the 'baby-faced' Breton when she accompanied her former mistress, Henrietta, Duchess of Orléans, Charles's adored youngest sister, to the signing of the secret Treaty of Dover. The reunion between Charles and Henrietta (who was married to Louis' spiteful younger brother, the Duke of Orléans) took place at the end of May 1670 and lasted fifteen days. Charles was accompanied by Arlington and Sir Thomas Clifford, while Henrietta (known in France as Madame) chose Louise as her maid of honour. So impoverished was Louise, that Henrietta had to give her money to go and buy new dresses for the trip. To outsiders, this was an innocent reunion between devoted siblings, filled with balls, sea-trips and the theatre; to those in the know, negotiations of national importance were taking place behind the scenes.

The Treaty, whereby Charles agreed to make a public declaration that he was a Catholic (in return for two million crowns) and to aid Louis in his war of aggression against the Dutch Republic, was signed on 1 June 1670. Henrietta had acquitted herself perfectly and achieved all of Louis' aims while spending a blissful time in the company of her brother.

On the eve of what was to be their final farewell, Charles gave Henrietta, his 'dear Minette', two thousand crowns to build a monument to their mother, Queen Henrietta Maria. Henrietta beckoned to Louise to open her jewel box and let her brother choose whatever he wanted. Charles, with a twinkle in his eye, motioned towards Louise and said, 'This is the jewel that I covet.' Louise blushed and stood speechless as Henrietta smiled at her brother and gently scolded him, saying the girl was under her protection and she could not dream of upsetting Louise's parents, the prim and proud Guillaume and Marie de Penancoët, Comte and Comtesse de Keroualle. Little did Charles know that when he embraced his sister on board the ship that was to take her back to France, it would be the last time that he saw her; three weeks later she was dead.

Rumours were rife that Henrietta had been poisoned by her husband, Philippe, Duke of Orléans, who was openly homosexual and flaunted his relationship with the Chevalier de Lorraine in front of her. In fact, she probably died of peritonitis but it left Charles distraught with grief and Louise without a job. However, Charles's attraction to Louise had been noted by all parties and, at the English king's request, she was offered a position in the English court as maid of honour to Queen Catherine. This suited all parties – Louis would have someone at his beck and call at the heart of the English court while Charles could seduce the pretty young girl he had met at Dover.

Other courtiers, such as the Duke of Buckingham, had their own personal motives for bringing Louise to England. The Marquis de Saint-Maurice, ambassador of the Duke of Savoy to the French king, wrote to his master: '. . . the Duke of Buckingham . . . has taken Mlle de Keroualle, who was attached to the last Madame, to serve the Queen of England; she is a beautiful girl, and it's believed the plan is to make her mistress of the King of Great Britain; the Duke would like to supplant his enemy Madame Castlemaine [Buckingham's cousin Barbara], and the King's Most Christian Majesty would not be displeased to see one of his subjects in that lady's role, for women, it is remarked, have great power over the mind of the said King of England.'[2] Buckingham clearly believed he could make Louise his pawn, displacing his feisty cousin, Barbara – recently ennobled as Duchess of Cleveland – in the king's affections.

Louise's presence was soothing for Charles as it brought back happy memories of Henrietta. Coupled with that, Louise was an undoubted beauty, despite her childish looks. Long dark tresses tumbled over her shoulders while her round face was blessed with porcelain-white skin adorned with sensuous lips and alluring eyes, a combination that Charles found irresistible. Although she might appear coy and inno-cent, Louise had witnessed at first hand in the French court the scheming and intrigues that went on and there was an underlying intelligence that belied her appearance.

In early October 1671, Colbert reported to the Marquis de Louvois, Louis' war minister, that 'the King of England shows a warm passion for Mademoiselle Keroualle . . . His Majesty goes to her rooms at nine o'clock every morning, never stays there for less than an hour, and often remains until eleven o'clock. He returns after dinner, and shares at her card-table in all her stakes and losses, never letting her want for anything . . . I believe I can assure you that she has so got round King Charles as to be of the greatest service to our sovereign and master, if she only does her duty.'[3]

And there was the problem – Louise had been resisting the king's advances ever since her arrival in England. Arlington persuaded his wife to speak to Louise and urge her to either 'yield unreservedly to the King, or to retire to a French convent'.[4] Lady Arlington connived with Colbert and together they hatched the Euston plot, with which Louis was 'vastly amused . . . and will have pleasure in hearing of the progress she makes in the King's favour'.[5] By inviting Louise to Euston, Lady Arlington was hedging her bets on Louise replacing Barbara Cleveland in Charles's affections. Isabella, the Arlington's only child, was betrothed to Barbara's son, so by aligning herself with Louise, Lady Arlington was taking a big risk. Future support from Louise would insure Lady Arlington against any loss of patronage which might follow in the wake of Barbara's fall from grace.

Euston Hall was a magnificent country house just over twenty miles east of Newmarket. Arlington had purchased the run-down estate in 1666 and had only just finished rebuilding the house in the French manner, recalling his time spent in exile with the king. From a distance, it resembled a French château with flags fluttering on top of its four domed pavilions. The diarist John Evelyn, who was one of the house party, described it as 'very magnificent and commodious, as well within as without, nor lesse splendidly furnish'd'.[6] He gazed in awe at the magnificent ceiling paintings executed by the Italian baroque painter, Antonio Verrio, and advised Arlington on the landscaping of the gardens and park. Great avenues radiated from the east and west, linking the house with the surrounding landscape. Evelyn ordered for Arlington 'plantations of firs, Elmes, limes &c. up his parke, and in all other places and Avenues.'[7] Formal pleasure gardens were laid out closer to the house with elaborate waterworks and an orangery.

During the Euston house party, Charles travelled from Newmarket to Euston every other day, sometimes staying overnight. The Arlingtons entertained on a lavish scale with all of the great and the good from the surrounding counties descending on their stately residence. Evelyn was amazed at the spread of food, noting in his diary 'such a furnished Table had I seldome seene, nor any thing more splendid & free', and goes on to say how for fifteen days at least two hundred people were entertained, along with horses, servants and guards.[8] In between horseracing, the mornings were spent hunting and hawking and the afternoons in playing cards, often carrying on until the early hours of the morning.

After Louise had been ravished by Charles in the mock wedding ceremony, she relaxed her guard and, according to the prudish Evelyn, the 'young wanton' was in a state of undress for much of the day, indulging in 'fondnesse & toying' with Charles.[9] They went racing at Newmarket where Charles 'seemed more than ever solicitous to please Mlle. Keroualle' as Colbert reported back to Louvois, continuing, 'Those small attentions which denote a great passion were lavished on her; and as she showed by her expressions of gratitude that she was not insensible to the kindness of a great king, we hope she will so behave that the attachment will be durable and exclude every other.'[10] Back in France, Louis was delighted with her conquest, ordering Colbert to present his congratulations to Louise, and eager to use Charles's new mistress to further his own political ambitions.

Meanwhile Louise was vilified by the English pamphleteers; she was said to have coyly exclaimed about her seduction, 'Me no bad woman. If me taut me was one bad woman, me would cut mine own trote.'[11] Whatever her feelings, seclusion in a convent was now out of the question – Louise was pregnant. Nine months later, a baby boy was born, destined to become the first Duke of Richmond.

*   *   *

As Charles's mistress, Louise became a prominent hostess, entertaining many at court. On the evening of 24 January 1682, she hosted a magnificent reception for the Moroccan Ambassador in her apartments at Whitehall Palace. Located at the south-west end of the famous Stone Gallery, her apartments occupied a prime position in the palace.[12] Over the last decade as Charles's mistress, she had redecorated them several times until they outshone even those of the queen herself. They were richly furnished in the latest style with silver tables, stands, vases and sconces, interspersed with japanned cabinets and screens. An exquisite marquetry cabinet, with matching pier table and candle-stands, now at Goodwood, was presented to her by Charles. The walls were hung with superb French tapestries depicting French royal palaces, including Versailles and Saint Germain, along with some of the best paintings from Charles's collection. Expensive clocks ticked and chimed in every room. Evelyn, who was present at the reception, was bowled over by the 'rich & splendid furniture'.[13]

In honour of the ambassador, Louise laid on a great banquet with musical entertainment and the guests were seated at a long table. Evelyn describes how the Moroccans were seated alternately with ladies of the English court, predominantly the king's natural children and mistresses. Although he dismisses the latter as 'catell [cattle] of that sort', he does concede that they adorned the proceedings, 'as splendid as Jewells, and Excesse of bravery could make them'. The Moroccans, or 'Moores' as he called them, seemed to take everything in their stride and he was struck by their good manners, 'decently tasting of the banquet: They drank a little Milk & Water, but not a drop of Wine, also they drank of a sorbet & Jacolatte [chocolate]: did not looke about nor stare on the Ladys, or expresses the least of surprize, but with a Courtly negligence in pace, Countenance, & whole behaviour, answering onely to such questions as were asked, with a greate deale of Wit & Gallantrie.' Towards the end of the evening, the king appeared just as the ambassador was leaving. Evelyn goes on to describe how the ambassador and his retinue often went to Hyde Park where they demonstrated their superb horsemanship, flinging and catching lances while galloping flat out.[14]

That Louise was hosting such an important reception shows how far her star had ascended over the course of the preceding decade. She was no longer the blushing Breton, dutifully attending the queen and shyly resisting the king's advances. Now, she was *maîtresse-en-titre* of Charles and a vital link between him and his cousin, Louis XIV. Of course, she was not without her rivals and they put up a spirited fight for Charles's affections. Barbara Cleveland, who had been Charles's mistress since 1660, still had apartments at court. Famous not only for her beauty but also her tantrums, she was the mother of at least five of Charles's illegitimate children. Barbara had a strong personality coupled with a passionate nature and her bed was by no means reserved for Charles.

Louise's other main rival was the actress Nell Gwyn. Unlike Barbara and Louise, she was not of aristocratic birth, but rose from humble origins to become the most famous Restoration actress. 'Pretty, witty Nell', as Samuel Pepys described her, was the people's heroine. In her, Charles found relief from politics and the petty squabbles of court life; she amused him and he loved her for it. A well-known story relates how Nell was travelling through the streets of Oxford in the royal carriage; mistakenly thinking it contained Louise, the crowds started hurling abuse at the passenger. Quick-witted Nell responded by thrusting her head out of the window and screaming out, 'Pray, good people, be civil . . . I am the *Protestant* whore!' much to the crowds' delight.[15]

Charles visited Louise's apartments daily, often interviewing the French ambassador, and even his ministers there.[16] Honoré Courtin, Colbert's successor as French ambassador, reported back home that 'the king was frequently at the Duchess of Portsmouth's, where there were card tables for three different games – hombre, basset, and thirty-and-forty; and that he promised to attend her Sunday routs at which she dispensed the most charming hospitality.'[17] At these intimate supper parties, Louise flattered Charles through his love of music and arranged for the best singers and musicians to play his favourite airs.[18] Soon after his arrival at the English court, Courtin realised that '. . . one must be a man of pleasure to get on here, otherwise it is useless to come to England'.[19]

Unlike Barbara and Nell, Louise was playing a risky political role. As a French Catholic, she was hated by the common people. Courtin warned his government that 'The soldier, the sailor, and the civilian, but particularly . . . the middle and lower classes, [are] imbued with hatred for France.'[20] Many people saw Louise as a pernicious influence on the king and feared that England would become a Catholic country once again. Little did they know that their king was already a closet Catholic and huge sums of money were flowing into his coffers from the French king. Charles wrote: 'I have received from his most Christian Majesty [Louis XIV], by the hands of M. Courtin, the sum of a hundred thousand crowns, French money, for the second quarter, ending on the last day of June, and to be deducted from the four hundred thousand crowns payable at the end of this year. Given at Whitehall, September 25, 1676. Charles R.'[21] Between March and September the following year, he drew a staggering £40,526 at the French Embassy and then signed a treaty in which he engaged to remain neutral in return for an annual payment of £80,000.'[22] These covert payments enabled Charles to remain independent of Parliament and not rely on it for money.

Louise was also reaping handsome rewards for her services. In the Exchequer archives, the paymaster's clerk set down 'in reverential verbiage the sums paid her'. Her regular pension was £12,000 sterling a year, which was swollen by supplements up to £40,000 a year. In the year 1681, 'the French slut' drew from the Treasury £136,668.[23] One clerk noted that Louise was paid £8,773 over seven months in 1676 whereas Nell was only paid £2,862. The following year, Louise pocketed £27,300 and Nell only £5,250. These figures were a far cry from her annual salary of £150 that Louise received as maid of honour to Princess Henrietta.[24]

Money was not the only thing Louise was given; both Charles and Louis showered her with jewels. When Charles inadvertently gave her venereal disease, he consoled her with a pearl necklace and an enormous diamond. Earlier, via his Treasurer, the Earl of Danby, Charles had given her the cash to buy a pearl necklace costing £8,000 and a pair of earrings costing 3,000 guineas. Not to be outdone, Louis sent her a pair of earrings worth £18,000, the most important gift sent to England in 1675.[25] As a more intimate sign of his affection, Charles presented her with an emerald ring encircled with diamonds, engraved with their initials entwined below a duchess's coronet.[26] This coronet celebrated her elevation as Duchess of Portsmouth, Countess of Fareham and Baroness Petersfield in 1673. Later that year, Louis granted her the Aubigny estates in the centre of France. These lands had an ancient association with the Scottish Stuarts, having been granted to John Stuart in 1422 for helping the French fight the English. They had descended in the Stuart family until the death in 1672 of Charles Stuart, third (and last) Duke of Richmond, also prosaically known as the eleventh *Seigneur* of Aubigny. His heir was technically his distant cousin, Charles Stuart, king of England. However, the ownership was pending as no French king would allow an English monarch to possess land in France. Giving Aubigny to Louise was a satisfactory compromise as Louise was of French aristocratic birth and in the service of both monarchs.[27]

Louise was shrewd enough to realise that her position at court entirely depended on Charles's affection for her and she made every effort to please him. Apart from one dalliance with Philippe de Vendôme, Grand Prior of France, a handsome French nobleman known for his powers of seduction, she remained faithful to Charles and he found peace and contentment in her company. His nickname for her was 'Fubbs' (meaning 'chubby') on account of her fashionably plump face, signing off a letter to her: '. . . I love you better than all the world besides, for that were making a comparison where tis impossible to expresse the true passion and kindnesse I have for my dearest dearest fubbs.'[28] Louise could see that many members of Charles's famously louche court would stab her in the back given half a chance. For that reason, she nurtured friendships in the right places including Charles's brother, James, Duke of York, next in line to the throne, and William of Orange, husband of James's daughter, Mary, who followed in the line of succession. James was Catholic and William was Protestant along with Charles's eldest illegitimate son, the Duke of Monmouth, whom Louise also befriended. Monmouth gave Louise a full-length portrait of himself by Sir Godfrey Kneller that still hangs at Goodwood, a poignant reminder of this dashing hero of the people whose attempt to seize the crown resulted in his execution in 1685. There is also a full-length portrait by Sir Peter Lely of Barbara Cleveland, who Louise took great pains to get on with, at least superficially. Faced with the beauty and charm of Hortense, Duchess Mazarin, who threatened to lure Charles away from her completely, Louise held out an olive branch and asked her to dinner.[29] In these astute manoeuvres, not only with the king's family and mistresses but also his chief politicians, Louise was paving the way for her future and, more importantly, that of her son.

*   *   *

Among the treasures on display at Goodwood is a tiny plain linen shirt with simple silk collar and cuffs, laid out beside a little jerkin in linen damask with a geometric pattern. It is accompanied by an old typed label: 'The 1st Duke of Richmond's first shirt and jerkin'. Designed to be worn together, these baby clothes are a tangible reminder of the precious baby who was born to Louise on 29 July 1672, nine months after the Euston house party. He was named Charles after his father and, judging by the number of child portraits at Goodwood (seven), his mother was exceptionally proud of him. At first, Charles did not recognise him officially and, to make matters worse, Louise's father sent her his solemn curse, such was the shame of this illegitimate child to the proud old Breton.[30] Three years later, when her parents visited England in the spring, they did not ask to meet their grandson, a snub that must have hurt Louise considerably.

In the summer of 1675, Charles, always attentive to Louise, made amends by creating his bastard son Duke of Richmond, Earl of March and Baron Settrington in the English peerage.[31] As a sop to Barbara Cleveland, her sons were made Duke of Southampton and Duke of Grafton respectively. In a comic move of one-upmanship, Louise rushed the official document to Danby in the middle of the night, to obtain his signature before he left London for a few weeks, thereby leaving Barbara to wait until his return. This manoeuvre ensured Louise's son took precedence over Barbara's sons. When having the patent drawn up, Charles changed his mind about his son's surname, and rather than giving him the traditional surname of illegitimate Royal offspring – FitzRoy – he decided, 'Upon better thoughts I do intende that the Duke of Richmonds name shall be Lenox . . .'[32] A month later, the young boy was also created Duke of Lennox, Earl of Darnley and Lord of Torboulton in the Scottish peerage.[33] The surname and titles were carefully thought out by Charles; Henry VIII had first used the title Duke of Richmond for his illegitimate son and it was created on another two occasions for the Stuart family, before dying out in 1672 with the death of Charles Stuart, third (and last) Duke of Richmond. Louis had already granted Louise the Aubigny estates, so giving Charles's natural son the Richmond and Lennox titles, as well as the surname, neatly tied all the different strands together.

As well as the titles, the young Duke of Richmond was also given Richmond Castle in Yorkshire, a ruined fortress in a commanding position overlooking the River Swale and the town of Richmond, from whence his title derived. Although of little practical use to the young child, its romantic history as a powerbase of the north under the Earls of Richmond, dating back to the Norman Conquest, did add a certain mystique to his ennoblement. Coupled with that, Louise herself was descended from one of the Earls of Richmond.[34] To help maintain his position at the top of the aristocratic tree, young Charles Richmond was given a comfortable income of £2,000 a year and a Scottish governess to keep him in check. For this vital role, the Countess Marischal was paid a salary of £200 a year, supplementing her £150 salary as a Lady of the Bedchamber to the Queen.[35] A couple of years later, by now aged five, Richmond's income was topped up by Charles granting him and his heirs 'twelve pence of lawfull money' for every cauldron of coal leaving Newcastle by sea.[36]

On top of everything else, Charles Richmond was blessed with good looks, combining his father's dark swarthy features with his mother's beauty. Evelyn, who was not a fan of his mother and referred to her as the 'prostitute Creature', had to admit that 'what the Duke of Richmond, & St. Albans, base sonns of the Dutchesse of Portsmouth a French Lasse, and of Nelly, the Comedian & Apple-womans daughter, will prove their youth does not yet discover, farther than that they are both very pretty boys, & seems to have more Witt than [most of] the rest.'[37] John Macky, the Scottish spy, described him as 'well shaped, Black Complexion, much like King Charles'.[38]

As a child, Charles Richmond was spoiled by both of his parents. Aged nine, the king made him a Knight of the Garter, Britain's oldest and most prestigious order of chivalry. When the king came to bestow the blue ribbon around his neck, it was too long, so he placed it over his left shoulder, starting a tradition that has continued to this day.[39] During his father's lifetime, he was often called Prince Charles Lennox and he looks quite the prince in his portrait by William Wissing. Commissioned to celebrate his investiture, it now forms the focal point of the Ballroom at Goodwood. Seated in his robes beside a magnificent ostrich-plumed hat and wearing a pair of high-heeled silk shoes with frilly rosettes and jewelled buckles, he was an extremely good-looking youth with a 'butter wouldn't melt in his mouth' air. Louise was intensely ambitious for her son, her determination partly springing from her own insecurity at having made her way in the world by becoming the king's mistress. Just one example of jealousy rearing its ugly head was when Louise visited Tunbridge Wells to take the therapeutic waters. On arriving in town, she discovered that the Marchioness of Worcester was occupying the house that she herself had planned on renting. Furious, Louise sent Lady Worcester a message chastising her in no uncertain terms for pulling rank (a marchioness was one rung lower than a duchess on the ladder of precedence). Lady Worcester, extremely well bred herself, replied that 'titles gained through prostitution were never recognised by persons of birth and breeding' and refused to move out. Indignant and embarrassed, Louise called on Charles to help. His response was to send a company of Guards to escort her back to Windsor, not daring to expel the arrogant marchioness.[40]

Not content with her English titles, Louise craved a French dukedom to go with her lands at Aubigny. This would entitle her to sit on a *tabouret* (an elaborate stool) in the presence of the queen at Versailles, the ultimate honour at the French court. Louise used Charles as her envoy, who called aside Paul de Barrillon, Courtin's successor as French ambassador, and told him that 'the Duchess of Portsmouth and her son, the Duke of Richmond, are the persons above all others in the world whom I love the most, and would be deeply obliged to the King of France if he agreed to reconvert the estate of Aubigny into a duchy for her, with the reversion to her son and his future issue.'[41] Barrillon was indignant and said as much to Louis, but the French king saw things differently and immediately ordered the letters patent to be drawn up, granting her the Duchy of Aubigny. When told of the news, both Charles and Louise were overjoyed, and she dashed off an immediate thank-you letter to Louis. Part of her motivation for the French dukedom was paving the way for her son and laying the foundations for a future dynasty. As a precaution, she asked Louis to give her son the same privileges as a French gentleman, enabling him to inherit the money she had invested in France.[42]

In her ambitions for her son, Louise overstretched herself when she tried to marry him, aged eight, to Elizabeth Percy, the twelve-year old daughter of the late Duke of Northumberland and the greatest heiress in England. Elizabeth's guardian, her grandmother, was having none of it, harbouring a grudge against Louise to whom she had once been forced by her gambling losses to part with her earrings at a very low price.[43]

While Louise schemed on her son's behalf, his father simply enjoyed playing with him. As a boy, Charles Richmond shared his father's love of horseracing, a legacy that would be passed down the generations and ultimately lead to racing at Goodwood. Charles II was a brilliant horseman and rode successfully in races himself. He visited Newmarket twice a year, taking the court with him. Both his father, Charles I, and grandfather, James I, had enjoyed horseracing at Newmarket, the latter being credited with introducing the sport to the town.[44]

So it was fitting that Charles Richmond should ride in his first race aged ten. Unfortunately, Louise was tucked up in bed with a cold so missed the event. The previous year, the king had made his son Master of the Horse, another slightly ridiculous appointment for a nine-year-old boy, but a hugely prestigious post in the royal household. The post had formerly been held by his half-brother, the Duke of Monmouth, and was a clear sign of the king's favour and affection for his son. In practice, three commissioners were appointed to carry out the duties required until his majority.

*   *   *

On the night of Thursday, 5 February 1685, the twelve-year-old Charles Richmond knelt beside his father's bed to receive his final blessing. The king spoke with special affection to his son. One by one, his children passed through the gilded rail and approached the great canopied bed hung with crimson damask to say their farewells. The king's bedchamber at the palace of Whitehall was packed with dignitaries; seeing his children receive a blessing, they cried out that he was their common father and dropped to their knees to be blessed. At six o'clock in the morning, Charles asked for the curtains to be opened so he could see the dawn for the last time. As the morning sun began to rise over the Thames and light filled his bedroom, so Charles's life ebbed away and, at noon, he breathed his last.

Only six days before, Charles had been partying hard, shocking the disapproving Evelyn who wrote in his diary: 'I am never to forget the unexpressable luxury, & prophanesse, gaming, & all dissolution, and as it were total forgetfullnesse of God (it being Sunday Evening) which this day sennight, I was witnesse of; the King, sitting & toying with his Concubines Portsmouth, Cleaveland, & Mazarine: &c: A French boy singing love songs, in that glorious Gallery, whilst about 20 of the greate Courtiers & other dissolute persons were at Basset round a large table, a bank of at least 2,000 in Gold before them, upon which two Gent: that were with me made reflexions with astonishment, it being a sceane of utmost vanity; and surely as they thought would never have an End: six days after was all in the dust.'[45] After sleeping badly, Charles had collapsed the following morning into the arms of Lord Bruce while he was being shaved. Louise rushed into his room in a state of disarray but soon composed herself and spent the morning tending him like a wife. Later, she retreated, as she said to Barrillon, 'I cannot with propriety go back into the room; besides the Queen is there almost all the time'.[46] Fraught with anxiety over Charles's salvation, on the Thursday she called for Barrillon and told him, 'Monsieur l'Ambassadeur, I am now going to tell you a secret, although its public revelation would cost me my head. The King of England is in the bottom of his heart a Catholic, and there he is, surrounded with Protestant Bishops! There is nobody to tell him of his state or speak to him of God ... The Duke of York is too busy with his own affairs to trouble himself about the king's conscience. Go and tell him that I have conjured you to warn him that the end is approaching, and that it is his duty to save without loss of time, his brother's soul.'[47]

A Catholic priest was duly found; he was none other than Father Huddleston, who had helped Charles once before in his hour of greatest need, when he aided his flight after the Battle of Worcester, during the Civil War. At huge personal risk to himself, Father Huddleston was smuggled into the king's bedchamber after it had been cleared of almost everyone, numbering some seventy-five people.[48] The Duke of York said to his brother, 'Sire, here is a man who saved your life and is now come to save your soul.'[49]

'He is very welcome,' murmured Charles and, after confession, received the last sacraments and took communion. Huddleston then left as he had come, through a secret door.

Owing to her position as the king's mistress, Louise was unable to be with Charles during his final hours. However, she was never far from his thoughts, and he urged his brother to take care of her and 'not let poor Nelly starve'.[50] An hour after Charles died, the new king, James II, broke the news to Louise and assured her of his protection and friendship. For several years, Louise had been courting James's friendship for just this eventuality when she was at her most vulnerable. She knew James was keen to maintain Louis XIV's support but, as a French Catholic who was hated by the people, her sharp instincts told her it was not wise to stay at Whitehall and she fled to the French embassy, along with her son and some of her more precious possessions.

Over the coming months, Louise made preparations to leave England with her son. Louis assured her that he would protect her, writing at the end of February: 'I sympathise deeply with the proper sorrow you feel at the death of the late King of Great Britain. And as I know that you have not failed over the last years of his life to act in every way as you found befitting the duty of your birth and the advancement of your services to me, not only am I anxious to extend the protection you ask of me into whatever part of my kingdom you may choose for your retirement, but I shall also be most pleased to fall in with your wishes on whatever matters may present themselves, and to show you how deeply your good will and its effects have gratified me'.[51] Louis' use of the word 'retirement' only served to emphasise the dramatic change in Louise's circumstances and she took every measure to make sure she was not only safe, but financially secure.

James dealt a blow when he stripped the young Duke of Richmond of his position as Master of the Horse, using the excuse that he was too young and inexperienced. Louis expressed his displeasure and James softened his approach to Louise, keen to keep the French king on side. Louise pushed to get the £19,000 income that Charles had given her, leaning on her friend the Earl of Rochester who was Lord Treasurer. Eventually, she settled for an allowance of 2,000 guineas with a further 3,000 guineas for her son, asking that they all be paid to her son, her pride prohibiting her from accepting so paltry a sum. She also had an income of 2,000 guineas from the confiscated estate of Lord Grey in Ireland, which was to pass to the young Charles Richmond when he reached his majority.[52]

With the execution of the Duke of Monmouth for treason, the political climate in England was getting very hot. Louise feared an attack by Parliament on top of the blatant lies the pamphleteers were spreading about her. Thus, in August 1685, she set sail for France, along with her son, Charles Richmond, her jewels, and 250,000 francs' worth of gold that she had drawn the instant Charles had died. Several other ships were needed to transport her furniture and belongings from her Whitehall apartment, which James had allowed her to keep.[53] After fifteen years on English soil, Louise's native France beckoned.

Charles, first Duke of Richmond, painted by William Wissing to commemorate
his investiture as a Knight of the Garter aged only nine
(© Trustees of the Goodwood Collection)

2

Exile

*'. . . Good looking, if good-for-nothing-else, first Duke of
the new creation . . .'*

The eighth Duke of Richmond
about his ancestor[1]

Safely in France, Charles Richmond knelt on the exquisite inlaid
marble floor in front of the high altar of the Royal Chapel at
Fontainebleau, dedicated to the Trinity. The angelic voices of the choir
soared up into the great vaulted ceiling whose six painted scenes represented the doctrine of Redemption. Further paintings of Old
Testament kings, patriarchs, prophets and sibyls, framed by magnificent gilded plasterwork, gazed down upon the assembled members of
the French court. The king and his brother, Monsieur, were seated
high above everyone else in the upper tribune, where they had the best
view of the richly carved marble altar adorned with statues of Henry
IV as Charlemagne and Louis XIII as St. Louis, flanking Jean Dubois'
painting 'The Holy Trinity at the Descent from the Cross'. Richmond's
great grandfather, Henry IV, had commissioned the decoration in the
early seventeenth century using the finest artists of the day: Martin

Fréminet (painter); Barthèlemy Trembley (*stuccadore*); and Francesco
Bordoni (sculptor). After Henry's assassination, his son (and Richmond's
great uncle) Louis XIII, oversaw its completion.

All eyes in the chapel were fixed on Bishop Bossuet, court preacher
to Louis XIV and a brilliant orator. Amidst wafts of incense, Bossuet
celebrated mass and, during his sermon, the 'whole court was in tears,
moved by the thought of the grace of God, Who calls those He loves
to Him'.[2] Everyone was gathered there to witness Richmond's
conversion to Catholicism, renouncing the Protestantism of his youth.
Louis and Monsieur both signed the document of renunciation and the
young boy stole the hearts of everyone watching. A song was written
especially for the occasion:

> 'It is not your face that charms so well
> Dear child, which holds me in this spell.
> Your mind it is, so quick to engage,
> Drawn from your mother's breast, and gay,
> Which, even when fifty is your age,
> Will please as it has pleased today.'[3]

No one was more proud than his mother, Louise. Before leaving
England, James II had urged him to embrace the Catholic Church
while Louise had assured Louis 'that she will beseech him [Richmond],
when the time comes, to agree to put the finishing stroke to the
matter'.[4] By becoming a Catholic, he was following in the footsteps of
his great grandfather, Henry IV, who was famous for issuing the Edict
of Nantes, whereby Huguenots (French Protestants) were granted the
right to practise their religion without persecution from the state. In a
twist of fate, the following day, 22 October 1685, Louis XIV signed the
Revocation of the Edict of Nantes leading to widespread persecution
of the Huguenots, many of whom sought refuge in England, bringing
their skills with them.

Since his arrival in France, Louis had treated Richmond like a
prince, presenting him with a superb flintlock-sporting gun made by

Bertrand Piraube, the French Royal gun-maker. The workmanship is exquisite, with a solid silver barrel and chased classical ornament incorporating figures of Mars and Jupiter and Louis himself portrayed as a Roman emperor. When it was sold from Goodwood by Richmond's descendant, the ninth Duke of Richmond, in 1958, it was described as 'probably the finest fire-arm ever offered for public auction in this country' and was eagerly snapped up by the Royal Armouries for a world record price.[5] Louis was an ardent lover of the chase and invited Richmond to join his hunting-parties, presenting him with magnificent hunting clothes trimmed in gold and silver braid as a member of his élite wolf-hunting club.[6] Galloping through the forests of Versailles and Fontainebleau, Richmond basked under the protection of the great Sun King. When William of Orange ousted his cousin, James II, from the English throne in 1688, William refused to allow Richmond his allowance. Louis stepped in and granted him an income of £20,000 from the French coffers.[7]

As a teenager, Richmond's pride swelled and he longed to see active service. He had asked his exiled uncle, James, if he could join him on his invasion of Ireland, only to be rebuffed by the reply that he was 'too small and too young'.[8] This only served to make him even keener to take up arms; Louis gave him his chance in August 1689 by allowing him to serve as a volunteer in the French army in the attack on Walcourt in the Spanish Netherlands (now Belgium). However, on this occasion Louis overreached himself, and the French suffered a heavy defeat against the Grand Alliance, which included the Dutch and the English armies. The latter was commanded by the young John Churchill, later Duke of Marlborough, who would have been known to Richmond from the English court. Richmond must have acquitted himself well as the following year he was appointed aide-de-camp to Louis' brother, the Duke of Orléans. He suffered a temporary setback when he was laid low by smallpox at Neustadt, but soon recovered and, in September, Louis gave him a company in a cavalry regiment.

Despite the kindness shown to him by Louis, Richmond yearned for more. As a child, he had been spoilt by both parents and lacked nothing material. The tragic loss of his father at such an impressionable age left him without the anchor an adolescent boy needs to mature into adulthood. Within his character, Louise's Breton pride was coupled with Charles's selfishness and endless pursuit of pleasure. This potent combination convinced him that he was being short-changed in France and could do better in England. Richmond longed to return to the days of his idyllic childhood in the English court, where he was, to all intents and purposes, a prince. The irony is that by blood he was more French than English (three of his grandparents were French) and his next move would plunge his mother into despair and exasperate Louis.

*   *   *

Meanwhile, Louise was trying to rebuild her life in France. Shrewdly, she had been building up reserves in France for many years but she was a born spender and a compulsive gambler; money slipped through her fingers like water. True friends were hard to find, although Courtin and Barrillon both remained on friendly terms with her. At the French court, Monsieur and Madame behaved graciously towards her, Madame remarking, 'The Duchess of Portsmouth is the finest lady of her kind that I have ever met; she is extremely polite and interesting in conversation.'⁹ A pleasant enough remark but barbed with the words *of her kind*. Louise was not without enemies in the French court; on one occasion, she was a hair's breadth from exile when it was reported to Louis that she had been gossiping about Madame de Maintenon behind her back (Louis was by this time married to Madame de Maintenon), when, in fact, she was innocent. On another occasion, she was said to have cast doubt on the legitimacy of James II's son, the Prince of Wales (rumours were circulating that a stillborn child had been substituted for a boy, smuggled into the bedchamber in a warming pan). The source of the rumours was tracked down – two young gentlemen at the French court – and Richmond protested his mother's innocence directly to the French king. He also denounced those that had claimed he was going off to join William of Orange. 'It is all false,' he swore, to which Louis replied, 'I know you both well enough not to have suspected you for a moment.'[10] Louis would remember these words three years later as he learnt of Richmond's duplicity.

Following the Glorious Revolution in England, Louise trod a delicate path between being deferential to the exiled Stuarts and trying to win William III's favour, reminding him that she had advised Charles to accept his proposal to marry his niece, Mary. However, William was not easily won over and her English pensions were stopped. To make matters worse, her apartment at Whitehall was destroyed by fire in 1691. Evelyn felt it was just deserts for the life she had led, writing in his diary: 'This night, a suddaine and terrible Fire burnt downe all the buildings over the Stone Gallery at W-hall, to the waterside, beginning at the Appartments of the late Dutchesse of Portsmouth (which had been pulled done & rebuilt to please her (no less than) 3 times & Consuming the lodgings of such lewd Creatures, who debauched both K. Char: 2nd & others & were his destruction.'[11]

On 2 February 1692, Richmond secretly left France and embarked on an intrepid journey, via Switzerland and Germany, to England. This was no easy trip and would have taken him several weeks, travelling no doubt on horseback with exposure to temperatures around zero degrees centigrade. We know very little about the route he took, other than he passed through Basel where he wrote to the pleasure-loving Marquis de Barbezieux, who had succeeded his father, Louvois, as war minister the previous year, telling him that 'he was going where he would have higher rank and a more plentiful revenue'.[12] Louise was distraught and told a furious Louis 'that she could not doubt her son's foolishness, that she believed he had gone in search of the Prince of Orange, and that she was in despair'.[13] Louis was gracious enough not to hold her responsible for her son's actions and transferred to her a substantial portion of the allowance he had been giving Richmond, to the tune of £12,000. Further salt was rubbed into the wound when a rumour was circulated that Richmond had stolen his mother's jewels.

*   *   *

Three months after his flight from France, on Whitsunday, 15 May 1692, Richmond reconverted to the Church of England. In a formal ceremony at Lambeth Palace, the Archbishop of Canterbury's residence on the south bank of the Thames, he declared 'in the presence of Almighty God', his 'hearty contrition and repentance of having publicly renounced and abjured the Reformed Religion professed in the Church of England'. He solemnly renounced 'all the errors and corruptions of the Church of Rome' and promised 'before God and this congregation' that he would 'continue steadfast in the profession [he had] made to the end of [his] life'. A written declaration was signed by him, in the presence of six witnesses, including the politician Sir Stephen Fox, whose son would one day marry Richmond's granddaughter.[14]

We do not know the background to Richmond's defection to England, but he promptly swore allegiance to William III and took his seat in the House of Lords in November 1693. William recognised his courage and made him one of his aides-de-camp, Richmond serving with distinction at the battles of Steenkerque and Landen in 1692 and 1693 respectively. The irony of fighting shoulder to shoulder with his former enemies against his former allies cannot have escaped him, especially as both resulted in victories for the French.

Richmond seems to have been very much his own master, ploughing his own furrow and taking little notice of those seeking to guide him, including his mother. Six months after his arrival in England, when he was just twenty, he married Anne Brudenell, a young widow of twenty-three. Her first husband was Henry, Baron Belasyse of Worlaby in Lincolnshire, and Anne came from neighbouring Northamptonshire where the Brudenells had lived since the fourteenth century. Both William III and Richmond's mother disapproved of the marriage, probably because the Brudenells were a well-known Catholic family; Anne's father, Francis, Lord Brudenell, was a Jacobite and had spent four years in the Tower of London for high treason.[15] Anne's aunt, Anna Maria, Countess of Shrewsbury, was a famous court beauty who had caused a scandal after her lover, the Duke of Buckingham, fought her husband in a duel from which he later died of his wounds. Buckingham then ensconced her at his country seat, Cliveden.

In hindsight, Anne, Duchess of Richmond, was the saving grace of her reprobate husband, and her kind and gentle character won the hearts of all his family, including Louise. More immediately, she had good looks and probably plenty of money (her sister's dowry was £12,000).[16] Her portrait by Kneller hanging at Goodwood shows an intelligent-looking woman who seems content in her own skin; her husband's, on the other hand, shows a proud-looking young man with a storm brewing under the surface and an arrogant air.

Anne seemed oblivious to her husband's faults, or at least chose not to notice them. She wrote to Louise, assuring her 'that I shall always behave my self as becomes his Wife'. A few months later, she was defending her husband:

'He has in some things bin much misrepresented and injured, for I doe protest with all the truth imaginable, that since I have had the happiness to know his grace, he has never bin from me twice after nine o'clock at night (which is far from leading a debauch life) all that truly knows my Lord Duke's way of living is in a wonder to see him that is so young so very regular and discreet, but what I believe may in some measure occasion all this faulce report, is that my Lord Duke will when he is in company be always in the best (which truly is a very commendable thing) and then it is impossible sometimes to avoid drinking a little too much, all the men of the greatest quality at the present here in England doeing it extreamly at their dinner, and then the Duke of Richmond has ye misfortune to expose himself in all publicke places, and perhaps though this may be but wonce in six months, it will make a noise all over the Kingdome, all those that are so handsome as his grace to be sure will have enemies upon the account of envie. Indeed it is the only thing I have to wish changed in

> him, *except that of his not persuing to gain the fame his quality and*
> *qualities deserve, for here no man has it in his power to make himself*
> *so considerable in the world as he has, being master in his person and*
> *understanding of all fine qualities, and esteemed so by all sides here.*
> *Indeed I have often desired him to take it in his consideration and*
> *forgitt some little things (it may be) he had reason to resent, but I*
> *found it was a disagreeable discourse so my part was to let it fal. I*
> *thinke my self very happy to find your grace has the same sentements*
> *and desire, who I am sure aught and will I hope prevail, for indeed*
> *my Lord Duke has all the duty and tenderness for your grace*
> *imaginable, and I found your last letter was a most sensible trouble*
> *to him.'[17]*

In Anne, Louise had found a dutiful daughter-in-law, who could keep her informed of her son's activities and defend his reputation whatever the truth may have been. John Macky's brief description of Richmond does not give much away: 'He is a Gentleman Good-natured to a Fault; very well bred, and hath many valuable Things in him; is an Enemy to Business'.[18] Perhaps the last comment was a veiled reference to his spending habits.

Like many noblemen of his standing, Richmond spent a great deal of his time hunting – a passion that he inherited from his father. He visited Sussex regularly to enjoy the pleasures of the chase with the Charlton Hunt, the most fashionable hunt in the country. It was to follow the Charlton hounds that he rented and later bought Goodwood as a hunting lodge, conveniently situated just over the hill from Charlton.

The name Goodwood probably originates from Godwin's Wood, named after Godwin, Earl of Wessex, who was the father of King Harold, famously killed at the Battle of Hastings by an arrow in the eye. King Harold's Sussex land holdings were granted by William the Conqueror to Roger de Montgomery, first Earl of Arundel. The earliest mention of the name is in the twelfth century and, by the last quarter of the sixteenth century, there was a house and deer park, as seen in a map drawn up for the Earls of Arundel.[19] At that time, Goodwood was leased to Sir Thomas Palmer who lived in the 'faire mansion house' with its 'fayre garden and one fayre orteyard [orchard]'.[20] It then passed through a quick succession of owners, before being bought by the 'Wizard' Earl of Northumberland who built a simple rectangular house between 1616 and 1617, adding gabled wings at a later date. The Wizard Earl's house then changed hands several times again, being owned by John Caryll, Anthony Kemp, the Earl of Middleton, the Earl of Shrewsbury and William Rowley, before being bought by Richmond in 1697 for £4,100. Richmond had been renting the house for a few years prior to this and, typically, the purchase – which had begun in 1695 – took over two years to complete.[21]

Like all hunting lodges, Goodwood was modest in scale, with the minimum of accommodation, and only opened up for sport. Most of the servants would travel with their master from London – some in advance – so the house would be a hive of activity when he was in residence. Grooms, coachmen, postilions, stewards, footmen and maids – everyone rushing about here and there as they carried out their duties in cramped conditions. The house would have looked old-fashioned to Richmond's smart friends with its Dutch gables at the end of each wing, but they were more concerned with the sport and were content as long as they had a comfortable bed and were well fed.

Very little survives in the Goodwood archive relating to the first duke apart from a number of receipts, mostly from a flurry of activity in the early 1700s.[22] They reveal that Goodwood was Richmond's main residence and that it was very expensively furnished, despite its fairly small size. Rich fabrics were used for curtains, upholstery and bed hangings, while tapestries hung in some of the rooms. It is enlightening to compare a receipt for 'a Weeks milk' costing 'two Shillings nine penc' with a staggering bill totalling £516 5s 4d from Mr Wright, the upholsterer, which includes a set of twelve velvet-covered chairs, ten walnut chairs covered in Spanish Leather – the very height of fashion – and cushions filled with 'fine Swans downe'.[23] £47 14s was spent at the fashionable cabinet maker and looking-glass maker, John Gumley, and just over £39 was paid for two items of 'East India Goods' from Mr King (Chinese porcelain and lacquer furniture was all the rage).[24]

Large amounts were being spent on clothes and fabric: twelve 'fine holland [linen] shirts' and twenty-four 'fine Muslin Neckcloths' for the duke were bought from Mr Daval on 22 December 1702 and, together with some lace, cost just over £31, while a further £42 was spent with 'Mr. Elliot the Laceman'.[25] Richmond must have been a bit of a dandy: £24 was paid to the periwig maker in 1705 and a bill for shoes 'for His Grace The Duke of Richmond' lists seventy-one pairs, bought between December 1699 and February 1703 from Charles des Pres and totalling £20 14s.[26] Sometimes he was buying as much as a pair of shoes a week, not only for himself but also for his servants, including a black page whose shoes cost four shillings a pair compared to six shillings a pair for his master. The large quantities of yellow cloth purchased may have been for servants dressed in the yellow Richmond livery.[27] Linen for the table was no less expensive: £79 was spent on napkins and tablecloths in 1703.[28]

Other receipts cover food (from the butcher, baker, fishmonger, 'poulterer', 'fruiterer', grocer and cheesemonger) and drink (from the brewer, wine merchant and 'Master of the Cellar').[29] Clearly, the Richmonds were being well fed and watered as their diet included salmon and oysters washed down with champagne and burgundy.

Expenses for Goodwood poured in – Richard Griffin, the gardener, was on an annual salary of £25 in 1717.[30] Without a permanent London base, the Richmonds rented various houses including one in Haymarket and another in Arlington Street. The half-year rent for the former was £50 in 1703.[31] Household expenses mounted up when bills for lighting (candles) and fuel (charcoal) were added, let alone those of cabinet makers (£163 was spent with Mr Rymell in 1706).[32] A team of staff was needed to run the household and look after the family including footmen, a cook and a doorkeeper.[33] Ned the footman was paid thirty shillings for three months' work.[34]

Travel was another heavy expense, including the use of horses and sedan chairs (for getting around London). Mr Phillips, the coach maker, supplied a new coach in 1695 for £52 18s 9d but the poor chap was not paid for it until November 1704.[35] A duke must live according to his status and a smart coach was an essential accoutrement, especially when making the long journey from Goodwood to town. Another coach maker, John Chapman, also struggled to have his bills settled; over the course of five years, by 1707 Richmond had racked up a bill of £527, despite part payments along the way. Chapman had supplied six new coaches decorated with the duke's coat of arms, the most expensive being £85; four old coaches were taken in part exchange at £8 each.[36]

With all these bills pouring in, it was not surprising that the Richmonds were always strapped for cash. We do not know Richmond's income from the coal tax dues, but he would have struggled to settle these bills from the £2,000 income he had formerly received from his father. When the Restoration court beauty Frances Stuart, widow of the last Stuart Duke of Richmond, died in 1702, he inherited the Lennox estates in Scotland, which he promptly sold.[37] By 1713, Anne had resorted to pawning items to pay off the creditors who were hounding them. In a letter to her husband, she mentions a 'gold box you sent me, which I value so much I never dare carry it in my Pocket' but fears she must soon have to 'Pawne it or something els'. Coal dues were down and she was eating at her sister's house to save money.[38] The following year, she pawned 1,569 ounces of silver plate engraved with the duke's coat of arms in return for £350 to be repaid a month later.[39] Meanwhile, her husband borrowed £600 from Sir John and Lady Betty Germain; the debt (plus interest) was not fully repaid until after Richmond's death ten years later.[40]

Anne's chief duty was to provide a son and heir, and with Louise anxious to see the dynasty continue, the pressure was on. A daughter, Louisa, was born in 1694, not long after their marriage, but it was not until seven years later that they finally had a son, christened Charles after his father and grandfather. Another daughter, Anne, was born in 1703 and, with her birth, the family was complete. The children are often referred to in letters between their mother and grandmother,

even though Louise seldom saw them. 'Lady Anne is extremely proud
of your graces naming her in your letter', Anne wrote to her mother-
in-law, chatting away about her youngest daughter. She continues,
'... she has certainly very pretty little features, and wou'd be much
handsomer if Lord Duke [her husband] wou'd give me leave to part
her Eye-brows, for their meeting gives her a cloudy looke, which
makes her sister and Brothere for ye generality be more liked, but
theire features are nothing so exacte as hers, for theirs grows large and
much of King Charleses and ye Royal Family!'

By the time of this letter, the eldest daughter, Louisa, was already
married. Her husband was James, third Earl of Berkeley, a well-known
admiral and member of an old established family, so the match would
have been deemed very suitable. She was clearly the apple of her
father's eye, as in the same letter, Anne says 'he [Richmond] is very
partial to them two [Louisa and James], especially Lady Berkeley, who
writs me word she is perpetually afflicted with the Chollick; I was in
hope it would have left her ... She has youth and strength so I hope
will overcome it.'[41] As their darling daughter, Louisa was painted twice
– once when she was twelve by Charles d'Agar, and again just after her
marriage, by Charles Jervas. With the birth of her first child, Augustus,
Louise de Keroualle became a great-grandmother. Tragically, Louisa
died the following year while giving birth to her second child,
Elizabeth. She was only twenty-three.

*   *   *

In July 1714, Richmond was travelling through the streets of Paris in
his coach. As it trundled over the Pont Neuf, the newly built arched
bridge linking the left and right banks of the River Seine to the Île de
la Cité, three men jumped out of the crowd, grabbed the footmen and
forced the duke out. He was then subjected to a torrent of abuse by
Richard Hamilton, an Irish officer and a prominent member of the
Jacobite Court in France. Hamilton accused Richmond of badmouthing
the exiled court at 'an assemblée in his presence' and 'after much

threatening to beat him if he would not draw', wounded him twice in the stomach.[42] The incident raised more than a few eyebrows and underlined the fact that Richmond had his enemies as well as his friends. It was not the first time that he was fodder for the press; two years earlier, he had given refuge to General Macartney, a friend of his who had acted as second to Lord Mohun in his fatal duel in Hyde Park with the Duke of Hamilton. Both Mohun and the Duke of Hamilton were mortally wounded, the duke expiring as he was being carried to his coach. The Duke of Hamilton's second, John Hamilton, accused Macartney of having dealt the fatal thrust as Mohun and the Duke were rolling around on the ground. Macartney then fled the country with a price on his head. The duel was given political impetus as Macartney was a staunch Whig and Protestant and the Tory party was out to get him. In a letter to his mother, Richmond tried to defend himself against accusations in the newspapers:

> '. . . what is this fresh thing that I have done to make the world and the Gazettes accuse me of siding with the Queen's enemies? I know nothing of it, thank God; and if I did, I should be their enemy as staunchly as I am loyal to my Queen. In God's name how have I shown my inclinations to be otherwise, my dear Duchess? Parliament is not yet assembled; there is no contest for any Election; in what have I shown want of regard to Her Majesty? When folks accuse me, they should at least tell me of what . . . but if my crime is what I suspect, from your letter mentioning the Gazette, it is that I have shown myself so much a friend to Generall Macartney. Ah, my dear Duchess, if that is my crime, I confess it with pride. What! Is it enmity to the Queen to try to save one's intimate friend that has been unfortunate enough to be second to poor ill-fated Lord Mohun? No, no, dear Duchess, you cannot blame me in your heart, for I am sure that when poor Macartney asked my protection you would not have had me betray him. Think well of it; you would have saved him as I did, and I would think myself the meanest of men had I done otherwise. Remember that all I did to help Macartney was done

before the Queen's Proclamation was issued. I will trouble you no
further upon this point, but leave you to judge if I am right or not.

'One word more and I have done. I do not understand why,*
because the Duke of Hamilton and Lord Mohun killed each other
because they could not agree, it should be made a matter of State
importance. I cannot make it out.'[43]

Unfortunately, Richmond lacked judgement in his choice of friends.
The French ambassador, the duc d'Aumont, put it succinctly when he
said to Louise, that 'bad companions often spoil the best intentions'.[44]
Lord Mohun was a notorious rake and gambler and even association
with him would have cast Richmond in a bad light. There was a
shallowness to his character that clearly worried his mother. He had
changed his allegiances to monarchs and countries and swayed
between Catholic and Protestant beliefs, with the result that people
did not quite trust him. He was suspected of some complicity in
Jacobite schemes in 1696, although there is no evidence that he was
ever involved in anything treasonable. After William III's death, he
remained loyal to his successor, Queen Anne, carrying the Sceptre
with the Dove at her coronation. However, he drifted away from the
Whig Party, only to return opportunistically at the accession of George
I in 1714.

Louise, who with the stealth of a cat had always supported the right
party, needed reassurance that he would not do anything stupid.
Writing to her in 1712, he assured her, 'You know well that I have
always been attached to the Whig Party, and that for four years in
succession in Parliament I have always obeyed the Queen's commands.
It is not for me to enter into the reasons for changing the Ministry, for
so long as the Crown is well served I shall be content.' The irony shines
through when he continues, 'But permit me to remind you that, as I
have the honour to be a King's son, and an English Duke, I cannot
change with whatever wind may blow; when I tell you this you may
assure yourself that there is no man in the world, of either party, that
has more respect and veneration for the Queen than I have, and always

shall have. As for the interest I may have in France, I trust in a great king that has never done an injustice.'[45]

*   *   *

With a new monarch on the throne, Louise paid a visit to England in 1715, still hoping she might get her English pension resurrected. Despite the time that had passed since Charles II's death, she was still a well-known personality at court, where she was received by George I and presented to the Princess of Wales, later Queen Caroline. Among others present at the drawing room were the Countess of Dorchester (James II's mistress) and the Countess of Orkney (William III's mistress). When Lady Dorchester, noted for her sharp tongue, saw Louise, she exclaimed, 'By Jove! Who would have thought that we three whores should meet here!'[46] Memories of taunts from Nell Gwyn came flooding back, but she held her head high and smiled graciously.

Like her son, Louise was perennially short of cash. She had tried unsuccessfully to extract a pension from William III on a short visit to England in 1698. However, lack of funds had not stopped her from travelling in style; on that occasion her son had hired a coach pulled by six horses to transport her from Rochester to London, a stately progress lasting four days. The bill, presented to Richmond, came to £7 but was not paid until nearly five years later.[47]

Since her arrival in France, Louise had lived mainly at fashionable addresses in Paris, surrounding herself with rich furnishings including chandeliers, looking glasses and tapestries.[48] Burdened with the upkeep of the Château of Aubigny and its romantic hunting lodge, the Château de La Verrerie, she pleaded successfully that it was for the French Crown to maintain it.[49] Right up until his death, Louis XIV kept her creditors at bay and each year suspended all lawsuits against her, no doubt ruining innocent tradesmen in the process. After Louis' death, his nephew Philippe II, Duke of Orléans, acting as Regent, increased her pension from £12,000 to £20,000 and then to £24,000. Finally, anticipating a crash in the Regent's finances, she managed to persuade him to give up her pension in return for a lump sum of £600,000 to be used to buy a life-annuity, 'in consideration of the great services she had rendered France and to give her the means of keeping up her rank and dignity'.[50] Thereafter, she settled at Aubigny and turned her attention to charitable works. She established a hospital administered by nuns, who cared for the sick and provided education for the young. Voltaire met her on one of her visits to Paris and recalled, 'Never did woman preserve her charms so late in life. At the age of seventy she was still lovely, her figure stately, her face unfaded.'[51]

In the twilight of her life, one of Louise's chief pleasures was her growing family. Her daughter-in-law Anne and her three grandchildren delighted her and kept her informed of all that was happening at Goodwood. In contrast, her son continued to vex her as he slid into greater debt and dissipation. A brawl with a gentleman in Chichester was reported in the press causing Louise great distress. He wrote to reassure her that it was nothing serious: 'But, my dear Duchess, permit me to scold you for being frightened at what the Gazettes tell you concerning the great fracas which has taken place. The fact is that a person named the Chavalier Miler [Sir John Miller] at Chichester attempted to be insolent. I took him by the scruff of the neck and told him that if he didn't leave the room I would have him given a hundred strokes with a stick by my servant! He took my advice, retired, and that's the whole story; I swear to you that there was nothing more!'[52] It is not surprising that Jonathan Swift, the satirist, called him 'a shallow coxcomb'.[53]

To pay one of his gambling debts, Richmond settled on an ingenious solution. The money he owed was considerable – £5,000 – and the man he owed it to was none other than the Earl Cadogan, a strong-willed general who had been Chief of Staff and right-hand man to the Duke of Marlborough. Richmond and Cadogan agreed that Cadogan's daughter, Sarah, would marry Richmond's son, Charles, then known by his courtesy title, the Earl of March.

Unlike his gambling partner, Cadogan had had great success in the past, making large amounts of money betting on the outcome of sieges in the War of the Spanish Succession. Sarah's dowry would therefore pay off the debt and, to Cadogan's delight, his daughter would one day become a duchess, occupying the highest rung on the ladder of the English aristocracy. Their children had no say in the matter and were still young – March was eighteen and Sarah only thirteen. When March first set eyes on his bride at her home in The Hague, where her father was ambassador, he exclaimed, 'Oh no, they're not going to marry me to that dowdy!' After the ceremony, he was quickly packed off with his tutor, Tom Hill, to go on the Grand Tour, while Sarah went back to her mother to complete her education.[54]

*   *   *

It was at Goodwood that Anne spent much of her time, while her husband attended Parliament up in London. Her daughter Anne was still at home and Anne herself was content to lead a quiet life in the countryside, away from the gay existence of London and all its temptations that were a constant drain on resources. The peacefulness of rural Sussex and its fresh air were in stark contrast to the hurly-burly of court life. In an attempt to modernise the old Jacobean house, the façade had been given a facelift, making the windows symmetrical and adding *oeil de boeuf* windows to the attic storey.[55]

Richmond returned for Christmas 1721 but was clearly very ill. Anne's letters from Goodwood tell of his slow demise. Writing to March on his Grand Tour on 3 January 1722, she tells him, 'Papa brought from London an intermiting Feaver and with it most violent Histerik Fits that he has been all this Fortnight that he has favoured Goodwood most extreamly ill, Mr. Peakhamne with the Barke has stopd the Feaver, but his othere Fits were attended with such convulsions that I sent for a Docter from London who asurs Lord Duke unless he intirely leaves of strong waters his recovery is impossible . . . I never remember Lord Duke so broke & decayed as he is at present: in his Fits he raves after you and says he is sure if he did but see his Dear Boy he should be well . . .'[56] Towards the end of the

month, he was still no better: 'I wish he may continu as well as he was
when he first left Goodwood, but I fear it, for he is extremely decay'd,
and continus the cause of all his illnesses to a greater degree than
ever . . .'[57] A week later, she writes, 'I have had so much affliction, and
in Lord Duke's Long sickness so little sleepe, that my memory is quit
gon . . .'[58] Poor Anne was then taken ill herself; her daughter, Anne,
wrote to her brother on 21 February: 'I must Trouble my Dear Brother
again with my sille Letters, but mama is not well and is not able to set
pen to paper She is so weak . . . Mama tho not at all well gives her Love
to you.'[59] This gentle lady, who had been such a devoted wife to a very
difficult husband, died on 9 December later that year and was laid to
rest among her ancestors in the Brudenell family vault at Deene,
Northamptonshire. Less than six months later, her husband followed
her to the grave, 'worn-out with debauchery, he had become no longer
the handsomest creature in the world, but the ugliest'.[60]

*   *   *

At the end of May 1723, a funerary hatchment, a wooden or canvas
lozenge-shaped plaque emblazoned with the duke's coat of arms on a
black background, was hoisted above the front door of Goodwood
House where it would remain until the autumn. It was just one of the
many funeral trappings that commemorated Charles Richmond's
death. Against both his 'Uncle Brudenell' and father-in-law's wishes,
the new duke decided that his father should be buried with all the
pomp and ceremony possible in Westminster Abbey.[61] Perhaps the
irony of this sad reprobate being laid to rest with the full honours of a
duke and Knight of the Garter was too much for them to bear.

The cortège, including a hearse drawn by six horses, accompanied by
two coaches and four horsemen dressed in mourning, took two days to
make the journey from Goodwood to London. There, the coffin was
placed in the Jerusalem Chamber near the west doorway of the abbey.
The chamber was 'hung deep in mourning' and an elaborate catafalque
erected with velvet drapes, silk streamers and black ostrich plumes.

Ducal coronets, stars, crests and garters were liberally strewn all over the chamber. One hundred and twelve candles flickered as six 'mutes in mourning' stood by the coffin. For the funeral service itself, one hundred and fifty men in mourning, carrying as many candles, lit the procession. All the main rooms at both Richmond House (his London residence) and Goodwood were elaborately decked out with grey cloth hangings, including walls, curtains, chairs and beds, to remain in situ for a year. The total cost of these lavish funeral expenses was just over £656, a substantial sum, especially when one considers that a labourer's wage in 1725 was about 10 pence a day.[62]

For all his faults, the first duke had some redeeming qualities. He inherited a love of the chase from his father which led to the purchase of Goodwood and subsequent hospitality to his friends and family. Clearly a bon viveur, his hard-drinking friends enjoyed his company. In war, he proved himself a brave soldier and had a streak of daring. But beyond that, his merits trickle out. Unlike his father, he lacked self-control and lived way beyond his means, racking up huge debts. From both of his parents he inherited a desire to keep up appearances, something his mother took particular care over; but this was at the expense of others, with lowly tradesmen suffering as a result. He did not have the monetary resources of a royal prince but he behaved as if he did.

His mother passed on her pride in birth and rank, a reaction against those who had looked down on her for her impoverished childhood and role as the king's mistress. Both Charles and Louise spoilt their son, which made him arrogant and selfish. He was not a shrewd judge of character like his father nor could he manipulate people like his mother. Instead, he was swayed back and forth on the stormy seas of religion and politics, lacking the intelligence to steer the right course and heed wise counsel. Thomas Hearne, a contemporary diarist who met him in Oxford, was singularly unimpressed considering him 'a man of very little understanding, and tho' the son of so great a king as king Charles II was a man that struck in with everything that was whiggish and opposite to true monarchical principles'.[63]

Louise outlived her son by eleven years and Charles II by almost half a century. The final nine years of her life were spent at her château at Aubigny where her thoughts increasingly turned to her eternal salvation. Her ever-growing family visited her and were a constant source of comfort. In October 1734, she was taken ill and travelled to Paris to consult doctors. It was to be her last journey. She died in Paris on 14 November and was buried in the Church of the Barefooted Carmelites. Her body was laid to rest in the chapel of the des Rieux family, her grandmother's noble family through whom she was related to Charles II.

Fubbs, the yacht that Charles had named after her, underwent some small repairs that same year. Seaworthy again, she rode the waves until 1781, by which time Louise's great-grandson was duke and her legacy was firmly established.

John Wootton painted a series of pictures of the second Duke of Richmond's hunters in the 1740s; Goodwood House can be glimpsed in the background along with the Temple of Neptune and Minerva
(© Trustees of the Goodwood Collection)

3

The Charlton Hunt

*'Mr Roper has the reputation of keeping
the best pack of fox hounds in the Kingdom.'*

Alexander Pope, 1712

On 14 October 1651, four men passed surreptitiously through Charlton forest. One of their party was the most wanted man in England – Charles II – who was fleeing for his life. Following the Royalists' defeat at the Battle of Worcester, Charles had been on the run for six weeks with a huge price on his head. Now, they were just a few hours from his escape across the Channel. Moving quickly on, they passed over Arundel Hill, taking refreshments at Houghton Bridge, followed by a close shave with a party of Roundheads at Bramber. Thereafter, they made their way to Brighton for supper at the George Inn, before finally slipping away from Shoreham on board a small coal barge, the *Surprise*.[1] It would be nearly nine years before he set foot on English soil again.

To eighteenth-century ears, the Charlton Hunt was synonymous with some of the best sport in the country and Mr Roper was its celebrated huntsman. It is the earliest documented pack of foxhounds in the country and its fame drew the cream of society, including Charles's dashing illegitimate sons, the Dukes of Monmouth, St Albans and Richmond. Given their father's escape through Charlton forest, it held an added emotive pull. Monmouth is reputed to have declared, 'When I am king, I will keep my court at Charlton.' A poem entitled *The Historicall Account of the Rise, and Progress of the Charleton Congress*, written anonymously and mysteriously delivered by a porter to the second Duke of Richmond in 1738, credits Monmouth with the founding of the hunt, together with his friend, Ford, Lord Grey.[2]

Charlton is a hamlet three miles north of Goodwood and lies in a shallow valley at the foot of the South Downs. To its north spreads the vast Charlton forest, extending to over 800 acres. In former times it had been part of the extensive tracts of land owned by the Earls of Arundel. They had a hunting seat nearby at Downley from where they enjoyed the thrilling sport that the area offered. Lord Grey, later created Earl of Tankerville, lived not far away at Uppark where his family probably kept some hounds; it is likely that Grey moved some of these hounds to Charlton. Prior to hunting the fox, deer hunting – an exclusively aristocratic pursuit – was all the rage but it gradually went into decline during the seventeenth century as land was fenced in and deer forests were cut down. Hunting the crafty fox provided an exhilarating alternative.

Grey was implicated in the Rye House Plot of 1683, a scheme to murder Charles II and his brother the Duke of York at Rye House on their way from Newmarket to London. Having given his captors the slip, Grey fled into exile where he joined Monmouth. Following Monmouth's unsuccessful rebellion and beheading, he managed to obtain a pardon and probably continued hunting at Charlton. Roper fled the country, too, and went to live in France to hunt with St Victor, a celebrated French huntsman who kept a pack of hounds at Chantilly. It was only after the accession of William and Mary in 1688 that he dared show his face again.[3]

Roper, who came from Kent, was an extremely able huntsman and became something of a sporting celebrity. The fame of the Charlton

Hunt grew and the nobility and gentry flocked to Sussex to follow the hounds. Among them was the Duke of Devonshire who, on one occasion, galloped his horse down Levin Down and flew over a five-barred gate at the bottom, a daring feat that was long remembered, as jumping fences while out hunting at that time was practically unknown. Unfortunately, Roper managed to upset 'The Proud Duke' of Somerset by hunting too close to his palatial seat at Petworth.[4] Jealous of the attention that the Charlton Hunt was attracting, Somerset established his own hunt in the hope of luring away some of the fashionable Charlton followers. After months of petty squabbling, Sir William Goring, a local landowner, acted as mediator and Somerset threw in the towel and gave up hunting.

The call of the hunting horn proved irresistible to the young Charles, first Duke of Richmond, then in his early twenties. His half-brother, Charles Beauclerk, the bastard son of Nell Gwyn who was made Duke of St Albans, joined him in the chase, as did his nephew, the second Duke of Grafton. For these hot-blooded young men, foxhunting became an obsession and, in Richmond's case, his small hunting lodge at Goodwood would one day form the heart of an extensive ducal estate.

*　　*　　*

Richmond's son, March, returned fresh and tanned from his Grand Tour in the summer of 1722, having been travelling for nearly three years. Everyone was anxious to see how he would get on with his wife, Sarah, none more so than March, who had last set eyes on her as a gawky teenager. Arriving at The Hague, where Sarah's family lived, March decided he would have one last night out before the inevitable sentence that awaited him. He and Tom Hill, his faithful tutor and confidant, decided to go to the theatre. There he spied a ravishing young lady, admiring her from across the stalls. Over the course of the evening, his gaze constantly returned to the young beauty and he was smitten. What should he do? Should he introduce himself, if only to suffer in purgatory for the rest of his life as to what might have been? Instead, he asked those around him if anyone knew her name. They responded in astonishment that such a well-heeled young man did not know the reigning toast, the beautiful Lady March – his wife.[5]

After their joyful reunion, March and Sarah returned to England to pass the summer at Goodwood and Caversham, the Cadogans' estate in Berkshire. Throughout his travels, March had dreamed of Goodwood and the happy times he had spent there as a child. In his memories, it was always summer with the mellow red brick of the façade warmed by the sun and the deer lazily grazing in the park. It had been a paradise for a child to grow up in, free to roam and explore the neighbouring pastures and woods. The antiquary Jeremiah Miller, when visiting Goodwood a couple of decades later, wrote: 'The Park is but small. It rises behind ye house up the side of the Downs, from whence there is a most beautiful view of Portsmouth, St Helens, ye Isle of Wight & Chichester.'[6] Goodwood House itself was surveyed soon after March's return by the fashionable classical architect Colen Campbell, architect to the Prince of Wales. The floorplan is surprisingly simple, with the house being only one room deep; four bedrooms are accessed from the main staircase and a further two from the back stairs.[7]

March could not wait for the hunting season to begin and to get back into the saddle. Like his father, he adored hunting and had done so ever since he was a child. Despite suffering a serious accident as a boy while out hunting, his spirits were not diminished. At the time, his anxious mother wrote to his grandmother Louise in France to try and exert some pressure on her son not to take his 'only son' hunting, 'as he is very young, weake, and extreamly ratle-headed, his liffe upon those horses ["fine Hunters"] will be in the greatest of dangers, and since he has so lately escaped with liffe and limbs, through God's great mercy, twou'd be presumption to run him in ye like danger again. Hunting being a qualification not necessary to make a fine gentleman . . .' Needless to say, Richmond ignored both his mother's and his wife's pleas and continued to take March out hunting, regaling him with stories of wolf hunting with Louis XIV in France. Their mutual love of the chase helped to form a special bond between them at a time when fathers and sons were often emotionally distant from one another.

By 1721, Roper was getting on in years and took on a joint Master to share the burden of running the hunt, although he still hunted the hounds himself. The person he chose was Charles Powlett, third Duke of Bolton, a wealthy nobleman from Hampshire.[8] Together, they focused on the breeding of successful hounds, which was key for the Charlton Hunt to maintain its reputation.

On Shrove Tuesday, 1723, Roper mounted his horse for the final time. His beloved hounds quickly found a fox and, as he cried out, 'Get on!' he collapsed in the saddle and died instantly, aged eighty-four. It was an entirely fitting end for this hunting hero. Bolton was now sole owner of the hounds and the hunt increased in popularity. That same year, the 'Great Room' – or 'Dome' as it was sometimes called – was completed in Charlton. This was a banqueting house paid for by the followers to replace 'a small Dark Cell' where they had been meeting. Here, after a hard day in the saddle, the hunt followers could dine in style without having to leave Charlton – the social side of the hunt being just as important as the sport. It was designed by the 'architect earl', Richard Boyle, third Earl of Burlington, and is described in the poem, *The Charleton Congress*:

> '. . . then Boyle, by instinct all divine began
> is this an Edifice for such a band?
> I'll have the Honour to erect a Room,
> shall cost Diana's Train, but such a Sum;
> they all agreed, and quickly paid it down,
> and now there stands a sacred Dome, Confes't
> the finest in the Country, most admired.'[9]

The building was probably of one storey surmounted by a dome. There has been some suggestion that the Great Room (and its predecessor) was used as a covert meeting place for Jacobites, however nothing conclusive has been proved.[10]

That same year, Richmond also died, leaving his son and heir saddled with huge debts. Under the watchful eye of Uncle Cardigan, the young duke became a keen supporter of the hunt. More leading figures in society journeyed to Sussex for the sport, including the first Duke of Montrose who travelled all the way from Scotland. Some of them, including Richmond, Grafton, the Earl of Halifax, Lord Walpole and Lord De La Warr, built for themselves small hunting-boxes in Charlton where they could stay the night, since hunting in those days started at the crack of dawn. Devonshire shared a double-fronted one, occupied by him on one side of an archway and Lord Harcourt on the other, with William Fauquier lodged in the attic between the two. Richmond used his winnings from a horse race at Tunbridge Wells to pay for his hunting-box, probably to the designs of Roger Morris, who was working at Goodwood at the time. Named Fox Hall, it was described in the poem, *The Charleton Congress*:

> *'A warm, but small Apartment, each one has,*
> *the Duke's alone appears magnificent,*
> *conspicuous, it stands, above the rest*
> *And uniform, & nearest to the Dome.'*

An avenue led away from its elegant pedimented front façade and the Great Room was conveniently across the lane in front, enabling Richmond to stagger home in the early hours.[11] Inside, the principal (first) floor contained a single room with a bed alcove. Richmond kept the bare minimum in the way of furnishings, really only using it to sleep and breakfast in. For his wake-up call, he kept a coffee pot, a pair of candlesticks, six teaspoons, a strainer, a pair of tea tongs and a cream pail and, for eating, a knife, fork, spoon and tumbler, all in silver.[12]

The previous year, Lord Grey's grandson, the second Earl of Tankerville, had inherited Uppark and established a rival pack of hounds, much to the annoyance of the Charlton Hunt and the detriment of their sport. As a result, Richmond decided to give the 1728 season a miss and travelled to Europe. When he returned home a year later, Bolton had resigned; he had fallen for the charms of the beautiful Lavinia Fenton, a leading actress who had appeared as the star of *The Beggar's Opera*. Bolton managed to persuade her to give up acting but it was agreed only on the condition that he gave up hunting. So, in 1729, he resigned as Master of the Charlton Hunt, leaving a vacancy that needed filling urgently. Richmond's friends encouraged him to take on the hounds as proprietor. Living nearby at Goodwood, he was the obvious choice. Reluctantly, Richmond agreed but on condition that De La Warr would be Master in his absence. The aggravation with Tankerville rumbled on until eventually everyone called it quits and a lengthy agreement was drawn up between the two proprietors. It was called the 'Treaty of Peace, Union and Friendship' and was written on a parchment scroll seven feet long and signed and sealed by Richmond and Tankerville with a quartet of dukes as witnesses: Grafton, St Albans, Bolton and Montrose. In essence, the two parties agreed to merge their packs and share the costs. For the 1730-31 season they took on a third Master, Garton Orme of Woolavington, probably to act as mediator should things become difficult again.

The convivial Richmond threw himself into his new role and, in 1730, purchased the manors of Singleton and Charlton from the Earl of Scarbrough.[13] These lands included forests and coverts within easy reach of the kennels in Charlton. In the centre of Charlton, he erected a flagpole at the top of which fluttered a flag depicting a yellow fox in a green field. After one season, Tankerville resigned, taking half the pack with him, much to Richmond's relief. Meanwhile, Richmond was building Fox Hall and more noblemen were flocking to Charlton. All seemed rosy until Richmond broke his leg early in 1732.

Fortunately, Richmond had chosen a good deputy in De La Warr and the latter's correspondence provides an insight into the trials and tribulations of running a pack of foxhounds – troubles with the hunt servants, breeding hounds, buying horses, good and bad days hunting

– all is discussed. Richmond was back in the saddle by November and his new hunting-box was finished.

The cost of running the hunt was considerable. The expenses for 1739 totalled £841, of which £169 was for wages.[14] That did not include the expense of Richmond's own hunters, which in 1746 cost him £418, a sum that included wages for grooms. Five hunt liveries, in the distinctive blue and gold, cost an additional £35.[15] Over the course of eight years (1739-46) Richmond worked out he had spent £7,180 on the hunt, excluding his horses.[16]

*   *   *

The flint façade of Goodwood House glistened in the autumn sun. Although it was by no means a large ducal seat, it still commanded respect for its neatness and was pleasantly situated in a small deer park studded with oak and chestnut trees. Above its columned front door, the first duke's Garter star was proudly displayed, skilfully carved in stone. Closer inspection revealed a tiny lead 'sun in splendour', the insignia of the Sun Insurance company that insured the house.[17] When he had inherited the house from his father, Richmond had dreamed of rebuilding it, employing Colen Campbell to design a new house in the Palladian style. Plans were drawn up and costs listed; Campbell even went so far as to publish three plates in his *Vitruvius Britannicus* of 1725. However, Richmond decided not to go ahead, probably for financial reasons. Instead, Campbell's assistant Roger Morris remodelled the existing house and it was his hall into which the front door opened.

The smell of wood smoke greeted the visitor upon entry into the Great Hall, fires crackling away in the grates of a pair of classical chimneypieces that stood opposite the windows; candles in glass sconces lit the room at night and the chiming of an eight-day clock marked the time. Ionic columns screened each end of the room and horse paintings by John Wootton hung on the walls. Richmond had commissioned the foremost horse painter of the time to immortalise his favourite hunters on canvas, each with a local landmark in the background and held by a liveried groom. In addition, he had his favourite hound, Tapster, painted, clearly branded 'R' and proudly standing with a view of Chichester and the Isle of Wight in the distance. Wootton's first commission for the duke was a charming painting of his eldest daughter, Caroline, aged about ten, standing beside her smart little pony and attended by a groom. Wootton wrote to the duke after sending him the picture:

'My Lord Duke
    'I hope your Grace has rec'd the little Picture of Lady Caroline safe and I wish it answers your Grace's expectation, if any dust should be upon it pray make use of a clean Spunge and water and nothing else and now my Lord give me leave to return your Grace my moste hearty thanks for the noble present of Venison you pleas'd to send me, it came safe and sweet and proved a delightfull repast, I invit'd some friends to partake of your Grace's bounty and wee did eat and drink your Grace's good health and each man look'd like a new-varnish'd portrate, I had some artists with me but they were observ'd to draw nothing but Corks, thus my Lord your Grace sees where ye Wines in ye Witt's out but I know your Grace is so good as not to expose the nakedness of your Graces most oblig'd humble Servt. to Command
    J. Wootton.'18

Although Goodwood House was not large, it was fitted up to a high standard, worthy of the grandest of visitors. In the Great Dining-Room they would have sat on damask-covered settees, dined at a mahogany dining table with four leaves and taken their food from a marble-topped sideboard. Looking out of the windows of the Drawing Room, the view would have been framed by blue silk window curtains; a 'large India [lacquer] screen' stood on one side of the room. Upstairs, the duke and duchess's bedroom had 'flower'd India [chintz] Hangings' on the walls, bed and windows. The duchess's dressing room had red damask curtains and the duke's closet had yellow mohair hangings.

Guests would have been lodged in one of the other principal bedrooms: the Little Tapistry Room (as it's name suggests with tapestry hangings); the White Bed Chamber (with more 'flower'd India Hangings'); the Great Tapistry Bed Chamber (with more tapestries); the Red Bed Chamber (hung with red damask); and the disturbingly named Haunted Room (again with 'flower'd Indian Hangings'). The children were housed separately in the 'Little House' along with the senior household servants.[19]

Despite the children not sleeping under the same roof, Charles and Sarah Richmond were devoted to them. Caroline was born in London in the spring of 1723, an occasion celebrated back at Goodwood by Richmond's sister, Anne, Tom Hill and another friend who 'testified our joy in a bowl of punch' while the servants got drunk dancing to a fiddler playing 'in an ecstasy of delight'.[20] Nobody was more eager for a boy than Louise, praying from a distance in France that her legacy would continue with the birth of a great-grandson. Twice her hopes were dashed. After the death of the first boy in 1724, she wrote: 'She [Sarah] has not kept her word to me though! For in her last letter she promised me a little son, but – the dear child! – I'm sure she is very sorry to have failed in her promise! But I hope that the third will be an increase of the right sort in your family, which I pray the Almighty to bless!'[21] After the birth of a second boy in 1730, a messenger was despatched post-haste to Aubigny, arriving, according to Louise, 'at 5 in the morning half dead! I never recollect in my life having had so pleasant an awakening as when I learnt of the birth of your little son and happy delivery of the charming Duchess. Embrace my charming Caroline for me, tenderly; did she receive her brother graciously? For it seemed to me that when she was here she was none too anxious for one!'[22] A few days later the boy was dead and Louise was left to grieve in solitude.

Richmond's great friend, the colourful courtier Lord Hervey reported to Stephen Fox in 1731: 'I write to you from the Duchess of Richmond's, where I am to dine. She has a belly up to her chin and looks mighty well. His Grace is in great anxiety for her welfare, and a boy.'[23] Alas, it was a girl. She was named Emily and, for her christening, her godfather, George II, presented her with a magnificent christening bowl made by the Huguenot silversmith Edward Feline.[24]

In 1735, a third son, Charles, was born and much to Richmond's relief he was 'a fine child and likely to live'.[25] Sadly, Louise had died only three months earlier so she never saw her prayers answered. Two years later, another son, George, was born; the 'heir and a spare' would be inseparable companions throughout their lives.

The children charmed their parents' friends, to the extent that Sir Thomas Robinson, later Governor of Barbados, threw a ball at his London house in honour of Emily when she was only ten years old. Horace Walpole told a friend that there were 'an hundred and ninety-seven people, yet no confusion; he had taken off all the doors of his house, and in short distributed everybody quite to their well-being. The dancers were the two Lady Lenox's (Lady Emily Queen of the Ball, and appeared in great majesty from behind a vast bouquet) . . . A supper for the lady dancers was served at twelve, their partners and waiting tables with other supper stood behind. Oh I danced country dances, I had forgot myself. The ball ended at four.'[26] To another friend, he gossiped: 'The beauties were the Duke of Richmond's two daughters, and their mother still handsomer than they; the Duke sat by his wife all night kissing her hand.'[27]

The Richmonds were absolutely devoted to one another, she addressing him in one letter as 'My dearest angel' and signing off, 'Dearest life adieu believe me your most sincere affectionate wife'.[28] In another she ends, 'adieu my dearest dearest love I am yours for ever & ever'.[29] Even the worldly Walpole could hardly believe it was genuine: 'I drove to the other end of the town, where I heard lived a constant couple – I found a man and woman, Duke and Duchess of Richmond, both handsome enough to have been tempted to every inconstancy, but too handsome to have ever found what they would have lost by the exchange. I begged this happy charming woman to tell me by what art she had for twenty years together made herself beloved; and that I was persuaded from that air of heavenly good nature in her countenance that she would tell me, when she knew my happiness depended upon it. She coloured with a sort of mild indignation that made her ten times more beautiful, and replied, she knew not what I meant by art – that she had always obeyed, been virtuous, and loved her husband; and was it strange he should return it?'[30]

For much of their married life, Sarah was pregnant. Walpole informed a friend of his in the summer of 1748 that 'the Duchess of Richmond . . . does not go out with her twenty-fifth pregnancy.'[31] Two years later, he reported: 'The Duchess of Richmond . . . again lies in, after having been with child seven-and-twenty times: but even this is not so extra ordinary as the Duke's fondness for her, or as the vigour of her beauty: her complexion is as fair and blooming as when she was a bride.'[32] Of the twelve babies she gave birth to, seven survived infancy. Caroline, Emily, Charles and George were joined by three more daughters – Louisa, Sarah and Cecilia – with Cecilia being the baby from Sarah's twenty-seventh pregnancy.

Like their father, the boys loved hunting and spending time at Goodwood. George even had a pet fox named Fanny who narrowly escaped death when she was pursued by the Charlton hounds. Despite wearing a collar identifying her, she was chased within an inch of her life, the anxious mounted followers unable to stop the hounds until they got on to a fresh fox.

During the winter months, life at Goodwood revolved around hunting. Aged twelve, Emily sympathised with her mother: 'I am afraid my Dr Mama finds it a little Dull being alone, for as for *Papa*, his hunting takes up most part of his time.'[33] Sarah herself was a keen follower of hounds. The septuagenarian 'Proud Duke' complimented her hunting prowess: 'I did perceive by the lookes of the Dutchess of Richmond's horse to bee very well rode by soe noble and soe Great a Huntress to the very death of many ffoxes & soe entirely to Her Grace's satisfaction.'[34]

*   *   *

In the pale light of dawn on Friday, 26 January 1739, Charles and Sarah Richmond mounted their horses and rode down the narrow lane in front of Fox Hall into the heart of Charlton. The winter of 1738-39 had been a particularly mild one and that morning a soft mist lay over the village, concealing it from the surrounding Downs. Richmond felt a tinge of excitement about the day ahead; they had already had thirty-six days' hunting that season and had killed a fox on thirty-three of those. As both the local landowner and proprietor of the hounds, he took a keen interest in every detail of the hunt, recording each day's sport in his hunting diary.[35] The hunt's fame was such that they had had to create a club the previous year with membership strictly limited to only those who had been elected; rule 4 stated that 'one black Ball is an Exclusion'.[36] That morning, he was mounted on Slug, while his huntsman, Tom Johnson, was on Badger. The other hunt servants were Billy Ives, David Briggs and Nim Ives mounted on Sir William, Pickadilly and Walker respectively, all in Richmond's keep. They had previously been out on Wednesday, two days before, when they had found but had not killed a fox and, in his own words, 'the day altering to very bad weather, the scent dying every minute, wee took off & came home'. However, the sport did not end there and he continued, 'Nim dug out a bitch fox, which we turn'd out of the window at Fox Hall.'[37]

In Charlton, the Richmonds greeted the rest of the field, a total of eighteen followers plus the four hunt servants resplendent in the Richmond livery of yellow with scarlet collars and cuffs. Among the blue-blooded field were three of Richmond's cousins, all grandsons of Charles II: the gargantuan Charles Fitzroy, second Duke of Grafton, known to his friends as 'Old Puff'; and the brothers Charles Beauclerk, second Duke of St Albans, and Lord Henry Beauclerk. The Biddulph brothers, Richard and Charles, were also present and Lords Harcourt and Ossulstone, both in their twenties and keen followers of the chase. Keeping an eagle eye on these young bloods was Brigadier Henry Hawley, a severe army officer in his late fifties, who would later find fame as 'Hangman Hawley', a sobriquet resulting from his ruthless severity to the Jacobite insurgents after the battle of Culloden in 1746. Sarah Richmond was the only lady present; the Charlton Hunt was undoubtedly a male preserve and its members were all high-born gentlemen. However, ladies did occasionally hunt and Sarah's husband owned the hounds. It was also probably one of the rare occasions when she was not pregnant and she was making the most of it.

Hounds and huntsman did not hang around for long; as soon as everyone had met up, the huntsman, Tom Johnson, cracked his whip and headed towards East Dean wood in the chilly morning air. At 7.45am, a fox was found, the huntsman blew his horn and they were off, crashing through the woodland with hounds in full cry. In Richmond's own words:

> 'At a quarter before eight in the morning, the hounds found a fox in East Dean Wood, & ran an hour in that cover, then into Charlton forest, up to Punters Copse, through Herringdean to the Marlows, up to Coney Copse, back through the Marlows to the west gate of Charlton forest, over the fields to Nightingale bottom, Drought house, up Pine Pit Hanger, over by Downley ruins, through Lady Lewknor's Puttocks, by Colworth down, through old Read, all along Venus wood, to the hacking place, through the Marlows, cross Cocking road to Herringdean copse.'

Somewhere between Pine Pit Hanger and Lady Lewknor's Puttocks, St Albans took a tumble, while Lord Harcourt blew his first horse at the corner of Colworth down. Richmond continued – his hunting journal entry clearly written in a state of euphoria:

> 'Then into Singleton forest, where they ran several rings, for near an hour, in that covert and Punters Copse, & were several times at a fault, then from Punters Copse they ran through Charlton forest and East Dean wood to the lower Tegleaze, Buckleys, down between Graffham & Woolavington, through

Mr Orme's park & paddock, Northwood arm, over the heaths to Selham furze, Fielder's hop garden, by Selham barn, through the enclosed fields belonging to Selham & Ambersham, to Ambersham furzes, Todham furzes, over the brook by Dunford farm, to Aukers furze, cross Cocking causeway by the lime kiln to Paddock wood, Henley copse, Halfpenny wood, then cross Cocking highway.'

At this point, Lord Harcourt's second horse collapsed and he retired for the day, accompanied by the charming William Fauquier, a leading member of the fashionable Dilettante Society. Meanwhile, the hounds ran on, in hot pursuit of their quarry, 'up by Herringdean barn, to Suncombe, over Cocking course, to Punters copse, into Charlton forest at the north gate' where Brigadier Hawley changed horses and Billy Ives, helping out that season, jumped on to one of Sir Harry Liddell's hunters. The fox dashed on 'quite through the forest by the stone table, to Nightingale bottom, to Drought house, up Pine pit hanger, by Downley ruins, to Whistling Alley copse, Heydon barn, cross the south end of West Dean warren, down to Binderton farm' where Sir Harry dropped out, 'cross the Lavant, up Binderton, down, through Haye's bushes, Bickley bushes, cross the enclosures into the Valdoe, through Goodwood park, where the fox was seen'. Here, Richmond took the chance to swap on to Saucy Face, a fresh horse in the stables at Goodwood, and provide another fresh mount for his cousin, St Albans. Galloping off on Saucy Face, they continued 'out at the upper Charlton gate, to Strettington road upon the downs, through Seeley copse' – where Richmond did a somersault over his horse's head – 'to Lady Derby's rook wood, over by Halnaker windmill to Seabeach farm' at which point Ralph Jenison, Master of the King's Buck Hounds, Cornet Honeywood, Tom Johnson and Nim Ives had exhausted their horses and went home 'thoroughly satisfied'. Richmond, however, was not going to give up and took off, 'over Long down' (where his written account ends and another scribe takes over) 'through Eartham common field, quite through Mr Kemp's high wood'. Here, Billy Ives tired his second horse and, as St Albans was not wearing a warm overcoat, he decided to call it a day and gallantly handed over the horse that he had just picked up from Goodwood to Billy so he could continue with the hounds. Billy galloped after them to try and catch up, while the fox shot 'through the enclosures to Slindon in-down, to Madehurst parsonage' when he finally caught up, following them 'over Madehurst down to Fairmile, through the enclosures to Madehurst church and so to Houghton forest'. Richmond caught up here – following his fall – and they continued 'cross the road by the waypost, over Houghton down to South wood, through the enclosed fields of South Stoke down to the brooks, where they killed her, a bitch fox'. The 'official' transcript of the day ends with a more prosaic 'where the twenty three hounds put an end to the campaign and killed the old bitch fox ten minutes before six. Billy Ives, his Grace of Richmond and Brigadier Hawley were the only persons at the death.'[38]

Richmond recognised the significance of the day and immediately ordered his men to measure the distance with a cartwheel, a task that took them two whole days. The distance covered was a staggering fifty-seven miles and had lasted just over ten hours. It was christened 'The Grand Chase' and the hounds that were present at the end proclaimed 'The Glorious Twenty-Three Hounds' and individually named. On Sunday, 4 February, thirty-six members of the Charlton Hunt gathered in London at the Bedford Head Tavern for their annual dinner, and having waxed lyrical about 'the greatest chase that ever was', they proposed that an official account should be written up and circulated for posterity. Thus, the Grand Chase entered the annals of foxhunting history.

*   *   *

'Temperance and Regularity are still necessary for me to observe, and at Goodwood I believe no one ever heard of either of them, for my part I am determined not to come within a house that has a French Cooke in it for six months,' wrote the Whig politician William Pulteney politely declining an invitation to Goodwood. He added that he hoped he would 'have the honour of eating many a good dish with you again, & swallowing many a bottle of popping Champaigne, but for the present a little discretion is absolutely necessary'.[39]

Pulteney, later first Earl of Bath, loved coming to Goodwood. Indeed, Goodwood was fast becoming a mecca for hospitality. Carrying on in the tradition started by his father, Richmond invited friends and family to come and stay, and enjoy the sport on offer. As owner of the hounds, he was allowed 'to bring whoever he pleases from Goodwood to Dinner at Charlton'. Given the exclusivity of the Charlton Hunt Club, this was quite a coup. Sarah, as mistress of the house, made all of the necessary arrangements, although she would often run things by her husband. In anticipation of one house party, she wrote to him in London to tell him that she needed 'a chest of Lemons & half a one of oranges . . . also more burgundy & champain to serve us the rest of the summer . . . & that Will Maning must buy 30 hams att 7 pence per pound att Jullians in the haymarket or Suffolk Street' and worried that it would not arrive at Goodwood in time: 'I imagine that the chest of oranges & the adition to the wine may take up both to much time & room in the waggon so as they are not absolutely nessesary for the treat, as the hams are, I had rather be contente with the first quantity of wine & with 60 dossin [dozen] of Lemons & 6 or 8 of oranges than have the waggon set out late . . .' She also ran the guest bedroom situation past him: '. . . now as to beds for people, there is Lord Midlesexs new room, two good field beds in his outward room, the red bed, the haunted room & one in Sr. Thomas's outward room, six upon that floor, above there is Carolinas, Mr Hills & Mrs Pitts at the gardeners house one & St. Pauls, in all 11'.[40]

John Collis, Major of Hastings, waxed lyrical about a dinner Richmond gave at Vanbrugh Castle, Greenwich, which he rented for a short time: 'there were 27 Sussex gentlemen, amongst the rest, the Duke of Newcastle, Earl of Wilmington, Lord Abergaveny, Lord

Ossulston, who is the Earl of Tankerville's son. The entertainment vastly splendid, and served all in plate [silver], dishes and all, and a fine desert. There were 24 footmen waiting at table, and as he is master of the horse to the king, 16 of them in the king's livery and the rest in his own, which is very handsom. In short, the dinner, side board, desert, and grandeur, surpassed almost everything I ever saw, and the house vastly rich finished.[41]

It was not just foxhunting aristocrats that Richmond entertained at Goodwood. Tom Hill, his old tutor, remained a life-long friend and became part of the family to the extent that he had his own room at Goodwood. Another Goodwood regular was Mick Broughton, who later became Richmond's chaplain. Mick was a highly amusing correspondent, often poking fun at Richmond. Knowing Richmond's obsession with hunting, he began a letter in 1747: 'I presume you are . . . returned from the pursuit of the Old Fox in the green Cops, to that of the Old Fox in the white Tower [a reference to the menagerie at the Tower of London]; and let him be earth'd, Headed, or Escape I doubt not but your Grace and your noble Compeers will acquit your-selves as honourable and Skilful Hunters.'[42] The actor-manager and playwright Colley Cibber was a regular guest who enthused: 'For who can want spirits at Goodwood? Such a place, and such company! In short, if good sense would gratifye a good Taste, with whatever can make life agreeable, thither she must come for a Banquet.'[43] Richmond's old friend the Irish impresario Owen McSwiny, who he had first met in Venice while on his Grand Tour, was another frequent guest. McSwiny was very entertaining company and may well have brought the actress Peg Woffington with him; Emily raised her eye-brows at the 'extraordinary Match' and exclaimed, 'How can he [McSwiny] be such an old foole!'[44] When he died, McSwiny left Peg his entire estate.

The celebrated beauty, Peggy Banks, was a bosom companion of Richmond's daughters. Following her departure from Goodwood, Sam Chandler, Mayor of Portsmouth and nicknamed the 'Sussex Laureate' by his friends, penned the following lines:

> *'See how the Fawns surcease their wanton pranks*
> *Grieving the loss of pretty Peggy Banks,*
> *The woods, too, murmur, and the warbling grove*
> *Is silent, and endites no tale of Love.*
> *All Goodwood mourns . . .'*[45]

One gets a picture of a much-loved host and hostess who relished the company of lively and entertaining guests from diverse walks of life. The first duke's party-loving blood pulsed through his son's veins; however, it was tempered by his mother's gentleness, sincerity and sense of duty. His mother's brother, Uncle Cardigan, kept a close eye on his nephew and was anxious he did not slide into debt like his father. Six months after the first duke had died, Cardigan wrote from Deene (where Anne's body had recently been interred in the family vault) to his nephew to warn him of the perils that might engulf him if he continued overspending:

> *'I don't in the least doubt but you will easily forgive your poor Uncle Cardigan for the liberty he is going to take in laying before your Grace the state of your affairs, and the ill consequence that must attend if speedy remedy be not found. I am extremely concerned to find by your Uncle Brudenell that you have run very much into debt since the death of the late Lord Duke, when I had last the honour of seeing you, I took the liberty then to acquaint your Grace how much it wou'd redound to your honour to see your fathers debts payd, which you assured me was your full resolution of doing, and that you wou'd not run yourself into any expense till such a time as they were honestly and justly discharged, but your youth soon got the better of your intentions, tho I hope it is not too late to find out a way of making yourself and creditors easy, and the sooner it is done, the more happy you will be in all respects, for no man of honour can be easy when he sees his familys ruined for want of their just due, therefore I beg leave to make this proposal to your Grace, which I find by your*

> *Uncle Brudenell will be agreeable to you, and that is to borrow*
> *ten thousand pounds at Lady Day next, your Grace appointing*
> *two Trustees for the discharging of such Debts as shall be*
> *Specifyd, and for you to assign over £2,500 a year for five years,*
> *which will pay off both interest and Principal, it will likewise be*
> *necessary for your Grace to assign so much of your income to the*
> *Duchess of Richmond for her Pin-money, and housekeeping, and*
> *such a sum for your pocket money, and all these sums to be*
> *invested in the same Trustees hands, agane to be appointed by*
> *your Grace for the payment of your debts . . . By taking this*
> *method, you will find that all your Creditors will be easy and*
> *satisfied, and without doing something of this kind, they will*
> *soon become clamorous, and perhaps take such course of Law as*
> *may blast your reputation and character, which ought to be as*
> *dear to you as your life, and I make no doubt but your Grace has*
> *a just regard for both.'*

His letter did the trick although, a month later, Cardigan was urging
him to economise further on his household expenses.[46]

*   *   *

In Singleton parish church, the nearest place of worship to Charlton
and just over the hill from Goodwood, a conspicuous marble monument stands out. Unlike some of its neighbours, it commemorates
neither gentry nor clergy, but a huntsman: Tom Johnson. It was
erected by Richmond in memory of 'Old Tom' who had hunted the
Charlton hounds for ten very successful seasons before his death five
days before Christmas in 1744. Richmond may well have composed
the lines of Tom's epitaph himself:

> *'Here Johnson lies, What Hunter can deny*
> *Old, honest Tom the Tribute of a Sigh.*
> *Deaf is that Ear, which caught the op'ning Sound,*

> Dumb is that Tongue, which chear'd the Hills around.
> Unpleasing Truth Death hunts us from our Birth
> In view, and Men, like Foxes, take to Earth.'[47]

Various noblemen who had enjoyed hunting with Tom are inscribed on the monument, including the Duke of Marlborough and his brother, John Spencer, both of whom had initially recommended Tom as the replacement for John Ware, the drunken successor to Roper. Ware gets short shrift in the The Charleton Congress:

> 'that vilest Slave, the Huntsman, Ware, his name;
> alone, and drunk, went out and let the Pack
> kill fourteen Farmer's sheep, all in one day;
> Oh: fatall day!'[48]

Key to the success of the Charlton Hunt was the huntsman and Ware had never lived up to Roper's reputation. John Smith was chosen to succeed Tom, although he does not seem to have had the same celebrity status as Roper or Tom. Given the calibre of the Charlton Hunt members, only the best hunt servants would do.

Throughout the 1740s, the hunt membership swelled with illustrious names. The Earl of Lincoln was elected in 1742, joining his uncles, the Duke of Newcastle and Henry Pelham, both of whom were subscribers to the Great Room. Newcastle was Secretary of State and a staunch ally of Richmond. Three of Richmond's nephews – George, Augustus and William Keppel – were elected in 1745, 1748 and 1750 respectively. Both George and William were generals, the latter Commander-in-Chief in Ireland, and Augustus was later First Lord of the Admiralty. Henry Legge, who was elected in 1742, later became Chancellor of the Exchequer, while Robert Darcy, Earl of Holdernesse, who was elected in 1743, was the future Secretary of State for the North. William Cavendish, fourth Duke of Devonshire, became a member in 1745 and went on to become Prime Minister. The same year, John Lindsay, Earl of Crawford and the veteran of many continental campaigns, was elected. Another officer who was elected in the 1740s was the soldiers' hero John Manners, Marquess of Granby, after whom public houses up and down the country were named.

All of these leaders – political, social, military and naval – were brought together by a shared love of the chase and many of them were invited to stay at Goodwood. Understandably, Richmond was 'fitting up the old house, & endeavouring to make it as convenient, & comfortable as he can'.[49] This included building a new kitchen block in the classical style to cater for all the entertainment he was laying on. Some believed the new building was the commencement of Campbell's grandiose plans for a new house but an amateur drawing of the house at this date shows it to have been much simpler.[50]

Galloping over the South Downs in pursuit of the fox, the day-to-day worries that beset these leaders slipped away. Although noble birth bestowed on many of the followers huge privileges, it brought with it weighty responsibilities not only to family, households and landed estates, but also to the nation. Many felt this sense of duty keenly, none more so than Richmond himself. For Britain, the first half of the eighteenth century was far from peaceful with wars against Spain and France, the Hanoverian succession, the Jacobite uprisings and the South Sea Bubble all causing upset and anxiety. Many Charlton Hunt members were directly involved in some of these events, including the Jacobite Rebellion of 1745-46. Some of them played leading roles, including William Keppel, who was in charge of the front line at Culloden.

Many members would have known each other before they hunted together, particularly those involved in Government or Court, and business matters were no doubt discussed. Family members were always welcome; the day after Richmond consented to James Fitzgerald, Earl of Kildare marrying his daughter, Emily, he was elected a member at Charlton. At times, Charlton was filled to the gunnels with members, servants, grooms and horses and all the paraphernalia they entailed. In February 1748, Richmond made a note of where everyone was billeted in Charlton and the quarters for their horses; there was a total of 19 members and 143 horses.[51]

Richmond wrote to his wife from Charlton in March 1750: 'I am just come home from an exceeding fine Chase . . . This finishes the hunting season in Sussex for this time; & everybody butt myself goes away tomorrow', signing off, 'Adieu sweet love, I long to hear from you tonight, my love to all the Dear Children, your's my sweet angell, & only your's for ever & ever'.[52] Little did he realise that it was to be his last day's hunting.

Carné's Seat, the hilltop banqueting house built for the second Duke of Richmond in 1743 and described at the time as 'one of the finest Roomes in Britain'
(© The British Library Board)

4

Taming the Landscape

*'All my plantations in general flourish prodigiously . . . & our
verdure here is beyond what I ever saw anywhere . . . the whole
parke & gardens are in the highest beauty.'*

Charles, second Duke of Richmond to
Peter Collinson, 1746[1]

The sash windows of Goodwood House were thrown open on a
balmy summer's afternoon. Across the park you could just make
out a small gathering of people dotted around an expanse of grass,
their white shirts catching the light. A dull thwack followed by a brief
pause and a ripple of applause were the only sounds drifting back.
There was a cricket match taking place.

When the game had finished, the 'gamesters' strolled back towards
the house in the hazy sunshine, the two umpires sweltering in their
heavy frock coats and tricorn hats. Reaching the gravel sweep, the
gentlemen passed into the house through the front door, dropping
their curved willow bats in the Great Hall, while the estate employees
skirted round the back of the house in the direction of the Servants'
Hall. Refreshments beckoned – game pie and meats, followed by

plum pudding, for those in the dining-room; meat and vegetables, followed by apple pie and cheese, for those below stairs. To quench their thirst, their host, the second Duke of Richmond, provided endless glasses of claret for the gentry and brimming tankards of ale for the lower orders.

Richmond was a passionate cricketer who was bitten by the bug at an early age. His father had been a keen cricketer who enjoyed both the game and the entertainment that went with it; brandy (costing one shilling and sixpence) was handed out when he had 'plaid at Cricket with [the] Arundel men' in 1702.[2] Cricket was by no means new to Sussex; as early as 1622, some young men in neighbouring Boxgrove had been reprimanded for playing cricket in the churchyard on a Sunday.[3] But it was Richmond who really put organised cricket on the map in the county.[4] Challenging his friend Sir William Gage of Firle to a match in 1725, his team went on to play matches in London, Surrey and Kent as well as Sussex. In 1727, he organised two matches against Alan Brodrick of Peper Harow's team, drawing up on a small piece of folded paper some 'Articles of Agreement . . . (for two Cricket Matches) concluded the Eleventh of July 1727'.[5] They played twelve a side and a caveat was included for the captains – Richmond and Brodrick were allowed to speak out against the umpire. And, of course, there was a wager: 'Each Match shall be for twelve Guineas'. These sixteen 'articles' or laws are the earliest known written rules of cricket in existence.

Richmond's cricketing career came to an abrupt end when an iron fireback fell on him in May 1732, breaking his leg.[6] Despite access to the very best surgeons of the day, he did not recover until February of the following year when Colley Cibber wrote to him: '. . . heartily wishing that your leg may be able to run up and down stairs after my Lady Duchess as long as you live'.[7] However, the summer was not quite the same without his cricketing diversions, so he took the nearby Slindon team under his wing and under his patronage it became the greatest team in England. It was led by the three Newland brothers who all played for England. 1742 was probably their best year, when the

Slindon eleven won 43 out of 44 matches played. Two years later, following a match in London, Richmond crumpled up the scorecard, and popped it into his pocket. Little did he realise that one day it would be the earliest scorecard ever to have been recorded.[8]

This love of cricket was shared by all of Richmond's family. Sarah Richmond often sponsored matches and helped plan them, while their two sons enjoyed playing the game. Charles, the eldest, was a very capable cricketer, captaining Sussex against Hambledon at Goodwood in 1768. Even his gung-ho sister, Sarah, played cricket. When the diarist Hester Thrale saw Sir Joshua Reynold's bravura portrait of her sacrificing to the Graces, she remarked: 'She [Sarah] never did sacrifice to the Graces. Her face was gloriously handsome, but she used to play cricket and eat beefsteaks on the Steyne at Brighton.'

*   *   *

In the stillness of High Wood, a stone lioness reclines on top of a smart rectangular plinth, her gaze directed towards the spire of Chichester Cathedral glinting in the distance. The silence, only interrupted by birdsong, is a far cry from the sounds that resonated through the park nearly three hundred years ago when the lioness it commemorates was alive. Back then, her roar would have mingled with that of leopards and tigers, the howling of wolves and jackals, the barking of husky dogs, the snorting of wild boar, the grunting of Indian pigs, the laughing of monkeys and baboons, the meowing of cats, the chirping of ostriches, the screaming of vultures and the hooting of owls. All of these birds and animals at one time or another lived in the second Duke of Richmond's menagerie at Goodwood. Under his tenure, the house and grounds really began to flourish.

Richmond was born at just the right time for someone with an enquiring mind, coinciding as he did with the Age of Enlightenment, which transformed scientific thinking. He took a keen interest in natural history and his menagerie was the ultimate expression of this passion. Through his wife, he was related to Sir Hans Sloane, the

famous physician, naturalist and collector, who was president of the
Royal Society. Aged only twenty-two, Richmond was elected a Fellow
of the Royal Society, probably owing to Sloane's influence. When
Richmond or a member of the family was ill, Sloane was called upon
to act as physician; when one of his animals took a turn for the worse,
Sloane acted as his private vet.

The Goodwood menagerie followed a long tradition of mainly
Royal menageries, stretching back to the time of Henry I who had a
menagerie at Woodstock Palace in Oxfordshire. Botanical gardens
with menageries attached were created in Europe during the
Renaissance, the most famous being Louis XIV's menagerie at
Versailles. Richmond used his extensive network of contacts to send
him birds and animals from the most far-flung corners of the globe, so
his menagerie was stocked with beasts from both the East and West
Indies, Africa and Asia.[9] Lord Baltimore brought over a bear for him,
presumably from America where he was Proprietary Governor of
Maryland, while in 1744 Sir Thomas Robinson sent him 'one of the
most beautiful Civit Cats I ever saw' from Barbados.[10] The animals
arrived by sea, usually via London, and were then transported to
Goodwood at considerable cost. Unsurprisingly, some of them did not
survive the journey, the most unfortunate being an elephant that died
in a fire at sea in 1730; others lived only for a short time after their
arrival.[11]

With all of these exotic animals living in relatively close proximity
to one another, it was imperative that they were safely housed. The
larger animals were kept in iron cages, constructed at huge expense
– that for a tiger cost £93 and was 15 feet square. The smaller animals
and birds – such as eagles, monkeys, cats and dogs – were chained.[12]

Feeding the animals was a mammoth task. The meat-eaters ate 36
lbs of beef a day and 39 lbs of horse flesh. In 1729 and 1730, Richmond
was buying between 140 and 156 loaves of bread each week. The variety
of food was huge: barley and oatmeal for the fowl; greens, apples,
carrots and bread for the monkeys; sheep's heads, beef and bullocks'
hearts for the eagles; hay, oats and turnips for the sheep . . . to name

but a few. Often, food was in short supply, which led to the keeper of the animals, Henry Foster, exclaiming, 'I am afraid we shall have a famine amongst the animals.'[13]

When an animal was ill, Hans Sloane was called in as well as John Ranby, soon to be made surgeon to the king's household. Once dead, an animal was often sent to them for examination and dissection. This was all part of the spirit of the age where there was an endless quest for knowledge and understanding as hitherto unknown species arrived in England. It was also the age when biologists and botanists were classifying species, led by the indefatigable Carl Linnaeus, who visited England in 1736.

As well as sharing his beasts with his own circle of educated friends, Richmond allowed the general public to visit the menagerie. In April 1730, Henry Foster reported to Richmond that 'we are very much troubled with rude company to see ye animals. Sunday last week we had about 4 or 5 hundred good and bad . . .'[14]

Being of a jovial character, Richmond was often having his leg pulled about his menagerie. Writing to him in 1732, Lord Hervey likens 'the Loves, Courtship and Marriages of your Beasts' to 'the whole matrimonial World . . . The marriages of your bears, tigers, wolves and monkeys would certainly do for a representation of half the conjugal performances in England.' He goes on to make reference to mutual acquaintances of theirs:

> 'For example if you were to talk of a marriage between a great She-Bear and an old Baboon, in order figuratively to describe the sweet union of my Lord and Lady St. John, or if you told us in delineating the D. & D. of M—r, that one of your She-Tygers was wedded to a Jack-ass, People would immediately see that the Account was feign'd in order to satirize these People . . . If I was to take up Lady Hervey's visiting book I am sure I could, by that assistance to my memory, humanise as many beasts as Snyder ever painted, or as you and Noah every protected.'[15]

The menagerie was located at the top of the park. Surrounded by a high flint wall with a ha-ha at the front, it was the perfect distance from the house – far enough away to keep the family out of danger and away from any unpleasant smells and sounds, yet close enough for a vigorous morning or afternoon's walk with guests. Richmond enjoyed taking his friends and relations for a perambulation of his garden and grounds. One of the highlights was Rock Dell, a ruined hermitage, constructed in a sunken area in High Wood, the name of his pleasure ground. Here, unsuspecting guests would stroll nonchalantly with their host, admiring the garden features built into the banks. The peaceful scene was enhanced by the gentle trickle of water, emanating from a classical shell house and flowing into a glassy pool in the middle. Resting their hands on his arm to steady their progress down the steep slope, they would poke their noses into a tiny 'Hermit's Cell'. Taking a moment to adjust to the sudden darkness, a strange snuffling sound would suddenly sharpen their senses; as they peered through the darkness into an inner cell, horror of horrors, there was a live baboon staring, equally shocked, back at them. Shrill screams would ensue followed by hearty laughter on the duke's part; more was to come. Nearby, he had constructed a 'Ruined Abbey', a mock Gothic doorway using fragments of Gothic tracery. Here, his by now wary guests entered in trepidation. Moments later, many would come hurtling out in terror. For inside they had discovered, gently padding back and forth behind an iron grille, none other than the king of beasts.

The 'Ruined Abbey' forms the entrance to a small series of tunnels, neatly lined in brick. Richmond's exotic animals were released into the other end of the tunnels and would appear lurking behind the grille – an exhilarating and terrifying experience for any visitor. One tunnel ends in a long deep ditch, traditionally known as the Lion Run. Another tunnel comes out nearer the house where the entrance is lined with broken flints, giving it the appearance of a naturally-formed tunnel. These tunnels were turned to a more macabre use in the 1740s when the menagerie was clearly in decline. Richmond's daughter,

Emily, wrote from her home in Ireland: 'I find the fate of all the unlucky animals that come to Goodwood is to be burying them in the Catacombs . . .'[16] As her father's interest in the menagerie waned – probably for practical and financial reasons – the dead animals were buried in the tunnels in the manner of Roman catacombs. The tunnels were then filled in and, generations later, as fact morphed into myth, they became the subject of wild speculation.

*   *   *

George Vertue, the celebrated antiquary, sat beside Richmond in his chaise. It was drawn by a team of six miniature horses, their black glossy coats shining in the June morning sun. Vertue noted with enthusiasm that they were 'a set of so rare & so small that each horse (black plump & round) [did] not exceed 9 hands – about a yard high'.[17] This perfect little scene was completed by a petite postilion and a young coachman resplendent in the Richmond livery, their gilt buttons glistening in the sunlight. Despite the size of their steeds, they were drawn 'with great spirit and swiftness' through the grounds of Goodwood. Richmond's face was beaming as he sped along.[18] He was an ardent gardener and this was his favourite time of year.

The intoxicating scent of *Magnolia grandiflora* wafted through the trees. It had only been introduced into England thirteen years earlier and Richmond's specimens were among the best in the country so he was justifiably proud of them.[19] He was at the forefront of English horticulture and Goodwood was becoming well known for its flowers and trees. Richmond was among a select group of gardeners obtaining seeds and plants from John Bartram in Philadelphia via the cloth merchant Peter Collinson. Bartram found an eager audience with an insatiable appetite for hitherto unknown exotics imported from the newly explored territories in America. Through Collinson, Bartram supplied a small group of English subscribers with his seed boxes, one of whom was Richmond. Another subscriber was Richmond's friend, Lord Petre, a young and enthusiastic landowner who transformed his park at Thorndon in Essex by the planting of 40,000 trees. Petre referred to his fellow horticulturalists as 'my brother Gardeners', a tightly knit circle that included Philip Miller, curator of the Apothecaries' Garden in Chelsea (now the Chelsea Physic Garden). While Richmond and Petre provided wealth and land to experiment with, Collinson and Miller provided expertise and, in Collinson's case, the trade connection with America.[20] Miller was regarded as the best gardener in the country and he advised Richmond on the gardens at Goodwood. His extensive planting scheme, dated 1735, lists all the flowers for a border 430 feet long.[21] Not surprisingly, the gardens were a hive of activity with gardeners beavering away. This came at a cost – Miller estimated the annual cost (including staff) of both kitchen garden and pleasure garden to total an enormous £271 10s 10d.[22]

Tragically, Petre died aged only twenty-nine. On the one hand, Richmond was distraught at the loss of his 'brother gardener'; on the other, he could not refrain himself from trying to get his hands on some of Petre's young trees and shrubs that his widow was willing to sell. In one of his many chatty and humorous letters to Collinson, he says: 'The small magnolias are confounded dear, butt I must have them, though I believe nobody else will be fool enough to buy any at that price.'[23] They also betray the scale on which he was buying: 'I want some small cedars of Lebanon that is from six inches to three foot high . . . & about 100 of the Common Thuya . . . I don't so much as mention the number of cedars of Lebanon, because the more I could have the better, for I propose making a mount Lebanon upon a very high hill.'[24] Collinson reckoned Richmond's collection of 'Exotic hardy Trees' to be 'the best . . . that was then in England' and, just after his death, Bishop Richard Pococke was able to write that 'this place is most famous for a great variety of forest trees and shrubs; they have thirty different kinds of oaks, and four hundred different American trees and shrubs, which compose one wilderness. This place was very agreeable when it was inhabited by the most amiable couple in the world, the late Duke and Dutchess.'[25]

'Honest Peter', as Richmond sometimes called Collinson, was clearly great company and regularly stayed at Goodwood as well as a host of other stately homes, including Woburn Abbey in Bedfordshire, the Duke of Bedford's seat. Their friendship was close enough to giggle about a mutual acquaintance, John Hill. Writing to Collinson in 1741, Richmond says: 'Hill the apothecary is now with me, he's a well behaved fellow, butt between you and I is not he what wee call a *puppy*?'[26] The following year, Hill was staying at Goodwood again prompting Richmond to write: 'I shew'd your rime to Hill, & hope it may do him some good, butt he like a thousand other odd dogs pikes himself *most* upon what he knows *least*. Gallantry seems to be his favorite passion, which he is no more cut out for than a quaker is for dancing a minuet.'[27] Hill, the butt of their jokes, variously tried his hand at acting and journalism, whilst also helping Richmond with his garden and collection of dried plants (known as a herbaria). His book *Exotic Botany* still sits on the shelves of the library at Goodwood, although it would have arrived after Richmond's tragic early death.

Other books that still line the shelves include Miller's *Gardeners Dictionary* (1737), the first of its kind, and Mark Catesby's *Natural History of Carolina, Florida and the Bahama Islands* (1729-43). The latter was a groundbreaking publication that opened people's eyes to the beauty of American flowering trees and shrubs, meticulously observed in Catesby's coloured engravings. By subscribing to publications such as these, Richmond was encouraging talented individuals; the unprecedented colonial expansion of the age had exposed them to a whole new world of flora and fauna. It also had its perks for the duke – Catesby included his pet 'Java Hare', a sweet little Brazilian agouti, in his Appendix.[28]

Such was Richmond's clout, he also managed to get his 'Greenland Deer' included in George Edwards' *Natural History of Birds* (1743) in addition to some of the exotic birds he kept in his aviary at Richmond House in London.[29] Edwards was a talented young artist who had been introduced to Richmond by Hans Sloane. When Edwards published the French edition – French being the international language – he dedicated one volume to Richmond and one to his wife, Sarah, in gratitude for their support. After Richmond's untimely death, Edwards went on to publish *Gleanings of Natural History* (1758, 1760 and 1764), noting four patrons who were 'the greatest promoters of learning, science, and arts, of any in the present age'. The first of these was Richmond, 'noble in his lineage and descent from the Royal house of these kingdoms, but still more noble and great from the innate magnificence, generosity, and goodness of his soul . . . his doors were always open to men of learning, science and ingenuity.'[30] The other three patrons were Sloane, Dr Richard Meade and Richmond's great friend Martin Folkes, Sloane's successor as President of the Royal Society.

*   *   *

On Christmas Day, 1762, Emily wrote from Ireland to her husband:

> 'My dear Angel
>   'I wish you a merry Christmas and a happy New Year. If you are at Goodwood, and that the sun shines as bright as it does here, I hope you will take a walk up to Carne Seat, sit down in the little room, and think of that you took with Lady Emily Lennox, just return'd from Bognor Church, sixteen years ago, and believe that I love you sixteen times better now than I did then.'[31]

When Emily was seduced by her soon-to-be husband, she was only fifteen years old and he was a lusty twenty-four-year-old. They could not have picked a more romantic spot for their amour. Carné's Seat, a hilltop banqueting house in the park at Goodwood, had only just been completed for her father to the designs of Roger Morris. It commanded a magnificent view south across the deer-peppered park, over Richmond's beloved American grove with the roof leads of the house just visible, taking in the city of Chichester with its pointed cathedral spire, and fading away with the sea glinting on the horizon and the hills of the Isle of Wight rising to the west. Inside, on the raised ground floor, a handsome reception room with painted classical ceiling was used for dining. Emily and Kildare would have cosied up in the miniature arcade room below, designed for the use of Emily and her younger siblings, complete with diminutive fireplace.

Richmond had named his pavilion after Monsieur de Carné, a faithful retainer of Louise de Keroualle whose wooden cottage it replaced. Here, he could retreat from the hustle and bustle of the main house and entertain in privacy. It was approached from the north, via a ride cut through a plantation. Stepping out of their carriages, visitors would pass through a smart iron gate, walk down some steps, and enter under the dome of the portico painted with the planets as they were aligned on the day Richmond was born. As yet unaware of the view owing to the dense planting either side, it was only once inside that all was revealed through the octagonal glazed windows of the loggia.

Outside, there was a small pleasure garden planted up with flowering shrubs and laurels interspersed with meandering paths. Hidden in the trees was an elegant privy, a small octagonal building with a central door opening to reveal three fitted seats side by side.[32] Close by, emerging from the undergrowth, was Goodwood's secret jewel, the Shell House. This was the creation of Sarah, who had been collecting shells assiduously for a decade. Thomas Robinson, ever the attentive friend, wrote from Barbados to Richmond: 'The Vessel that carrys this, will bring Your Grace one of [the] most beautiful Civit Cats I ever saw. – and I am now making a Collection for the Dutchess of Richmond of Shells – as we hear her Grace is fitting up a Grotto under one of the finest Roomes [Carné's Seat] in Britain built lately in Goodwood Park by Your Grace.'[33] Although he got the precise location wrong, word had reached the West Indies about her creation. Other sea captains on voyages of discovery brought back huge quantities of shells for Sarah: 'I have a small ship load of shells for the Dukes of Bedford and Richmond', wrote Captain Charles Knowles of HMS *Diamond* from Jamaica.[34] By the time of its completion, Sarah had more than enough, prompting Richmond to tell Collinson: 'The Dss of Richmond thanks you, butt she will purchase no shells as she had more given her than she knows what to do with.'[35]

Like Carné's Seat, the Shell House was designed along strict Palladian lines, probably by Roger Morris. The exterior glistened in the sunshine like some kind of giant crustacean, the surface encrusted with myriad shells of all shapes and sizes. The asymmetry of the shell work on the outside contrasted with the strict geometry and near perfection of the interior: the walls and ceiling were completely covered with a brilliant array of shells formed into a pair of miniature fireplaces below elegant swags, niches containing urns and pedestals, overflowing baskets and cornucopia and a coffered ceiling alive with flower heads formed from shells. Professionals probably did most of the work, although Sarah and her daughters may have lent a hand. Four panels survive with Richmond, Sarah, Caroline and Emily's initials as a mark of their work. Perhaps Kildare was allowed a sneak preview of his wife's handiwork on Christmas Day 1746.

Emily was not the only member of her family to find romance in the gardens and grounds of Goodwood. Sarah wrote to her husband at the end of the summer in 1740:

> 'My dear Angel
>
> 'Of all the time that I have lov'd you I never felt more love and tenderness for you, than I did yesterday. I haunted all the places where you had been last, one was to go among your new trees where you stood so long on Sunday, and I sat in a little roome an hour, which you give me the Key of, my children I kis'd till they ware tier'd with it, a little for their own sakes but much more for their being yours . . .'[36]

Perhaps Richmond had given her the key to the 'Lapland House' which Lady Newdigate saw when she visited Goodwood in 1747, or even the Parrot House, a building 'in ye woods . . . for Macaws wch fly about and add infinitely to the beauty of them'.[37]

In Georgian England, much entertainment took place in gardens and parks, so it is no surprise to find Vertue being taken to Carné's Seat where he 'had the pleasure to accompany their graces – with other Gentlem. to drink tea & c their coaches & equipages attending in great magnificence & state'.[38] Long summer days at Goodwood might have ended with a dessert of syllabub and fresh strawberries in the classical Temple of Neptune and Minerva, standing on a man-made grass mound a stone's throw from the house.[39] Here, guests could quietly watch the sun setting as the soft evening light filled the temple. Vertue made a quick sketch of it in his notebook during his visit, showing the pedimented roof above a triple-arcaded front with balustrade; the trees and shrubs of High Wood close in around the back and the sides.[40] The statues of Neptune and Minerva are just discernible in their niches, flanking an ancient Roman tablet that had been dug up by workmen in Chichester in 1723 and acquired later by the duke when he erected the temple to display it. Like Vertue, Richmond was a keen antiquarian, being elected a Fellow of the Society of Antiquaries in 1736 and its president in 1750, just before he died. Vertue excitedly sketched a stone coffin from Tortington Priory near Arundel that Richmond had placed in the garden and an ancient standing stone erected near Rock Dell.[41]

*   *   *

Richmond's son, Charles, was a keen sportsman and loved nothing better than a hard game of tennis. Charles II had been a regular tennis player, so it was no surprise to find his great-grandson throwing himself around a 'royal' tennis court. Young Charles Richmond's appointment diary for 1761 reveals him playing as much as five times a week when he was up in London.[42] He often laid bets on the outcome of his sets, losing £21 on one occasion. It was not long before he built a 'royal' or 'real' tennis court at Goodwood, situated just outside the park, south of the house. A new kitchen garden was established around it to provide fresh fruit and vegetables for his ever-growing household and no doubt some on-the-spot refreshment after a tennis match.

By 1761, Charles Richmond was already married. His bride was the pretty Lady Mary Bruce, only child of the Earl of Elgin and Ailesbury and his much younger third wife, Caroline. When Mary was only six years old, her father had died and her socialite mother had gone on to marry Henry Seymour Conway, a well-known general and politician. Conway was very close to his cousin, Horace Walpole, who was delighted with the Richmonds' union: 'it is the perfectest match in the world; youth, beauty, riches, alliances, and all the blood of all the kings from Robert Bruce to Charles II. They are the prettiest couple in England . . .'[43]

Orphaned as a teenager, Charles had had to engineer his own marriage, writing to his prospective step-father-in-law: '. . . ev'ry time I see her [Mary] I like her better & find in her ev'ry thing I could wish, I am eager to know if there are no obstacles to my Happiness, that if there are not I may accelerate it as much as possible'.[44] He goes on to ask Conway and his wife to sound out Mary, thereby preparing her for a verbal proposal. He need not have worried; they were married at the Conways' house on 1 April 1757 when he was twenty-two and she was seventeen. Mary's portrait by Sir Joshua Reynolds shows a demure, gentle creature quietly doing her needlework and dressed in a plain brown riding habit. Emily told her husband that she 'is most excessively pleasing . . . is sweetly pretty . . . as tall as me and very fair; quite girlish, unaffected and merry. I like what I see of her hitherto mightily.'[45] There was much amusement when Emily's boys were playing with Mary's nine-year-old half-sister, Anne: 'There is a vast friendship between William and Miss Conway; they play all day at being the Duke and Duchess of Richmond, and kissing eternally as they do.'[46]

Charles's overly protective eldest sister, Caroline, could not quite work Mary out. A year and a half after their marriage, she confided in Emily, 'She is so simple! It provokes one, but at the same time so excessively good-humoured, one is angry at feeling provoked with her.'[47] Used to stimulating intellectual conversation and analysing every situation that came her way, Caroline found her new sister-in-law baffling. A few weeks later, she wrote to Emily: 'The Duchess seems made to pass thro' life more happily than most people, very good health, great good humour and very little sensibility . . . there is a roughness in her that is not pleasing at all, and a very good opinion of herself . . . Altogether she is an odd character and not the kind of woman I should have thought my brother would have chosen; but I dare say they will be very happy.'[48] Charles seemed blind to his wife's failings, telling Caroline that she was being 'very kind to his Duchess', entertaining her while he was away, when in reality Caroline was trying to keep her on the straight and narrow. Caroline confessed to Emily that this naivety in her brother 'drew tears from my eyes, which is foolish, for its much better surely to have him deceive himself that way'.[49]

Mary's innocent charm and *joie de vivre* got her into trouble in the early years of their marriage. While her husband was abroad with the army, she was gallivanting about town. Charles's siblings were alarmed at what the gossips were saying. Caroline, writing to Emily, reported:

'George is much disturbed at some little imprudence of the Duchess of Richmond's among others. T'other night when Louisa and she were at the play together, the former went away before the farce, which the Duchess having a mind to see stay'd, the only woman in the box, with a Mr Medows and some other gentleman. George was out of town, and heard of it as an extraordinary thing, and told her of it; she insists upon it, he is such a prude, and that there is nothing in it. She means no harm, she says, and there is no persuading her a young woman's character may be vastly hurt without her meaning the least harm . . . George thinks too and I agree with him, that racketing about to the degree she does, my poor dear brother abroad, is not quite decent; you have no idea how she routs about. We don't mean she should shut herself up, but it's too much. She is beautiful this year, more admired by the men than anybody, which she likes. Prince Edward and Mr Thin always at her ear in public. George says always five or six men about her, she laughing loud and talking a great deal, all this in public from morning till night, and her husband abroad. I really *fear, poor thing, with the most innocent intentions (for I'm sure she loves my brother of all things) she will hurt her character. . . . I can't bear the thoughts of my brother's wife and the Duchess of Richmond's being on the footing of the fine flirting ladies about.'*[50]

Mary did not seem unduly concerned and admitted she preferred the company of men, telling Caroline that 'she knew the women hated her because the men liked her, and would be glad to get any stories of her'.[51] Caroline tried to show her the error of her ways, only for Mary to respond that 'she meant no harm, that 'twas mighty natural for her who loved being in public to divert herself as much as she could, when my brother was away, that when he was here she loved being with him better than anything else, and he not loving public places she prefer'd his company'.[52] Caroline was alarmed by the 'verses or love letters, *anonymous ones*, sent her continually' by her male admirers but admitted that men admired 'her good understanding because she has no foolish female delicacies'.[53] Still trying to fathom her character, Caroline goes on to say: 'She is an odd composition. George says she has good sense, which I doubt; that she has infinite good humour, no envy in her temper, nor no resentment is certain, and yet she has one quality that makes a sort of contradiction to the rest, a vast deal of pride. Feelings, what you and I mean by them, to be sure she has none.'[54]

Six months later, Caroline was relieved that her sister-in-law had calmed down: 'You can't imagine how much our Duchess improves; she seems to have discarded all her lovers. If my brother stays always at home for these next two or three years at least, she will do vastly well. She has the most perfect confidence in him, tells him everything in the world, the least trifling even, loves him as well as she can love anything, and grows more formed a great deal. He loves her ten times better than ever he did. It's vast pleasure to me to think that will be a happy marriage. She was so giddy when he was abroad last year I really was afraid about her.'[55] Caroline put the blame on her mother (who she felt was lacking in maternal devotion) and her upbringing: 'The more I see

Louise de Keroualle, the baby-faced Breton who captured Charles II's heart. She is depicted as Venus with her son, Charles, first Duke of Richmond, portrayed as Cupid in this double portrait by Henri Gascars.
(© Trustees of the Goodwood Collection)

The second Duke and Duchess of Richmond who were married to settle a gambling debt between their fathers. Their arranged marriage later became a union of love. Portrait by Jonathan Richardson. *(© Trustees of the Goodwood Collection)*

Charles, first Duke of Richmond, whose good looks belied his weak character, painted by Sir Godfrey Kneller. *(© Trustees of the Goodwood Collection)*

The saintly Anne, Duchess of Richmond, long-suffering wife of the first duke, by Sir Godfrey Kneller. *(© Trustees of the Goodwood Collection)*

Goodwood House painted by Samuel Grimm in 1782, a bucolic scene of horses lazily grazing in the park with the house and stables beyond. *(© The British Library Board)*

The Shell House was the creation of Sarah, Duchess of Richmond, who collected shells for nearly ten years before its completion in 1748. *(Photograph: Clive Boursnell © Trustees of the Goodwood Collection)*

Canaletto's famous view of Whitehall from Richmond House, commissioned by the second Duke of Richmond in 1746. *(© Trustees of the Goodwood Collection)*

Lady Caroline Lennox is among the children on stage in a performance of *The Indian Emperor* in 1732. Her father, the second Duke of Richmond, leans on the back of his wife's chair. Painting by William Hogarth. *(Private Collection)*

Racehorses Exercising at Goodwood, one of three sporting scenes painted by George Stubbs during his nine-month stay at Goodwood, 1759–60. (© *Trustees of the Goodwood Collection*)

THE WAY TO KEEP HIM AS PERFORM'D AT THE RICHMOND THEATRE &c.

Charles, third Duke of Richmond, watches a performance of the comedy *The Way to Keep Him* at his private theatre at Richmond House. (© *Trustees of the Goodwood Collection*)

Lord George Lennox, younger brother of the third Duke of Richmond, painted on his Grand Tour by Pompeo Batoni.
(© Trustees of the Goodwood Collection)

Charles, third Duke of Richmond, on his Grand Tour by Batoni. 'He loves dogs prodigiously,' said his tutor. *(© Trustees of the Goodwood Collection)*

Sir Joshua Reynolds's portrait of the third Duke of Richmond. Walpole admired his handsome and noble appearance.
(© Trustees of the Goodwood Collection)

Mary, Duchess of Richmond, by Reynolds, informally dressed in her riding habit.
(© Trustees of the Goodwood Collection)

The Tapestry Drawing Room, created by James Wyatt to display the set of Gobelins tapestries given to the third Duke of Richmond by Louis XV. *(Photograph: James Fennell)*

The Egyptian Dining-Room, restored to its former glory in the 1990s by the current Duke of Richmond. *(© Trustees of the Goodwood Collection)*

Part of the Sèvres service made for the third Duke of Richmond when he was ambassador in Paris, 1765–66. The birds were copied from George Edwards's *Natural History of Birds*.
(Photograph: Clive Boursnell © Trustees of the Goodwood Collection)

Waterloo memorabilia: the guest list for the Duchess of Richmond's ball; two Waterloo medals (for the duchess and the Earl of March); Napoleon's breakfast plate; two French hat badges; and a silhouette of Charles, fourth Duke of Richmond. *(Photograph: Clive Boursnell © Trustees of the Goodwood Collection)*

The Duchess of Richmond's ball at the moment the Duke of Wellington was told of Napoleon's alarming advance. Several of the guests were killed at Waterloo three days later. *(Photograph: Stephen Hayward © Trustees of the Goodwood Collection)*

The first horsebox designed to take Elis from Goodwood to Doncaster, where he won the St Leger in 1836. Painting by Abraham Cooper. *(© Trustees of the Goodwood Collection)*

the Duchess the more I blame Lady Ailesbury every day. Poor thing, she has I'm sure had no advantages from her education, and was quite a wild untaught thing turn'd loose.'[56]

*   *   *

A faint 'snip-snip' sound could be heard coming from the flower garden at Goodwood. Mary was gathering roses, lost in her own thoughts as she pulled the heavy boughs towards her. A gentle stroll down to the garden was part of her daily routine, especially in midsummer when the roses were in full bloom. In 1776, Sarah had remarked on a change in her sister-in-law: 'The Duchess has taken more to planting and Goodwood than ever I saw her do. She won't allow it, but I never saw her seem to enjoy home so much, and therefore I never saw her so comfortable – agreeable she always is.'[57]

In her thirties, Mary had built a charming 'Gothick' dairy, a short walk to the west of the house that could be visited as part of a tour of the grounds. Built in flint with neat stone dressings, the exterior is designed to look like a small church. Mary was probably inspired by her great friend, Horace Walpole, whose home Strawberry Hill was a perfect essay in the 'Gothick' style. Inside, a little refreshment room was decorated to evoke the atmosphere of an ancient monastic building – what Walpole called 'gloomth'. Figures bearing shields, emblazoned with the arms of Lennox, Keroualle, Brudenell and Cadogan, embellished the buttresses of the carved oak ceiling. Windows composed of 'ancient coloured glass' added to the effect.[58] A short flight of stone steps led down to a room with a large north-facing gothic window and vaulted ceiling. Stone shelves at waist height on three sides of the room were used for storing cream, butter and cheese in appropriate chinaware.

There was a tradition among aristocratic ladies for presiding over ornamental dairies. The dairy was seen as a suitably female preserve, conjuring up notions of purity, domesticity and abundance. Drinking milk became fashionable in the latter decades of the eighteenth century, fuelled by Josiah Wedgewood's range of dairy ware that became all the rage.[59] Mary could subtly demonstrate her feminine virtues by taking her lady friends for a healthy drink of milk in her dairy while also displaying her knowledge of the fashionable 'Gothick' style. Behind the scenes, servants could do the real hard graft and come and go unseen from the rear entrance, which opened on to Laundry Green, a square of lawn where the household laundry was aired and dried.

James Wyatt was probably the architect responsible for the design of the dairy, having worked at Goodwood since the 1770s. Wyatt also designed an Orangery for Mary's husband, Charles. Light and airy with tall arched windows, orange trees and shrubs could be brought inside over the cold winter months. Just outside stood a fine tulip tree planted by Mary's father-in-law, the second duke, in 1739. In summer, its profusion of tulip-shaped flowers emitted a subtle scent resembling cucumber.[60]

The trees at Goodwood were a lasting legacy of the second duke. A decade and a half after his death, Collinson wrote to a friend: 'As often as I survey my Garden & Plantations it reminds Mee of my Absent Friends by their Living Donations . . . Look Yonder at the Late Benevolent Duke of Richmond, His Everlasting Cedars of Lebanon will Endure when you & I & He is forgot. See with what Vigor they Tower away, how their Stems enlarge & their Branches extend . . .'[61] Young Charles Richmond took on his father's tree-planting mantle, using Collinson to buy trees, plants, seeds and shrubs. He wrote to Collinson from his London house in 1756: 'Friend Peter, I have several things to say to you about plantations & a long list of seeds which I must beg of you to procure for me . . . May I therefore beg of you to come & eat some Roast Beef with my wife & I tomorrow? We dine about four o'clock if you'l come an hour sooner we may do all business before dinner.'[62] In 1760, he asked Collinson to get him one thousand cedars of Lebanon for planting that autumn and the following spring at Goodwood.[63] Two years later and much to his frustration, there were 'not five of the five hundred left with one leaf on' in one of the plantations, so he ordered another hundred cedars.[64]

*   *   *

'Poor Mr Ogilvie has been near killed at Goodwood by an astonishing indiscretion of his own. He went, yes, and with one of his daughters, and without even a stick, into an enclosure where the Duke keeps an elk. The animal attacked him, threw him down, gored him, bruised him – in short, he is not yet out of danger.'[65]

William Ogilvie had a lucky escape. As the *London Chronicle* reported, 'had it not been for the loud and continued shrieks of his daughter, he would have been killed on the spot'.[66] It must have been a terrifying experience for the twelve-year-old Mimi standing powerless as her father was attacked by a moose (mistakenly called an elk). He was wounded in no fewer than fifty places.

Ogilvie, a dour Scot, was the second husband of Emily. She had married her sons' tutor after her first husband's death, and went on to have three children by him bringing the tally of her progeny to twenty-two. Over time, her family warmed to him and he proved a loving stepfather to those of her children who were still at home. The moose was owned by Emily's brother, Charles, third Duke of Richmond.

Although Richmond did not keep the menagerie after his father's untimely death in 1750, he did have some wild animals at Goodwood, including a wolf that once attacked him, ripping off the skirt of his coat as he fled from the scene.[67] From 1766, and over the course of the next seven years, he acquired four different moose from North America. The third one, a male obtained from General Carleton, Governor-General of Canada, was painted by George Stubbs for Dr William Hunter as part of a scientific study.[68] Hunter was the first Professor of Anatomy at the newly established Royal Academy. He was keen to prove that the North American moose was not descended from the ancient Irish elk, so he asked Stubbs to paint a pair of fully grown moose antlers in the foreground. Richmond was a keen supporter of Hunter and may well have given him Owen Farrell's (a famous dwarf) skeleton and portrait that had belonged to his father.[69] He was also an important early patron of Stubbs and later bought a painting of a lioness in a rocky outcrop with two lions prowling close by. The painting hangs at Goodwood to this day, a vivid reminder of the beasts that once roamed the grounds.

Richmond's interest in natural history was sparked by that of his father. However, it was his tutor, the scientist Abraham Trembley, who really sowed the seeds. On his Grand Tour, Trembley, who was one of the leading educators of the age, introduced him to some of the foremost intellectuals of the day, such as the scientist and naturalist René-Antoine Ferchault de Réamur. Richmond then studied science at the University of Leiden under the Swiss botanist Professor Frédéric-Louis Allamand.

Back at Goodwood, Richmond turned what had been the menagerie into the Pheasantry, a sheltered and enclosed spot to rear pheasants and house rare birds. Originally a chalk pit, the land formed an amphitheatre with steep wooded banks on both sides framing a simple classical folly at the rear. On the turfed terrace that ran around the top of the bank, Richmond added an urn-topped column as an eye-catcher in the park; it also served the practical purpose of a chimney for the folly and a marker for mariners at sea.[70] Like Carné's Seat, the Pheasantry commanded 'a beautiful and extensive prospect of the country to the sea' and formed another destination for amorous couples enjoying the pleasure grounds.

It also provided a place of solace for troubled times. In 1769, scandal shattered the family equilibrium; Richmond's sister Sarah ran off with Lord William Gordon, a dashing army officer who had swept her off her feet. Plucked from the misery of an unhappy marriage to Sir Charles Bunbury, she took their love child with them as society looked on in horror at the unfolding events. When she was persuaded eventually to give up Gordon, it was to Goodwood that she retreated, safe under her brother's protection and far removed from the court gossips.

The sensational fireworks display put on by the second Duke of Richmond in
May 1749 at Richmond House, London. Its pedimented façade is visible on the left
(© Victoria and Albert Museum Picture Library, London)

5

The Renaissance Duke

*'. . . His Majesty has always been extreamly kind & good to
me, & I should be the most ungratefull of men, if I did not love
& honor him with all the affection & duty that is due from a
servant & subject to a kind & good master . . .'*

Charles, second Duke of Richmond to the
Duke of Newcastle, 1743[1]

When the eighteen-year-old Charles March set off on his Grand
Tour in December 1719, he soon forgot about his child bride.
Although legally married, he regarded himself as without emotional
ties and therefore free to indulge in affairs of the heart. Ever the
charmer, he wrote to his mother from Vienna requesting her to send
'half a dozen or a dozen of ye best' English fans for 'the fine Ladys of
Vienna'.[2] Accompanied by his faithful tutor, Tom Hill, they travelled
on to Milan, Florence and Padua, before arriving in Venice in 1721,
in time for the annual Carnival. Here, March embarked on an affair
with a courtesan named Angela Polli, or 'Madame Angeletta' as
Johnny Breval called her. Breval was the eccentric tutor to Viscount
Malpas, another English aristocrat of similar age to March.[3] Breval was

smitten by her, describing her as a 'Divine Creature' and exclaiming, 'what eyes, what teeth, how much wit; and (the worst of the story is) how vast an affection for your L^dsp!'⁴ It was in Venice that March met the Irish impresario, Owen McSwiny, who arranged for Rosalba Carriera to draw pastel portraits of himself and Angeletta.⁵

Poor Angeletta was heartbroken when March left Venice in the spring of 1721. For the next six months, they wrote affectionate love-letters to each other and he showered her with expensive gifts, on one occasion getting McSwiny to buy her a hat 'with a very handsome black Feather in it' costing five sequins – about £2 sterling. When his dog, Dye, had puppies, he presented her with one. ⁶ But despite her protestations of love and his assurances that they were reciprocated, by February of the following year she had taken another lover, blaming him for dallying first elsewhere.⁷

Following Venice, the Eternal City beckoned. Here, March bought paintings and commissioned views of the Colosseum and the Roman Forum. The Grand Tour was seen as a rite of passage for young noblemen, providing not only an education in the culture of the Greeks, Romans and Renaissance but also exposure to fashionable society on the European Continent. Years later, when he was writing letters of introduction for Martin Folkes to eminent Italians, he told his friend that, 'Cardinal Albani is a very odd Curr, Ignorant enough & proud as Hell, butt has the finest library . . . in Europe, & without exception the very best collection of bustos in the world. You must flatter him upon his learning, & *bon gusto*.' He was equally scathing about the Princess Pamphili whom he described as, 'the ugliest woman in the world. Dam'd proud also, and stark staring mad, butt a Develish deal of Witt and some knowledge . . .'⁸ From Rome, the travellers spent time in Naples, Florence, Siena, Parma, Strasbourg and Lorraine before finishing in The Hague where the Cadogans had a house. March's father-in-law had footed the bill for his Grand Tour, although Cadogan was keen that his son-in-law did not follow in his father's footsteps and reminded him to be 'upon your guard against Play.'⁹

The exposure to classical art and architecture had a lasting impact on March that influenced him for the rest of his life. In Florence, he met the architect Alessandro Galilei and immediately asked him to design a new house for him. The dream house never materialised but Galilei did design the great Castletown House in Ireland that would one day become the home of March's daughter, Louisa.

*   *   *

The sound of merriment could be heard behind the closed door of the Great Dining-Room. The second Duke of Richmond was giving dinner to a group of his more colourful friends who were staying at Goodwood. Richmond was particularly proud of the decoration of the room, which transported the visitor away from the rolling hills of Sussex into the heart of the Roman Campagna. Framed in giant panels around the room was a series of ten paintings depicting allegorical tombs of celebrated Englishmen, encompassing recently deceased Whigs who had contributed to the Hanoverian succession. Each painting was executed by three Italian artists who focused on the architecture, landscape and figures respectively. By combining fictitious tombs of Englishmen in an Italianate setting, Richmond could link the glories of ancient Rome with English culture while making a bold statement about his allegiance to the Hanoverian dynasty.

The whole project had been the brainchild of Owen McSwiny, who had seen in the duke a suitable patron for the series. McSwiny orchestrated everything, commissioning the artists, arranging their payment, and shipping the pictures back to England. Among the artists was the young Canaletto who had almost certainly been talent-spotted by McSwiny and commissioned to paint the architecture in the *Allegorical Tomb of Archbishop Tillotson*. Over the course of eight years, Richmond bought eleven tomb paintings, resisting McSwiny's attempts to sell him more. McSwiny's correspondence survives, with a wonderful mix of salesmanship, excuses for delays and enthusiasm for the scheme. Although McSwiny had initially envisaged twenty-four tomb paintings, only twenty appear to have been executed. Hoping to capitalise on the series, McSwiny proposed selling prints of the pictures. However, the subscribers were not forthcoming and only nine were engraved.[10]

George Vertue sketched the picture-hang when he was staying at Goodwood in 1747.[11] In pride of place at the end of the room was the *Allegorical Tomb of King George I* which had been executed swiftly following the king's death in 1727. The other pictures included the tombs of King William III, the Duke of Devonshire and the Earl Cadogan (Richmond's father-in-law). John Wootton executed two overdoors of classical ruins to complete the dining-room scheme.

Through Owen McSwiny, Richmond also received four small views of Venice by Canaletto. They were painted on copper, which gave them an iridescent quality, and cost twenty-two sequins each (approximately £11 each). McSwiny shipped the first two paintings in November 1727, writing to the duke: 'I send your Grace by *Captain Robinson* (Commander of The Tokeley Gally) who sails, from hence tomorrow, *Two of The finest pieces*, I think, he, ever, painted, and . . . done, upon copper plates.'[12] The third painting, a view of the Rialto Bridge, was finished in January 1728. It is not known when it and the fourth painting arrived in England; however, two remain in the collection at Goodwood today: *The Rialto Bridge* and *A View of the Grand Canal*.

An inventory carried out in the summer of 1739 gives a glimpse of life at Goodwood during Richmond's tenure.[13] A 'card Table' in the Drawing Room and '2 Card Tables' in the New Drawing Room more than hint at evenings spent gaming. Likewise, 'a smoking table with a Marble top' in the Little Parlour speaks of whiling away the hours with a pipe. In the same room, 'a Box with a Bible' and 'one large and 6 quarto Common Prayer Books' tell of the central role of Christianity in society at that time. Richmond clearly used his dressing room as a study, as here we find '2 writing Desks' and 'a silver Lamp for sealing Letters' along with 'a Silver shaving Bason and Ewer' and 'a little silver Chamberpot'. Richmond must have been quite practical as there were also 'a hammer, chisel & Pinchers' and 'a Stick to measure Horses'.

The room also doubled up as an armoury with '12 Guns, 2 pair of large Pistols' and '1 pr. of small Pistols'. His interest in science is evident in a 'model of a Windmill', 'a reflecting Telescope & stand', '2 Globes' and 'a camera obscura'. One imagines he used the telescope at Carné's Seat to watch the comings and goings on the Solent and English Channel. George Vertue remarked on the panoramic view 'to Portsmouth, the Isle of White and the sea with the Harbour ships in it the fleet sailing out tho twenty miles in some part from this seat with the naked eye may be seen. But with a Telescope glass – every sail flags &c. of shipps are clearly discovered . . . in this place you have a view a Cemicircle of the sea for many hundred miles & nothing to intercept the sight.'[14]

*   *   *

The coronation of George II in Westminster Abbey was a magnificent affair. As the words of Handel's mighty anthem *Zadok the Priest* soared into the vaults, the second Duke of Richmond stood close to the new monarch and his consort; for the coronation ceremony Richmond was Lord High Constable, one of the Great Officers of State. This privileged position shows the high regard he was held in by the Hanoverian dynasty. Unlike his slippery father, the second duke was the epitome of loyalty and remained so for his entire life.

Three days after the coronation, on 14 October 1727, Richmond was appointed a Gentleman of the Bedchamber to the new king. Shortly afterwards, his wife Sarah was appointed a Lady of the Bedchamber to Queen Caroline whom she had already served as Princess of Wales.[15] The couple were to remain close to the royal family for the rest of their lives. The positions sounded glamorous but, in reality, they were quite tedious and demanded a certain level of physical stamina; the queen's ladies were not allowed to sit in her presence unless invited, or leave the room unless dismissed. For her services, Sarah was paid the princely sum of £500 a year.[16]

Richmond's great friend, Lord Hervey, helped to stifle the boredom with his constant gossip about court intrigues. In a letter to Richmond from Hampton Court, he jokes that there is a writ of *Habeas Corpus* issued 'from the Royal Bedchamber Office, for the removal of your's and my Lady Duchess's body forthwith to your respective waiting prisons in Hampton Court, where you are to suffer several weeks' imprisonment for diverse and sundry crimes of Omission towards the Lords and Ladies of Their Gracious Majesties' Bedchamber'. In other words, Hervey thought they were skiving and admitted that time would pass 'so much more pleasantly for your being here'.[17] Richmond himself confessed to the Duke of Newcastle that although he was ever ready to wait 'upon my Royal Master . . . when there is any real Duty that calls me', he could not help 'preferring foxhunting, & being with my family, to what is called fiddle-faddle waiting'.[18] At least they had a comfortable set of lodgings at Hampton Court. Here they had a dining-room that seated twelve; a drawing room with sofa and chairs upholstered in red caffoy (similar to damask); and a bedroom with checked linen curtains and matching bed hangings. There were a further eleven rooms for their staff.[19]

Richmond was recognised for his loyalty to the crown. Twelve years earlier, George I had revived the ancient Order of the Bath. In reality it was a ploy by the Prime Minister, Robert Walpole, to strengthen his own political position by granting favours to his supporters. Accordingly, Richmond's friend the Duke of Montagu (who was to be the Great Master of the Order) wrote to him asking him if he would become one of the thirty-six new knights.[20] Richmond hesitated, fearing it might mean he would never be made a Knight of the Garter, which his father had been and was the ultimate accolade. Through Montagu, Walpole allayed Richmond's fears and he duly accepted.[21] Unfortunately, he was unable to attend the installation ceremony as he suffered a mild attack of smallpox but he did manage to get tickets for some of his family and friends including Tom Hill. Hill had to break the news 'that his bauble, or honour, call it which you please, will cost yr grace five hundred fifty odd pounds six shillings and eight-pence'.[22] Regardless of the cost, Richmond was proud of the honour and had himself painted twice as a Knight of the Bath. He also commissioned William Chisholme, a carver and gilder, to make a frame for a charming double portrait of himself and Sarah by Jonathan Richardson; on each corner was carved the star of the Order of the Bath. It was invoiced on 18 December 1725 for the enormous sum of £27 7s 6d, just six months after Richmond had been installed. Less than a year later, Chisholme charged him a further £1 10s 'For Carving and Gilding the order of the Garter at the 4 corners of the fine frame'; Richmond had just received the much coveted Garter.[23] His Uncle Cardigan wrote immediately to congratulate him, cautioning him at the same time: 'I heartily rejoyce at it, and tho the expence is what you can't well afford, yet the thing is so becoming a Person of yr Rank, that the charge ought not to be grudg'd.'[24] Richardson's portrait depicts the young duke resplendent in armour with the collar of the Order of the Garter. One wonders whether Richardson, like Chisholme, had to redo the portrait replacing the collar of the Bath with the Garter. Either way, the complete ensemble of portrait and frame was probably intended for his grandmother, the aged Louise de Keroualle, who had begged him to send her a portrait of the two of them. The Aubigny buckle carved on each side may well have been a nod to her.

In January 1735, Hervey reported: 'The Duke of Richmond is at last declared Master of the Horse, and Lord Pembroke Groom of the Stole, each of them with a salary of £3,000 a year.'[25] This was a coveted position in the Royal Household, third in the pecking order after the Lord Steward and Lord Chamberlain. As well as the salary, it carried significant perks including the right to use the king's horses, coaches and attendants so he could travel in real style. He was responsible for all of the horses in the king's stables as well as his travel arrangements, so when the king visited Hanover, Richmond would be in attendance. For someone who had a genuine love of horses and good organisational skills, this was a plum job. Richmond was to be the longest-serving Master of the Horse of the eighteenth century.

Like many in his aristocratic circle, Richmond loved the theatre, a passion that he shared with his family. A painting by William Hogarth depicts a children's performance of John Dryden's play *The Indian*

Emperor or The Conquest of Mexico by the Spaniards. They are watched by a group of fashionably dressed adults including the second Duke and Duchess of Richmond and the royal children. One of the children on the stage is the Richmonds' eldest daughter, Caroline, who is gesticulating mid-sentence. The grand setting is the home of John Conduitt, Master of the Mint, who is depicted in a portrait hanging on the wall. The play was directed by Colley Cibber's son, Theophilus, and it was such a success that they were asked to perform it again in front of King George II and Queen Caroline at St James's Palace.[26]

Richmond also loved the opera. It may have been on his Grand Tour that he first took an interest in the opera, possibly encouraged by McSwiny. Back in London, he became the go-between for McSwiny and The Royal Academy of Music (a performing company), with McSwiny acting as a consultant at arm's length. In 1726, Richmond was made Deputy Governor of the Royal Academy of Music and stayed in his post until 1733 when he joined a rival company called the Opera of the Nobility at Lincoln's Inn Fields.[27]

From necessity, much of Richmond's time was spent in London. However, in the autumn of 1732, Lord Hervey wrote to Stephen Fox that, 'The D. of Richmond . . . is going to pull down and rebuild his house in town, and intends staying in the country all winter.'[28] The rebuilding of Richmond House in Whitehall was to be the second duke's major architectural achievement. It was actually the third Richmond House and replaced his father's house. Positioned near the banks of the Thames, it was perfectly located for attending court and parliament. The house was designed in the Palladian manner by Lord Burlington, who had designed the Great Room in Charlton. The interiors were almost certainly designed by Burlington's protégé William Kent with grand first-floor apartments sporting marble chimneypieces and damask wall hangings. The furnishings were also very grand and included giltwood seat furniture, marble-topped tables, mahogany commodes and old master paintings. During the next decade, Richmond built on a dining-room overlooking the river and created a terrace on the waterfront.[29]

Richmond's good friend, the Duke of Montagu, lived next door at Montagu House. It was at a drunken dinner there that one of Canaletto's most important commissions was dreamt up, as reported by Tom Hill:

> 'The only news I know to send you, is what I had this day from Swiney at the Duke of Montagu's, where we dined, & he, I think, got almost drunk. Canales, alias Canaletti, is come over with a letter of recommendation from our old acquaintance the Consul of Venice to Mac in order to his introduction to Your Grace, as a patron of the politer parts, or what the Italians understand by the name of virtù. I told him the best service I thought you could do him w'd be to let him draw a view of the river from y'r dining-room, which in my opinion would give him as much reputation as any of his Venetian prospects.'[30]

The result of this letter was Richmond commissioning two views of London from Richmond House: *Whitehall and the Privy Garden* and *The Thames and the City of London*. These were among Canaletto's first commissions in England where he had come seeking work. Seizing the opportunity to paint for such an important patron, Canaletto pulled out all the stops and the two paintings are exquisite in their execution. Unusually, they are almost square in format, almost certainly so they could hang above the mantelpieces in the hall at Goodwood where they were fitted into the panelling. Visitors to Goodwood could enjoy views over the Sussex countryside from one side of the room and views over London – as seen through the Richmond House windows – on the other. The commission successfully launched Canaletto's career on English soil.

*   *   *

On 27 June 1743, George II led the combined forces of Britain, Hanover and Austria to victory against the French at the battle of Dettingen. It was a close call – the allied army had managed to fight their way out of a French trap in Dettingen, eighteen miles east of Frankfurt on the banks of the river Main. At one point, George II's horse had bolted and was only stopped by the bravery of a young officer, Ensign Cyrus Trapaud. It must have been a worrying moment for Richmond, who had accompanied the king to Germany in his role as Master of the Horse, with responsibility for the monarch's huge transport train; six hundred horses had been shipped to Europe the previous autumn. On the day of the battle, Richmond was extremely miffed that the Hanoverian Master of the Horse, inferior in rank to himself, had failed to provide him with a mount for the day. General Honeywood, who was commanding one of the divisions (and was also a member of the Charlton Hunt), kindly lent him a horse. Richmond ended up attending the Earl of Stair – who was commanding the allies with George II – and seeing more of the battle than he would have done had he been with the king. That evening he 'had the honor to dine with him [George II] upon the field of Battle' and later had the satisfaction of the Hanoverian Master of the Horse being put in his place.[31] The battle of Dettingen was to be the last time a British monarch led his troops into battle. It was part of the ongoing War of the Austrian Succession (1740-1748), which involved nearly all the powers of Europe. Britain, Hanover and the Netherlands all supported Maria Theresa of Austria's claim to the Habsburg Empire; they were pitched against France, Spain and Prussia.

From the age of twenty, Richmond had served in the army. He was commissioned into the 'Horse Granadier Guards' while he was still on his Grand Tour and, like many noblemen at that time, was able to combine his military duties with all of his other responsibilities. When he returned home, he transferred to the Royal Regiment of Horse Guards (The Blues) as a captain. Two years later, in 1724 he was made aide-de-camp to George I with the rank of colonel. Thereafter, his rise through the ranks seems to have been on merit rather than social standing, for he was made a brigadier-general in 1739, major-general in 1742 (serving at Dettingen as such) and lieutenant-general in 1745. Finally, in 1750, he became Colonel of the Royal Regiment of Horse

Guards, an appointment that filled him and the regiment with delight. The Blues were particularly grateful to Richmond for defending their honour against an unjust charge of cowardice at the battle of Dettingen.

Shortly after Richmond's appointment as lieutenant-general in July 1745, Bonnie Prince Charlie landed on Eriskay, a tiny island in the Outer Hebrides. With only a handful of supporters, he had arrived on British soil to claim the throne for his exiled father, James. Events quickly gathered pace and in September, he entered Edinburgh unopposed with an army behind him. Shortly afterwards, government forces were routed at the battle of Prestonpans and the Jacobite army marched on England. George II's youngest son, the Duke of Cumberland, was speedily recalled from Flanders (where he had been fighting the French) to command the government army. Richmond wrote to him not long after Prestonpans to share his concerns about a French invasion: 'It is not the Scotch rebells that I fear, tho they have now got possession of Scotland, and have proclaimed the pretender at Edinburgh, butt I now look upon an invasion from France to be no longer a bugbear, butt a real danger, and a most certain thing if not prevented by force at home, and in the name of God Sir what is all Europe to us if your Royall father looses his crown, and wee consequently all our liberty, and every thing that is dear to us, which I am very sure wee can never enjoy butt under the government of your family.'[32]

Carlisle surrendered to the Jacobites in November and they continued south via Preston and Manchester to Derby. Meanwhile, Cumberland's army was marching north with Richmond – newly promoted to full general – in command of the cavalry. Richmond was in close contact with Newcastle throughout the campaign and they kept one another abreast of movements. Writing from Lichfield towards the end of November, Richmond said confidently, 'I hope & believe we shall have the honor of defeating & also destroying these villains', although he did express concern that his wife was on her way to Yorkshire to be nearer him, worrying that the 'Rebells' might reach that county.[33]

In the end, the Jacobite army decided to turn around and retreat back into Scotland and the comparative safety of the Highlands. Richmond had already considered this option for them, and admitted this was 'the worst of all' for the government forces as the rebels could then sit out the winter in the mountains whilst waiting for the French to invade. Newcastle momentarily panicked, writing from London in December, 'We are under the greatest alarms of an immediate Invasion from France.'[34]

Up north, Richmond was witnessing the siege and reduction of Carlisle, scribbling a postscript to Newcastle on 30 December: 'The Rebells have just hung out the white Flagg. Munday Night. Our Troops are now marching into the Town, pray send the enclosed quick to my dearest Taw [Sarah Richmond].'[35]

With Carlisle back in government hands, Richmond's duties were over and he returned to his hunting-box at Charlton to enjoy some winter sport. Friends and family kept him fully informed of events in Scotland as they unfolded. The Jacobites won the battle of Falkirk Muir defeating a relief force under General Hawley, another Charlton Hunt member. But this was the last victory they would have. After wintering in Scotland, Cumberland's army marched out of Aberdeen and defeated the rebels once and for all at the battle of Culloden on 16 April 1746. The news of the victory was brought to London by Richmond's nephew, Lord Bury, who was aide-de-camp to Cumberland. The reprisals were severe and Richmond's brother-in-law, the Earl of Albemarle, was given the task of pacifying the Highlands. Richmond himself, along with his fellow peers, sat in judgement at the trial of the 'rebel lords' in Westminster Hall. All were found guilty and condemned to death.[36] Bonnie Prince Charlie himself slipped away on board the French ship *L'Heureux* never to return.

* * *

'Wee then made at them, I came up to the women's side of the Chaise, and then thinking they were sure enough, went round to

secure my Cull and the Small coal man [vicar] . . . 'Dam you . . .
all', says I, 'deliver!' the Cull fell a Chattering, so rapt his knuckles
for him, which made him pretty obedient . . . 'Dam you', says I,
'do you collect'; which he imediatly did, and gave me the booty in
his hatt, that was about ten shiners, a couple of Smelts, a gold
tattle, Dust trunke and rolling pin (for so wee so call a Watch,
snuff box and tooth pick case); all this while the small coal man
satt and did nothing, upon that . . . 'Dam ye, the booty', says I.
Then he lugs out three or four hogs, . . . 'Dam ye', says I, 'your gold
and your watch'; upon which he fell a joaking; slap I let fly my pop
[gun], tho not with intention to kill the poor Dog neither, butt the
slugs whistled pretty close by his ears, which putt him in a most
confounded fright; 'take all', says he, upon which I whypt my
hand into his pocket, which I could hardly do for his paunch, butt
at last I lugg'd out his nett, that is his purse, with six shiners and
a smelt in it, butt the Dog had no tattle, upon which I cuss'd him
as he deserved. Then wee made off, butt took care to leave them
strict orders not to budge for half an hour; then away wee
went . . .'[37]

So reads a manuscript purporting to be the confession of a highwayman
of a dastardly robbery that took place in 1733 on the Trundle, otherwise
known as St Roche's Hill, in the Downs behind Goodwood. However,
closer inspection reveals the handwriting of the second Duke of
Richmond and further investigation shows it to have been a complete
hoax, instigated by Richmond. The innocent victim was Dr William
Sherwin, Canon of Chichester Cathedral. History does not relate what
he did to fall victim to Richmond but it was evidently the source of
much merriment in Richmond's circle. A few days after the supposed
robbery, Lord Albemarle wrote: 'I wish you and all ye Ladys privy to
ye Robbery my escape ye Law; ye Joke I like and wish I had seen
Sherwin in his fright.'[38] Tom Hill thought it was hilarious, writing
from London: 'I should have been vastly pleased to have seen the
Doctor's phyz at the time.'[39]

One imagines that Dr Sherwin was a puffed-up self-important cleric and his refusal to believe that it was a hoax only added to everyone's amusement. On a more serious note, Richmond was determined to stamp out smuggling in Sussex. It had become rife in the county owing to its proximity to the sea and smuggling gangs were terrorising the locals. In early October 1747, a gang met under the cover of Charlton Forest in the dead of night. Here, they planned an audacious robbery of the custom house in Poole where a recent haul of contraband tea was locked up for safekeeping. On the night of 6 October, armed with weapons, they broke into the custom house and made off with the tea. Several months later, John Diamond, one of the gang, was caught and held in Chichester Gaol. Now all that was needed was proof that Diamond was one of the gang members. A shoemaker called Daniel Chater knew him and was summoned to identify him; Chater knew enough of the custom house gang to hang them all.

On Sunday, 14 February 1748, Chater set out with William Galley, a custom-house officer, to make their way to a magistrate's house near Stansted (ten miles from Goodwood). On their journey, they stopped for refreshments in Rowlands Castle. Unfortunately, the landlady's suspicions were aroused and, being in league with the smugglers, she sounded the alarm. Members of the gang then tried to extract from Chater and Galley details of their mission. Failing to get any concrete answers, they plied them with drink and then carried them to a room to sleep. While they were slumbering, the gang decided to take drastic action. Rudely awaken from their sleep, Chater and Galley were bashed about the head and then forced on to the back of a horse. Their feet were then bound together under the horse's tummy and it was driven out of the village, while the poor victims on top were whipped and thrashed. A couple of times they rolled under the horse – their feet still tied – so their heads were hit by the horse's hooves. When they reached Lady Holt Park, they pulled Galley on to the ground and intended to throw him down a well. However, he was still conscious so his tormenters decided to carry on beating him. When they reached the Red Lion at Rake in the early hours of Monday morning, Galley appeared lifeless, so they buried him nearby in a fox's earth. Poor Chater had worse to come. He was chained up in a shed at Trotton, five miles away, where he was tortured mercilessly, his eyes and nose being mutilated. Two days later, on Wednesday evening, he was dragged from his prison and led back to the well at Lady Holt Park. There, his captors tried at first to hang him over the well and when that failed, they threw him head first down the well, piling rocks and bits of fencing on top of him.[40]

It was not until September that Galley's body was found by someone out hunting. Chater's body was discovered shortly afterwards. A month later, one of the gang members, William Steele, turned King's evidence and the gang was doomed. The Prime Minister, Henry Pelham (Newcastle's younger brother), wrote to Richmond in November that 'such a scene of villainy and barbarity I never before heard or read of. I conclude the Attorney General has seen it, for sure something may be done with those persons that seem concerned in this shocking act . . . I shall in my sphere pursue these villains to the utmost . . . I think we are all obliged to your Grace for the spirit you have shewn on this occasion, the next best thing is to use our endeavours to suppress the practice of smuggling.'[41]

At the time of writing, Richmond was one of the Lords Justices of the Realm during George II's absence in Hanover. He suggested the government take action and set up a special commission, as he was concerned that criminals were running riot and using intimidation to prevent justice taking its normal course. The special commission duly took place in January 1749 and seven of the gang were found guilty of murder and sentenced to death. One member eluded his sentence by dying in prison on the night that he was condemned. As a stern warning to all who might think of smuggling, his fellow murderers were hung in chains in prominent locations throughout the district; Benjamin Tapner swung from the gallows on the top of the Trundle. Pelham wrote to Richmond in February to 'return your Grace my hearty thanks, as a citizen of this country, for the unwearied and successful pains you have taken in detecting all sorts of villains and rogues in any shape . . . God bless you; you are born to do good to mankind.'[42]

Throughout his life, Richmond was a loyal Whig. He was elected Member of Parliament for Chichester in 1722 while he was still on his Grand Tour, mostly through the efforts of his father-in-law, Lord Cadogan. However, his parliamentary career was short-lived as his father died the following year and he took his seat in the House of Lords. This did not mean that he then sat back and relaxed; quite the contrary. He was a figure of considerable political importance in Sussex and actively campaigned in the west of the county on behalf of the Whigs. Together with Newcastle, they ensured that Sussex returned two government supporters unopposed throughout Richmond's life. His local involvement did not stop there. Richmond was mayor of Chichester twice and became High Steward in 1749.[43] Much of his time was spent at Goodwood where he constantly entertained people for both business and pleasure.

On the death of his grandmother, Richmond became Duke of Aubigny and inherited her estates, resulting in regular visits to France. Therefore, when the government needed a new ambassador to France after the Treaty of Aix-la-Chapelle, Richmond was the obvious candidate. Perhaps fortuitously for him – particularly in relation to the personal financial burden that Richmond had calculated the post would demand – he was never sent. The general protocol was that a Frenchman of equal rank would be sent to London as French ambassador. In the event, only a marquis was appointed so Richmond's brother-in-law, Lord Albemarle, was sent instead.

* * *

On the morning of 2 May 1744, Richmond's eldest daughter, Caroline, slipped out of Richmond House, anxious that nobody would see her. After a tearful farewell to her twelve-year-old sister Emily by the Cupola in Whitehall, she made her way to Charles Hanbury Williams's house in Conduit Street. There – against her parents' wishes – she was married to Henry Fox. When she broke the news to them later that day, they were apoplectic and she was banished. Very soon, everyone was talking about it. When Hanbury Williams went to the theatre that evening, he watched as the news spread from box to box, 'exactly like fire in a train of gunpowder'.[44] Horace Walpole, who was devoted to the Richmonds but also an insatiable gossip, informed his friend, Horace Mann: 'The town has been in a great bustle about a private match; but which, by the ingenuity of the Ministry, has been made politics. Mr Fox fell in love with Lady Caroline Lennox, asked her, was refused, and stole her. His father was a footman; her great-grandfather a King; *Hinc illae lacrimae* [Hence these tears]. All the blood royal have been up in arms.'[45] As far as the Richmonds were concerned, Fox was an upstart politician, much older than Caroline (she was twenty-one, he was thirty-eight) and totally unsuitable. Their darling daughter, always a model of virtue, had shattered their family happiness.

The public reaction to Caroline's elopement showed how much her family were in the limelight, whether they liked it or not. Richmond House was in many ways at the heart of court and political life. Having grown up in this atmosphere, Caroline was to become something of a political hostess herself, entertaining Fox's endless stream of friends at their home, Holland House in London.

It was to be four years before the family were reconciled. By then, the idea of Fox as a son-in-law had become more palatable. Writing to Richmond's old friend Princess Trivulci (with whom he probably enjoyed a brief flirtation on his Grand Tour), he tells her: 'The eldest girl Caroline, married against our wishes a man infinitely beneath her, so we do not see her; but I must also tell you that this man by his merit and talents is bound to make a name for himself in this country, and he holds one of the best appointments that a gentleman could have: he is Secretary for War. His name is Mr. Fox.'[46] In the end, Richmond held out an olive branch and, after berating Caroline's behaviour, gave his forgiveness and admitted: 'We long to see your dear innocent child, and that has not a little contributed to our present tenderness to you . . . When we meet, let our affection be mutual and you may be sure that seeing you is proof of the sincerity of ours. So, my dear child, you and Mr. Fox may come here at the time that shall be settled by yourselves . . . and both be received in the arms of an affectionate Father and Mother.'[47] As a reconciliation present, Fox presented his mother-in-law with a Meissen snuffbox, intricately painted with bouquets of flowers. It opened to reveal a portrait of Caroline, suitably demure, with a veil-like headscarf framing her sweet face. When Caroline gave birth to another son the following year, they named him Charles after both his grandfather and royal forebears.

To celebrate their renewed family harmony, Richmond threw a magnificent fireworks party at Richmond House on 15 May 1749 that was one of the most celebrated displays of the eighteenth century. Opportunistically, he had bought the remaining fireworks left over after the abortive fireworks display to celebrate the Peace of Aix-la-Chapelle in Green Park. No fewer than sixteen different types of firework illuminated the sky, some of which were launched from barges on the river. A grandstand, decorated to look like a Roman triumphal arch, stood lit up at the centre of the garden overlooking the river, while four illuminated pyramids framed the view, each topped by a crown in honour of the royal guests. Catherine wheels whirled on the terrace and showers of propelled stars rained down into the Thames. The king watched from the safety of the royal barge as the faces of the four hundred guests were lit up again and again. Afterwards, there was music and dancing. Walpole was ecstatic: 'Whatever you hear of the Richmond fireworks, that is short of the prettiest entertainment in the world, don't believe it; I really never passed a more agreeable evening.'[48] The party lasted until two o'clock in the morning.

*   *   *

In the spring of 1750, the Richmonds were planning a visit to their beloved daughter, Emily, in Ireland. They had never been to her marital home, the palatial Carton House in county Kildare, and looked forward to it with eager anticipation. However, Richmond became ill with bladder problems, the treatment of which prevented him from travelling. Keeping his son-in-law, Henry Fox, abreast of the situation, he confided at the beginning of June: 'my operations go on better & better every day . . . I piss extreamly well generally, & in a good stream, & with as good a spring as anybody of fifty years old . . .'[49] He was still not better by 19 June and Sarah was urging him to go to Paris to consult the famous French surgeon Jacques Daran. On 11 July, he dragged himself to the annual Garter Ceremony at Windsor before returning to Goodwood where he assured Newcastle that he was, 'better, butt not well yett, yett I am in a sure way of being well'.[50] At the end of the month, he caught a fever and the *Whitehall Evening Post* reported that 'His Grace the Duke of Richmond is very much indispos'd at his Seat at Goodwood in Sussex'.[51] In fact, Richmond had not quite made it to Goodwood and lay gravely ill in his bed at Godalming, where he kept a small halfway house to break the journey between Goodwood and London. His health had deteriorated rapidly from Monday, 2 August and Sarah had rushed to his side, arriving in the afternoon of the following day. Despite all their efforts, the doctors could not help him and he died on 8 August; he was forty-nine.

The autopsy that was carried out by Dr Middleton on the day of his death revealed various complications to his bladder and a growth around his hip and thigh that he believed was cancerous. However, a modern diagnosis of the symptoms reveals he died from blood poisoning as a result of the invasive treatment to his bladder; in other words, his doctors accidentally killed him.[52]

Ten days later, Richmond's body was carried in a crimson velvet coffin to Chichester Cathedral where it was laid to rest in a vault that he had not long ago had constructed beneath the Lady Chapel. On the same day as the funeral, his father's body was brought from Westminster Abbey to Chichester for re-burial, so father and son could be reunited in death.[53] Five of Richmond's children who had predeceased him were also moved into the vault. Just a year later, they were joined by his wife Sarah who went to the grave heartbroken, aged only forty-five.

The Charlton Hunt painted by George Stubbs during his nine-month stay at Goodwood;
the third Duke of Richmond is the tall figure in the centre speaking to his brother, George
(© Trustees of the Goodwood Collection)

6

The Radical Duke

*'Persons in your station of life ought to have long views.
You people of great families and fortunes ... if you are what
you ought to be, are the great oaks that shade a country and
perpetuate your benefits from generation to generation.'*

Edmund Burke to Charles, third Duke of Richmond[1]

Goodwood House was silent. The doors were locked, the shutters were closed, and the furniture covered in dust sheets. The new south wing, begun by the second Duke of Richmond a few years before his untimely death, lay empty and unfinished, its crisp Portland stone façade in stark contrast to its surroundings. The new wing was designed in a severe Palladian style, with a central pediment and unadorned sash windows. The architect was almost certainly Matthew Brettingham, who was employed by other members of the Charlton Hunt. At the centre of this new wing was the 'Great Room', a large chamber with a compartmentalised ceiling after a design by Serlio, a sixteenth-century Italian architect.

Unlike the house, the gardens and grounds were bursting with life; flowers, shrubs and trees, planted by the second Duke, matured under the care of a skeleton team of gardeners. Although their new master was young, they knew that he shared his father's interest in trees and took seriously his stewardship of the 1,100-acre estate he had inherited.

In March 1755, Charles, third Duke of Richmond and his younger brother, George, reached Rome. They were accompanied by their tutor, Abraham Trembley, who had overseen the young duke's education ever since his father's death. Indeed, it had been the second duke's dying wish that Trembley 'would be attached to the person of a son whom he was leaving at the age when a father is always necessary . . . I [Trembley] seized the opportunity with eagerness and gratitude...I followed it with delight; and my happiness increased when I found myself attached to both the sons of the illustrious father for whom I grieved.'[2]

Trembley, who had previously been tutor to the boys' Bentinck cousins, proved to be an inspired choice. Having achieved a certain amount of fame in the scientific world for his discovery that the marine polyp was not a plant but an animal, he had a profound influence on his young wards. He was a pioneering educationist who believed it was important not to overtax young minds. His approach was kind and caring, entering into his pupil's activities, allowing them time to relax and introducing ideas little by little. He believed it was crucial to excite their curiosity and wonder at the universe, often using natural history specimens. Leading by example, he instilled moral principles and stressed the similarities between men of different countries.[3]

After two years together in Geneva, Trembley and the seventeen-year-old Richmond had started the Grand Tour in earnest, meeting scientists and intellectuals wherever they went: Lyons, Marseilles, Montpellier, Bordeaux (where they met Montesquieu) and Paris (where they were entertained by Charles La Condamine, the Amazon explorer). After a few months back in England, they had continued their journey, visiting Tournai, Brussels, Strasbourg and Sarrelouis where Richmond was riveted by military manoeuvres. In the autumn, he was enrolled at Leiden University to study science, being joined by his brother, George, a few months later. They had set off again in the spring of 1754, meeting the Duke of Brunswick and Frederick the Great in Berlin. The summer had been spent travelling through Bohemia and Moravia; the autumn passed in Vienna; and in late winter, they travelled through Trieste to Venice before arriving in Rome.

Once there, both boys sat for the artist Pompeo Batoni. In a relatively short space of time, Batoni had established himself as the leading portraitist in the city and the go-to person for those on the Grand Tour.[4] Both boys chose to be painted with their pet spaniels who were travelling with them. Earlier, Trembley had remarked about Richmond: 'He loves dogs prodigiously. He loves also the human race and the *feminine* race.'[5] Richmond's portrait depicts a handsome young man with dark hair neatly parted in the middle and curls resting over his ears. He fixes on the viewer a confident look with his clear blue eyes while gently stroking one of his dogs. His erect posture in a suitably classical interior betrays something of the responsibility he was already carrying as the head of the family. George's portrait seems more informal, his striking military coat opening loosely over his gold-frogged waistcoat. His spaniel tries to jump up and is kept at bay by her master's hand.

Richmond was also painted by the German artist Anton Mengs, Batoni's main rival in Rome. Softer in manner, it has all the swagger of a Van Dyck portrait with the duke dressed in seventeenth-century costume alluding to both the great Flemish artist and the sitter's Stuart ancestry. In the shadows behind, a bust of Athena, goddess of wisdom, looms over his shoulder. Richmond was one of only a handful of travellers who were depicted by both Batoni and Mengs. His sister Caroline hung the Batoni portrait in her gallery at Holland House along with portraits of his siblings, while he kept an autograph replica for himself.

Like all young *milordi*, Richmond and George studied the ancient ruins in Rome and the masterpieces of painting, sculpture and architecture. It was probably in Rome that Richmond met a trio of young artists: William Chambers, Joseph Wilton and Giovanni Cipriani. Chambers was an architect, Wilton a sculptor and Cipriani a painter and each would be involved in an initiative of Richmond's back in London.

From Rome, Richmond and his brother made their way to Naples where they studied the ancient city of Herculaneum. The Roman city, which had been wiped out by the eruption of Vesuvius in AD 79, had been excavated recently. Richmond enjoyed surveying the ruins with original Latin descriptions to hand and, together with Trembley, made a careful study of an erupting Mount Vesuvius. Travelling north, they were entertained by Sir Horace Mann in Florence in May from where Richmond wrote home to his brother-in-law, Fox: 'I am in love with the Venus and take great pleasure to stroke her bum and thighs.' Florence was followed by Pisa, Turin and Bern where they met the mathematician Paolo Frisi, the natural historian Vitaliano Donati and the anatomist Albert Haller respectively. Haller, whose interests spanned physiology, natural history, politics and literature, made a profound impression on the young duke. They then began their journey home through the old duchy of Nassau and along the Rhine, finishing at The Hague in the autumn. Shortly afterwards, Richmond was elected a Fellow of the Royal Society. This must have been a proud moment for his tutor, whose task was nearly complete.

In February 1756, Richmond came of age. Trembley was given a handsome pension that meant he never had to work again. Speaking of his tutor, Richmond said, 'He really is the best and most honest man alive and has an infinite deal of learning and good sense.'[6] Trembley had taken a rebellious and headstrong teenager and, more than anything, nurtured his character so he could stand alone with confidence and ease.

*   *   *

Like his father, Richmond had high ideals and a strong sense of duty. The Whig aristocracy held the high moral and civic virtues of Republican Rome in high regard and collecting classical art was an expression of that. There was a subtle difference between the collecting habits of the second duke's generation and his son's – the second duke's generation had collected sculpture predominantly for who it represented; the third duke's generation primarily for aesthetic reasons.[7] The young Richmond believed that aristocratic taste could shape society and improve the nation. This civic-mindedness led to the creation of a sculpture gallery at Richmond House where artists could study copies of famous classical sculptures at first hand without having to travel abroad. The works in the gallery displayed ideals of the human body and a range of human emotions. At this period, the study of the human form underpinned artistic training.

The idea for the sculpture gallery was probably Wilton's and Chambers' who recognised the need for an academy in England.[8] For the gallery, Chambers designed a long room that ran down to the river, formed out of some old offices at Richmond House. Twenty-four statues stood in the room, including the *Apollo Belvedere*, the *Venus de Medici*, and the *Borghese Gladiator*. Busts on brackets adorned the walls and smaller pieces sat on the mantelpiece and tables. Another copy of the *Apollo Belvedere* by Wilton stood in a recess at the entrance to greet visitors.

Around the same time, Richmond was made vice-president of the recently formed Society of Arts. Walpole was very excited about both the Society and the sculpture gallery, writing to Horace Mann: 'There is now established a Society of the Encouragement of Arts, Sciences, and Commerce, that are likely to be very serviceable; and I was pleased yesterday with a very grand seigneurial design of the Duke of Richmond, who has collected a great many fine casts of the best antique statues, has placed them in a large room in his garden, and designs to throw it open to encourage drawing.'[9] As an encouragement to students, there was a prize system in place, based upon Continental models: 'There will be given at Christmas and Midsummer annually to those who distinguish themselves by making the greatest Progress the following Premiums. A Figure will be selected from the rest, and a large Silver Medal will be given for the best Design of it, and another for the best Model in Basso Relievo. A small Silver Medal for the second

best Design, and one for the second best Basso Relievo.'[10] Richmond
was one of the judges.

To begin with, all went well, with Wilton and Cipriani acting as
directors. However, when Richmond returned from abroad where he
had been engaged in military service, he found a sarcastic notice
pinned to the door by one of the students purporting to be from
himself. It apologized for his poverty and expressed his sorrow for
having promised premiums but not actually awarding them. Richmond
was incensed and immediately closed the gallery. He soon relented
but, two years later, Wilton and Cipriani resigned and Chambers
stopped working for him. Their resignation was probably prompted
by the formation of a rival organisation to the Society of Arts – the
Society of Artists of Great Britain. This new society charged entry for
its exhibitions and was just for artists and not craftsmen. The Society
of Arts continued to use the sculpture gallery but the society gradually
went into decline, to the extent that in 1770 the rival Society of Artists
were given exclusive access.

Under George III's patronage, the Royal Academy had opened in
1768, finally creating a proper academy for artists. The duke's sculpture
gallery continued to be used but its heyday was over. It had served its
purpose and, when some students maliciously mutilated some of the
statues by breaking off fingers, thumbs and toes, Richmond closed it
permanently. By 1782, it had been pulled down and the collection of
casts sat unused until they were dispersed.

Although the sculpture gallery was short-lived, Richmond publicly
demonstrated his interest in art and, through the human form, science.
The legacy of the sculpture gallery lived on in the lives of the artists
who had trained there and, when James Barry painted a mural at the
Society of Arts in 1780, Richmond was included as a patron of the arts.[11]

*   *   *

Thirty-four years after the second Duke of Richmond had stood beside
George II during the coronation ceremony in Westminster Abbey, his

son stood beside George III as he was crowned King of Great Britain and Ireland. The third Duke of Richmond and George III were both young; Richmond was twenty-six and George twenty-three. It seemed like the whole of London had turned out to witness the coronation procession and the abbey was packed with guests.

Richmond had been given the role of carrying the sceptre with the dove, a duty his grandfather had performed at Queen Anne's coronation. His wife, Mary, was also present, Walpole remarking that she was 'as pretty as nature and dress, with no pains of her own, could make her'.[12] Mary wrote her own description of the coronation in a letter to her sister-in-law Lady George Lennox, in her simple, prattling style:

> '. . . I . . . dress'd to the satisfaction of every Body altho' my hair was so short it wou'd scarcely make a Toupee; there was but two or three things in my dress I insisted upon which was going without Powder, (for with the bundle of false hair it wou'd have made my Head look as big as a House) wearing a ruff round my Neck, & not wearing some odious dropping curls of fair hair that wou'd have touch'd my shoulders; I asure you my dress was very much admired, which I must brag of as you know that does not often happen . . . I walk'd with The Dss. of St. Albans, which was horrid, for she is such a ridiculous sick looking Dwarf & unluckily a little humpish, that I was afraid the Mob wou'd say some thing shocking to her.'[13]

The Richmond family were still recovering from the fact that George III had spurned their sister Sarah for Princess Charlotte of Mecklenburg-Strelitz. At one point, it looked like he might propose to Sarah, but the Earl of Bute, his confidant and mentor, soon nipped those dreams in the bud and George resigned himself to marriage with a German princess. Two weeks before the coronation, Sarah had had to endure the humiliation of being a bridesmaid at George and Charlotte's wedding in the Chapel Royal at St James's Palace.

Relations had got off to a bad start with George III. Soon after his accession, he had appointed Richmond one of his Gentlemen of the Bedchamber. Just over a fortnight later, Richmond resigned after a row with the king. His sister Caroline was shocked and wrote to Emily to tell her the news: 'My dear siss will be surprised to hear my brother has resigned his Bedchamber already. Lady George told Sarah last Thursday she would set out Friday morning early for Goodwood, from whence she hoped to send up my brother as angry as she was, at the King making Lord Down and Lord Fitzmaurice his aide-de-camp, and their going over George's head. Accordingly, his Grace [Richmond] came, was twenty minutes with H.M., whom I believe is as much displeased with him as it's possible to be, and refused giving George rank; the particulars of the conversation are not known but that he has resigned is certain.' She continues that Richmond had retreated to Goodwood, 'where I hope he will stay till this storm is a little blown over, and time makes everything forgot, but it's vexatious to those who wish him well. The King's behaviour has been, by what I find, very sensible, very polite and very firm . . . I do think the King is in the right not to be bullied into these things by silly boys, who go over people's heads every day, and then are violent because he chooses to show a great mark of favour to a man he personally loves.'[14]

As he was to display repeatedly throughout his life, Richmond had acted impulsively without taking stock of the situation and seeking advice from those around him. Unfortunately, the king never forgave him and it tarnished a relationship that could otherwise have been so fruitful. Had his father still been alive, Richmond might have acted differently. But as it was, he had been his own master from the age of fifteen and carried with it all the responsibilities as head of an illustrious family; whenever a member of his family was under threat, he was the first to come to their rescue.

Not only was Goodwood a place of refuge from the stresses and strains of life, but it was also the place where Richmond could hunt to his heart's content. His pocket diary for 1761 has survived and it gives a glimpse of his love of the chase. On Friday, 13 November, he played tennis in London in the morning, attended the House of Lords until eight o'clock at night and dined back at Richmond House. At ten o'clock that night, he set off for Goodwood accompanied by his friend Lord John Cavendish. Travelling through the night, they arrived in Sussex early on Saturday morning, met the hounds at Singleton and spent the whole day foxhunting before dining that evening at Goodwood. Following a rest on Sunday (when it 'Rain'd almost all Day'), he hunted on Monday, Tuesday, Wednesday, Friday and Saturday of the following week. The week after that he hunted on three days and shot on the remainder.[15] It is little wonder that Goodwood's fame as a sporting estate grew and grew.

Despite his personal differences with George III, Richmond had an incredibly strong sense of duty and devotion to his country. Like his father, Richmond had entered the army while still on his Grand Tour in 1753 and quickly rose through the ranks. Both he and his brother were desperate to see military action and fight for their country. Their opportunity came in 1758 when both of them were involved in the successful raid on Cherbourg, part of the ongoing Seven Years' War which saw all of the great powers of Europe at war. The following year, Richmond saw action at the victorious battle of Minden, where he was commended by Prince Ferdinand of Brunswick who had commanded the combined Anglo-German army against the French.

Minden was to be the last action that Richmond saw. Although he continued to rise through the ranks, eventually becoming a field marshal, his attentions became more and more focused on politics.

*   *   *

The Goodwood stables were a hive of activity. The stable clock, chiming on the hour, kept perfect time; Richmond's servants all knew that their master was extremely punctual. The sounds of horses clattering over the cobbles or neighing across the red-brick courtyard mingled with the shouts of grooms and stable lads going about their business. Horses were the lifeblood of the estate and the stable block was filled with racehorses, hunters, hacks, carriage horses and workhorses. No fewer than fifty-four horses were housed under its roof and, by the end of the century, there were twenty-nine staff, including eleven grooms.[16]

As soon as Richmond had returned from his Grand Tour, he had commissioned William Chambers to design a stable block in the newly fashionable neo-classical style. This was an important commission for Chambers, coming as it did from one of the country's leading aristocrats; it was also one of Chambers' first commissions outside London.

Richmond's father, the second duke, had considered building a new stable block and had gone as far as having a plan drawn up by Colen Campbell. Although intended for the same site, this was never carried out so, in 1757, Chambers embarked on his design – a virtuoso performance in flint, brick and Portland stone. The stables are formed of a vast quadrangle entered through an imposing triumphal arch, proudly proclaiming Richmond's knowledge of Roman architecture. Entered beneath a coffered barrel vault, the red-brick courtyard is framed by simple pedimented façades with evenly spaced doors and windows. The garden side is centred by a rusticated and pedimented archway, topped by the clock.

When they were first built, the stables were far grander than the house itself. The new south wing was still incomplete, so Chambers was also tasked with finishing the 'Great Room', turning it into a grand library with painted bookcases and gilded pier glasses between the windows. No doubt his own book, *Treatise on Civil Architecture* (1759) sat on the shelves; one of the plates was dedicated diplomatically to the third duke. Richmond must have been keen to learn more about architecture as he paid Chambers to give him lessons. Chambers was also architectural tutor to the Prince of Wales, later George III, and later became Architect to the King, an unofficial position shared with his rival, Robert Adam.

While the third duke indulged his interest in architecture with the most celebrated exponents working at the time, he was also inclined to seek out and patronise the skills of the nation's finest artists. In April 1758, a year after their marriage, Charles and Mary Richmond sat for Joshua Reynolds, the fashionable portrait painter. While the duchess was painted seated, the duke was portrayed standing in a pose of commensurate ease, leaning nonchalantly against a stone balustrade with his huge pet dog beside him.[17] Reynolds was struck by the 'great beauty' of his dark blue eyes.[18] His portrait shows a man at ease with his situation in life; in the four years since he was painted in Rome he had both matured and grown more comfortable in his own skin. Both master and dog gaze in the same direction, the duke with an air of confidence and vitality and no hint of affectation. He wears a striking red coat with shiny buttons, generous cuffs and matching waistcoat and breeches. Like Mengs, Reynolds alludes to Van Dyck, this time in his sitter's pose.

Eight appointments for the duke are recorded in Reynolds' pocket book, including one in September, which was presumably when the finishing touches were added. It may well have been during these long hours of sittings that Reynolds told the duke about a talented young artist he had discovered called George Stubbs. Reynolds had recently asked Stubbs to paint him a warhorse for a portrait and was pleased with the result. Initially painting only portraits, Stubbs had spent the previous two years making detailed anatomical drawings of dead horses with the aim of having them engraved. Given the duke's interest in science and anatomy, originally sparked in him by his tutor, Abraham Trembley, and then fostered during his studies at Leiden University, it was only natural that he should be interested in Stubbs. He therefore invited him down to Goodwood where he was to stay for nine months and paint three sporting scenes on the estate.

The stay would also have enabled Stubbs to work on the engravings of his anatomical drawings; failed attempts to find an engraver in London resulted in him learning the skill himself and engraving his own plates, leading to the publication of *The Anatomy of the Horse* in 1766. While at Goodwood, he was probably lodged in the newly built stable block where there was extensive accommodation for visiting grooms and stable hands on the first floor; the ground floor was given over to loose boxes and stalls.

Stubbs's first painting depicts Richmond with the Charlton Hunt. The duke is mounted on a swanky black hunter looking towards his brother, George, and pointing his whip towards some of the hounds that populate the lower half of the picture. Both Richmond and George wear coats in the distinctive 'Garter blue' of the Charlton Hunt, with gold buttons. Captain Jones, Richmond's Groom of the Bedchamber, leaps over a post-and-rail fence to the left and nearby a hunt servant in the Richmond livery of yellow and scarlet doffs his cap on a rearing black horse, a French hunting horn slung over his shoulder. Another liveried hunt servant stands behind a grey hunter in the foreground, perhaps preparing the duke's second horse. In the middle distance, a further figure wearing his Charlton Hunt coat gallops towards the main party; this is probably Sir John Miller, an old family friend and hunt member. Miller had helped Richmond revive the hunt after a seven-year lull following the second duke's death. On the horizon, the hunt in full cry is visible; this artistic device of showing two activities taking place at the same time (known as continuous narration) was probably learnt by Stubbs on his Italian travels. The hounds are skilfully observed and Richmond would have known each one personally; he probably selected the best ones as two years earlier he had as many as fifty-seven couple. Stubbs painted separate studies of several of the Charlton hounds and they appear in his engravings.

In the second scene, *Racehorses Exercising at Goodwood*, Stubbs seamlessly combines three separate activities. At the centre of the painting, Mary, Duchess of Richmond, rides side-saddle in a beautifully tailored habit (in Charlton Hunt blue) beside Richard Buckner, the duke's steward who was responsible for the day-to-day running of the estate. Dressed in green livery, he points out three racehorses exercising, blanketed and hooded in the yellow Richmond livery with pet dogs racing along at their heels. On the other side of Mary is the profile figure of Lady Louisa Lennox, George's bride. She and George had eloped from her father the Earl of Ancram's house on

21 December 1759 and got married on Christmas day in Dumfries, so her inclusion celebrates their recent marriage.

Nearby to Louisa, in the right corner of the picture, a sweating grey horse is being rubbed down with straw by grooms and stable lads. They are probably members of the Budd family who worked at Goodwood around this time. The spire of Chichester Cathedral can be glimpsed in the distance, and beyond Chichester the pale hills of the Isle of Wight shimmer on the horizon.

The third scene shows Richmond's brother-in-law, Henry Fox, and his cousin, the Earl of Albemarle, shooting over pointers in the rolling landscape of the South Downs behind Goodwood. They approach some woodland with one spaniel on point, waiting for a partridge to spring up. Two green-liveried gamekeepers attend them, one of whom is mounted on an alert chestnut. Fox had been one of Richmond's guardians after his father had died, so his prominent position at the centre of the picture, smartly dressed in a gold-braided frock coat, shows the high esteem in which he was held. Observing from one corner of the painting is a black page dressed in the yellow Richmond livery. He holds an Arab hack, a highly desirable riding horse, while his colleague holds another skittish chestnut.

The Goodwood commission gave Stubbs a well-earned leg-up into the small circle of aristocratic patrons of the turf, all of whom admired his ability to paint horses in such an accurate and painterly manner. It also emphasised the central role of sport in life at Goodwood, the main legacy of the first and second dukes.

*   *   *

The Duke of Richmond's carriage wound its way through the cobbled streets of Paris. Inside, wrapped up against the chilly November air, sat Charles and Mary Richmond; opposite them was Horace Walpole, who was to act as their adviser on an important shopping spree. Their destination was the Sèvres porcelain factory just six miles south-west of Paris. Since 1759, it had been owned by Louis XV, to whose court

Richmond had just been posted (reluctantly) as ambassador. This visit, just a week after their arrival in November 1765, would be a welcome break from the meetings and formalities that the role demanded of him. In his hands, he clutched the two leather-bound volumes of George Edwards' *Natural History of Birds* dedicated to his parents. He had an idea in mind.

On arrival at the factory, the Richmonds purchased 'off the shelf' a garniture of three vases. They were decorated on each side with quayside and military scenes and were perfect for displaying on a mantelpiece or along the centre of a dining table. The visitors then got down to business, commissioning a bespoke dessert service of around 150 pieces for an eye-watering £500 (for comparison, Reynolds' portrait of Richmond had cost just over £31). Unusually, it was to be painted in both green and blue (*bleu lapis*) and decorated with birds copied directly from Edwards' books. This was the first time the Sèvres artists had painted real birds on china; up until then, they had dreamt up fantastical birds. The service was to include plates, ice-cream cups, sugar bowls, *compotiers* and wine-bottle coolers. Matching tea and coffee cups were included, accompanied by an unusually large teapot designed for English tea-drinking habits. Delicate simulated wicker-work baskets boldly combined the two colours.[19]

As Richmond was reluctant to leave the books behind, the Sèvres artists, François-Joseph Aloncle and Antoine-Joseph Chappuis, had to come to their Paris home, the Hôtel de Brancas, on the Left Bank. Here, the two painters painstakingly copied one hundred birds for which they were paid a *livre* per bird. Given Richmond's interest in natural history, nurtured by Trembley, it was essential that the birds were accurately depicted. He may also have been influenced by the Meissen dinner service that he had seen at his sister's home, Holland House; it was painted with birds copied from Eleazar Albin's book, *A Natural History of Birds*. Although he never intended it, Richmond was to be England's greatest patron of Sèvres porcelain.[20]

Richmond's embassy was short-lived. He had never really wanted to go and, when he was there, his heart was not in it. He had taken his brother George with him as Secretary and, together with their wives, they had formed a close-knit clique that raised more than a few eyebrows in Paris. Caroline, speaking like a typical eldest sister, disapproved of their conduct: 'I hear from all quarters, and indeed by their own account, can find, they treated the French with the utmost contempt and incivility; that contempt of everything but their own set of people is their fault in this country as well as France.'[21]

Another criticism levelled at Richmond was that he was simply not there but at Aubigny, his French estate, or back at home in England. He took his role as ambassador seriously but saw little point in fraternising with the French who had been enemies off and on for many hundreds of years. He also saw that the king's mistresses, particularly Madame du Barry, held sway and he was unlikely to have much real influence. However, Louis XV did present him with an important set of tapestries that would be a lasting legacy of his embassy.

Like the Sèvres porcelain factory, the Gobelins manufactory was owned by Louis XV. It had been bought by his great grandfather, Louis XIV, and since 1699 had supplied tapestries almost exclusively for the French court. In 1763, Richmond had bought a set of four tapestries from the *Portières des Dieux* ('Portals of the Gods') series, comprising Venus as spring, Ceres as summer, Bacchus as autumn and Diana as Earth. The four tapestries that Louis presented to Richmond three years later were from a series of thirty illustrating scenes from the story of *Don Quixote*. The complete series was intended initially for Louis' château de Marly on the outskirts of Paris, however only eighteen were needed. The tapestries are all woven with a comical scene taken from the novel, in a trompe l'oeil picture frame, surmounted by a peacock and supported by a shaped cartouche of a warrior. Garlands of flowers are hung over the surrounding pale golden mosaic ground, with a further outer trompe l'oeil frame. The upper corners bear entwined Ls for Louis while the lower right corners are signed and dated by Michel Audran or Pierre-François Cozette, in whose workshops they were woven. It was a prestigious gift that warranted a room worthy to display them, and Richmond had just such a room in mind.

At the Royal Academy exhibition of 1771, a young architect called James Wyatt exhibited an 'elevation of a house intended for a nobleman in Sussex'. That nobleman was almost certainly the third Duke of Richmond and the house Goodwood. Although it was never realised, it had clearly been Richmond's ambition to build a new house worthy of his status. In the mid-1760s, Robert Adam had drawn up some designs for a grand classical mansion.[22] Since inheriting the estate, Richmond had increased his landholding considerably from 1,100 acres. In 1765, he had purchased the neighbouring Halnaker House and its ancient park for £48,000 and he would continue buying up land well into the 1790s.[23] Wyatt was an up-and-coming architect who had discovered fame with his design for the Pantheon in Oxford Street, London. Richmond had a knack of spotting talented youngsters and later formed one of a trio of dukes who paid Wyatt £50 a year to stay in England when Catherine the Great of Russia tried to poach him.[24]

Wyatt's design shows a neo-classical palace with a central-columned rotunda, inspired by Robert Adam and James Paine's south front of Kedleston Hall (although Wyatt would never have admitted it, Adam being his chief rival). It would have fronted the original Jacobean house combining Brettingham's wing on the south and a new wing on the north. In the end, only the new north wing was built and this was where Richmond's new tapestries were hung.

The *Portières des Dieux* tapestries were displayed in the state bedroom. They were fixed to the wall with neat giltwood frames in the French manner. Richmond's ambassadorial cloth-of-state was incorporated into the bed hangings of a grand four-post bed. The four *Don Quixote* tapestries were hung next door in the drawing room, along with an overdoor tapestry of flowers and three large looking-glasses bought in Paris; all had the same delicate giltwood frame. The superb neo-classical ceiling was by the stuccoist Joseph Rose and the figural chimneypiece by the sculptor John Bacon; it represents 'male and female Beauty standing in the attitude of drawing aside a drapery which unveils the fire-place'.[25] French furniture and a Savonnerie carpet (also given by Louis XV) adorned the room, playfully mixing the French rococo with the English neo-classical style.[26] Robert Adam had done something similar at Croome Court and Osterley Park, although in these cases the tapestries covered the entire wall, almost like wallpaper.

The view from the drawing room was enhanced in 1787 by an architectural eye-catcher in the distance – the Kennels. Richmond had moved the foxhounds from Charlton to Goodwood and the pack was now known as the Duke of Richmond's Hounds. He commissioned Wyatt to design some kennels in a style appropriate to their ducal owner. The resulting building, which cost £6,000, was, as Viscount Palmerston remarked, 'in a style of elegance unknown hitherto to that species of building'.[27] Built in pale yellow brick and flint, it comprised a central square house for the huntsman with long low wings either side for the hounds. Wyatt incorporated an ingenious central heating system for the hounds who were kept warmer than the guests in Goodwood House itself. The neat classical ensemble was encircled on the park side by a bastion-like wall and a ha-ha. A Coade-stone plaque, with Richmond's coat-of-arms and the date 1787, centred the pediment above the front door. Never had hounds been so splendidly housed.

*   *   *

It was not for nothing that Richmond was known as the 'Radical Duke'. Aged seventeen, he had written to the Duke of Newcastle (one of his guardians), 'I prize liberty beyond anything.'[28] By the 1770s, he was championing the cause of the American colonists. When the king was reviewing the British fleet at Portsmouth, Richmond sailed in his yacht through the fleet flying the American colours at its mast-head.[29] Although his behaviour was antagonistic, it was not revolutionary. In closing a debate in the House of Lords in 1777, he said, 'The sincere wish of my soul is for peace – peace with America and the reunion of the empire. A firm alliance with America would be a favourable compact indeed. Should this unhappy war continue, the ruin of both countries will be inevitable. England will most assuredly fall.'[30]

The following year, Richmond moved an address for the removal of British troops from America. As the aged Earl of Chatham rose to reply, in a moment of high drama he fell back speechless 'in an apoplectic fit' and had to be carried out. He later died.[31]

As well as supporting the American colonists, Richmond also lent his support to the Irish in their grievances against the British government, declaring that 'he was for an union but not an union of legislature, but an union of hearts, hands, of affections and interests'.[32] In 1780, he tried to introduce a bill to reform Parliament that included manhood suffrage, annual parliaments and equal electoral districts. Unfortunately, the first attempt to introduce it was disturbed by the anti-Catholic Gordon Riots taking place right outside the Houses of Parliament. Shouts from the mob, some 40,000-60,000-people strong, for 'the noble Duke of Richmond' were fortunately quelled by Lord Mahon. Walpole described the dramatic chain of events to his friend the Rev'd William Mason, adding, 'The Duke of Richmond, who you and I lament is for toleration of popery, will please you by having yesterday offered a bill for annual Parliaments, and is gone out of town today, disgusted at its being rejected. Yet, though I differ with him on both points, I worship his thousand virtues beyond any man's: he is intrepid and tender, inflexible and humane beyond example. I do not know which is most amiable, his heart or his conscience. He ought too to be the great model to all our factions.' He ends, 'Jesus! if the Duke of Richmond had fallen a victim to a blind tumult, in which half the sacrificers devoted him to the Furies, while half adored him.'[33]

For most of his political life, the third Duke of Richmond was a Whig, although the political climate was very different to that of his father's time. George III resented the Whigs' power and their desire to keep him in check. He therefore allied himself to the Tory party and Richmond stuck resolutely to the opposition. When Richmond returned from his embassy in Paris, he was made secretary of state for the south in the Marquess of Rockingham's cabinet. However, Rockingham's administration was short-lived, and Richmond held the appointment for less than a year.

Although much of his life was spent in politics, Richmond was not a natural politician and his character, combined with George III's dislike of him, meant that the top positions of government eluded him. For all of his strengths there were some glaring weaknesses – he lost his temper all too easily and was apt to quarrel with people; he was easily distracted; and he focused on too many things in much too much detail at the same time. He worked best when he had a clear goal and end in sight. If he became disinterested, then the lure of Goodwood and sport became too great. Writing to Richmond in October 1768, Newcastle chastised him, 'that you were very unwilling to leave your Hunting and come to Town, to consider with our Friends the Plan of Conduct . . . For God's sake My Dear Lord, Don't let it be said that upon Points of this Infinite Consequence to this Nation, Your Grace has suffer'd Your Fox Hunting to deprive the Cause, and your Friends, of the Advantage of your Assistance, and most Material Support, and for the sake of a Fox Chase. That is not an Object for the Duke of Richmond, who deservedly stands in the Light he is now.'[34]

There were moments in Richmond's life when he suffered from depression and there was nothing left for him to do but to lie low. On these occasions, his kind-hearted sister Louisa fled to his aid and cared for him, spending the summer of 1769 together at Aubigny. When he suffered another bout in 1772, she stayed with him at Goodwood, writing to her sister Emily back in Ireland, 'I am really quite unhappy about my brother, I think him so ill . . . his nerves are so oppressed that he is quite miserable . . . I have seen [him] write a letter or two about business, and you can't think what an operation it was, and how much the worse he was for it. He says himself that he wishes he had nothing to do; certainly his eagerness about his works is vastly gone. He often seems to have no pleasure in the things that amused him . . .'[35] Fortunately, he pulled through and Louisa returned to her husband and busy life in Ireland.

*   *   *

'The principal objections to Lord Derby were his figure, face, and voice', wrote *The Town and Country Magazine* harshly when reviewing a play at Richmond House, conceding that 'his manner was excellent, and supported with spirit. Mrs Hobart, notwithstanding her corpulency, represented the widow Belmour with vivacity, and threw considerable humour into the comic scenes.'[36] Derby and Hobart had leading roles in the comedy *The Way to Keep Him* by Arthur Murphy. The aristocratic cast was made up of experienced amateur actors and members of Mary Richmond's family, including her half-sister, Anne Damer. It was directed by the famous actress Elizabeth Farren, with whom Derby was in love and would later go on to marry. Anne was also artistic director, commissioning scenery from Thomas Greenwood of the Drury Lane Theatre and full-length portraits from John Downman depicting Anne and her three best friends (Georgiana, Duchess of Devonshire, Lady Elizabeth Foster and Lady Melbourne). Wyatt had been called in to design a theatre, converting two first-floor rooms at Richmond House. The graduated seating was flanked on one side by the royal box – in anticipation of royal guests – with a gallery opposite. After the first performance of *The Way to Keep Him*, supper was served and the guests partied until four o'clock in the morning.

Going to the theatre was one of England's most popular pastimes in the eighteenth century and a celebrity culture grew up around actors and actresses such as David Garrick and Sarah Siddons, who rubbed shoulders with the aristocratic élite. Private theatricals became a favourite entertainment of the upper classes, often with children performing. The third Duke of Richmond had appeared in *Les Dehors Trompeurs (False Appearances)*, a comedy by the French dramatist Louis de Boissy, when he was only five years old. Other houses that had their own private theatre included Blenheim Palace, Oxfordshire; Cliveden, Buckinghamshire; Wargrave, Berkshire; and Wynnstay, Denbighshire.[37]

The first season at Richmond House was such a success that Richmond decided to build a new theatre. This time, Wyatt converted the house next door that Richmond had bought for his brother, George. There was a large box in the centre for the Richmond family and further boxes on the sides; the king had his own canopy suspended over the middle of the Richmonds' box. Rather than benches, there were proper seats in the stalls. Anticipation of the forthcoming season was high – Horace Walpole was bowled over by Lord Henry FitzGerald (Emily's son) when he saw him in a rehearsal of The Wonder. Walpole declared him 'a prodigy, a perfection – all passion, nature and ease; you never saw so genuine a lover – Garrick was a monkey to him in Don Felix – then he is so much the man of fashion, and is so genteel . . .'[38] When the play opened in February 1788, the ladies swooned over Henry, Walpole exclaiming 'he has raised a thousand passions'.[39] His death on stage as Varanes in the tragedy Theodosius caused two ladies to faint, one of whom was carried 'out of the theatre in a strong hysteric'.[40] Further drama ensued when the London mob gathered outside during one performance; stones were thrown, breaking some windows.[41] Such was the popularity of the Richmond House theatre that an important motion in the House of Commons was postponed so guests could attend.

Richmond left no detail to chance – everything was thought through. Tickets were strictly limited, cast lists were announced in The Times, high headdresses were banned, and ices and other refreshments were served in the intervals. The great Sarah Siddons gave the ladies advice on their costumes and the royal family were frequent guests. The final play to be performed in the 1788 season was False Appearances, the same play that Richmond had acted in as a child. It was translated from the French by Mary's stepfather, Henry Conway. The last night was slightly marred by the musicians (members of the Sussex militia) who petitioned Richmond for better refreshments. Richmond, never one to take criticism easily, refused.[42]

As in all things that interested him, Richmond had thrown himself into his theatre. However, a combination of challenges, not least the general gloom over the court following George III's mental breakdown, meant Richmond lost interest and the theatre was closed. It was subsequently converted into a house for George's son, Charles, and his wife, Charlotte, the future fourth Duke and Duchess of Richmond.

Through all the comings and goings, Richmond House remained at the centre of family life in London, but it could never be taken for granted. Four days before Christmas 1791, in the early hours of the morning, fire broke out at Richmond House. Upstairs, in Henriette Le Clerc's bedroom, a coal from the recently lit fire had set her bed hangings alight. Awakened from her slumbers, Henriette quickly put on her dressing gown and woke up the rest of the house. Richmond was downstairs writing a letter in the library; he sprung into action immediately, hurrying his wife and Henriette safely out of the house and summoning assistance from the dazed servants and onlookers. A group of brave helpers rushed to the first floor and started lowering the furniture from the windows; three precious mirrors and most of the paintings were whisked off the walls and carried downstairs. Two large cabinets containing Richmond's papers were lowered from the balcony and the books in the library were thrown out of the window on to mattresses. Busts from the bookcases and Wyatt's model for the new Goodwood were saved, along with the contents of the duke's 'museum'. Both the Dukes of York and Clarence assisted with the firefighting, directing soldiers and floating fire engines on the river. Clarence was 'frequently nearly up to his knees in water'. As the fire raged, Richmond spotted his favourite spaniel desperately trying to force his way out of an upstairs window. Offering a reward to anyone who would save him, one of the watermen precariously attached some ladders together, scampered up, threw up the sash and saved the dog. Relieved, Richmond gave him eleven guineas – more than a year's salary – and two guineas to the man who held the ladder. Around midday, the roof fell in, preventing the fire from spreading further and, by the evening, it had been extinguished. That night, Richmond and Mary slept at the Duke of Buccleuch's house next door surrounded by their furniture and pictures.[43]

Richmond House was not insured, nor for that matter were the contents. Richmond lived with his brother next door when he was in London and the collection was put into storage while he decided what to do. In the end, he chose to enlarge the existing house at Goodwood.

Always one to use the latest architectural style, Wyatt's original scheme was abandoned. Instead, Wyatt came up with a radical plan adding two wings to the Brettingham wing with copper-domed circular towers framing each façade and tying them all together. The resulting building was like a giant bay window, taking advantage of the sweeping views across the park and catching the sun at all times of the day. A giant double-height portico, with Doric columns on the ground floor and Ionic columns on the first floor, created a grand entrance with a balcony above. The new wings were faced with knapped flint, providing work for the poor.[44] Inside, the new rooms were on a much larger scale than the rest of the house, enabling the family to host large house parties. However, there was one problem – cost.

In 1799, Richmond had debts of £90,000 and annual outgoings of just under £11,500. The coal duties had risen by the 1790s to an average of £21,000 a year, although there were rumblings of public discontent over these payments. In addition, he had an income of just under £8,000 from the Goodwood estate and £2,500 from his military appointments. It was simply not enough, so he made the decision to sell his coal tax duties back to the government for the enormous sum of £728,333. This required an Act of Parliament but it gave him an annual income of £19,000 and enabled him to enlarge the house.[45] In the event, he never saw the house completed.

*   *   *

On 19 April 1782, Richmond was made a Knight of the Garter. Nathanial Wraxall picked up a titbit of gossip regarding the ceremony: 'A great person, who was present at the ceremony of the Investiture, observed with admirable discernment, that never did three men receive the Order in so dissimilar and characteristic a manner. "The Duke of Devonshire" said he, "advanced up to the Sovereign, with his phlegmatic, cold, awkward air, like a clown. Lord Shelburne came forward, bowing on every side, smiling, and fawning, like a Courtier. The Duke of Richmond presented himself, easy, un-embarrassed, and the dignity, as a Gentleman.'"[46] This great honour might have suggested that relations between the king and Richmond had warmed; the truth was that Rockingham was back in power and the leading Whigs were being rewarded.

When Rockingham formed his second administration, he made Richmond Master-General of the Ordnance with a seat in the cabinet. The Board of Ordnance was responsible for fortifications, distribution of armaments and military defence, so Richmond became one of the government's principal military advisers. This was a role perfectly tailored to him and he held on to his position after Rockingham's premature death three months later. It was not an easy ride. Anxiety about a French invasion revealed the defencelessness of the south coast in general, in particular Plymouth and Portsmouth. Richmond's plans for fortifications met with huge opposition, mainly to do with the cost, and his 'Fortifications Bill' was defeated in Parliament. Some of his ideas did come to fruition, although not immediately. One was for a chain of defensive towers along the coast, not begun until 1804 when the first 'Martello' tower was built. Another was for a set of land signals to be established on projecting headlands, so the alarm could be raised quickly and easily in the event of an invasion.[47]

Perhaps Richmond's biggest contribution to the Ordnance was in the area of mapping. As early as 1758, he had employed a young Dutch surveyor called Thomas Yeakell to map the Goodwood estate. Yeakell was joined a few years later by William Gardner and together they became two of the most important British cartographers, mapping the full seventy-two square miles of the Goodwood estate at six inches to a mile. They soon outgrew Goodwood and next planned a map of Sussex at a scale of two inches to a mile. Although they only completed the four southern sheets of the projected eight, their 'Great Map' set the standard for future map-makers.

With his interest in map-making – an essential component of defence – Richmond made the most of his position at the Ordnance. Yeakell and Gardner were given jobs at the Ordnance, working at the Tower of London where the Ordnance was housed. In 1785, he commissioned the first proper survey of Britain, starting with Guernsey and Jersey. Five years later, when General William Roy died, Richmond was spurred on to bring to fruition Roy's vision of a national military survey and, in 1791, what became known as the 'Ordnance Survey' was born.[48] In 1801, the first one-inch-to-the-mile map was published detailing Kent, but it was not until 1870 that England and Wales were finally completed when sheet number 108 (south-west Northumberland) was published.[49]

Richmond continued in his post at the Ordnance during the premiership of the Earl of Shelburne but, when that ministry collapsed, he resigned under the fragile coalition between Lord North and his nephew Charles James Fox. When that fell less than a year later, Richmond dramatically changed sides to the Tories and joined the ministry of William Pitt the Younger, resuming his role as Master-General of the Ordnance. The king changed his attitude towards him and is reported to have said that 'there was no man in his dominions by whom he had been so much offended, and no man to whom he was so much indebted, as the Duke of Richmond'.[50] Richmond ploughed on at the Ordnance, working tirelessly and pushing through his reforms. One of these was the introduction of two troops of horse artillery that could transport large wheeled guns at speed. Taking a personal interest in their training, he summoned 'A' troop to Goodwood, stabling the horses in Chambers' magnificent stable block and drilling the gunners on the South Downs.

Despite his conscientiousness at the Ordnance, Richmond was gradually eased out of government. In December 1790, Pitt appointed a new leader of the House of Lords, replacing Richmond. Three years later, he was made a scapegoat for the failed siege of Dunkirk – part of the French Revolutionary Wars – when heavy artillery failed to arrive. In defending himself (he was completely innocent) he was seen to be too vehement and was vilified in the press. Fed up with his non-attendance at cabinet meetings (which Richmond argued was because he had been ill and had been travelling with Ordnance work) and his argumentative manner, Pitt dismissed him from the Ordnance in

January 1795. He no longer had a seat in the cabinet and retreated to Goodwood to lick his wounds. It was not only the restorative surroundings of Goodwood that he craved, but also female company: 'For I confess I do want some of my females just now,' he wrote to Mary, who had been worried for his health.[51]

Mary had not been well herself. Her health had been declining steadily since about 1793 and she spent increasing amounts of time at Goodwood while Richmond attended to business in London, writing him chatty letters about the goings-on at home. After his dismissal, he stayed at Goodwood all the time and devoted himself solely to her. She died in early November 1796, prompting a mourning Walpole to write: 'I had loved [her] most affectionately from the first moment I knew her, when she was but five years old – her sweet temper and unalterable good nature had made her retain a friendship for and confidence in me that was more steady than I ever found in any other person to whom I have been most attracted. It is a heavy blow!'[52]

Richmond felt her loss keenly. Despite their dalliances, they had remained devoted to one another and she had willingly welcomed the little Henriette Le Clerc into their family. Although it was never formally acknowledged, Henriette was Richmond's illegitimate daughter by the Vicomtesse de Cambis. His affair with Madame de Cambis, a well-connected, intelligent and sophisticated French aristocrat, had lasted for much of the 1770s, with Henriette being born in 1773. Surprisingly, Mary did not seem all that bothered. Louisa, writing to Emily in 1776, commented: 'As to my brother's flirting, she don't mind it one bit, provided 'tis with what she reckons creditable and genteel. She is vastly comical upon that subject, for jealousy is not in question, but her pride is, & she is discomposed if she thinks he likes anything frippery or vulgar.'[53]

*   *   *

Tucked away on a high shelf in the Large Library at Goodwood sit three manuscript books of a curious nature to modern-day guests.

They record the weights of family members and friends who stayed at
Goodwood from 1784 until 1921. There was no apparent inhibition
about being weighed and sometimes the weights are annotated 'Before
Dinner' or 'After Dinner', with the occasional 'Boot, whip & hat'
thrown in. On 25 September 1786, children and adults were all weighed
before dinner. These included Mary (9 st, 5 lbs), Mary's half-sister,
Anne Damer (8 st, 13 lbs) and the twelve-year-old Henriette (6 st, 2 lbs).
A week later, Madame de Cambis (8 st, 12 lbs) was dining with the
family, including three of Emily's children: Sophia (8 st, 3 lbs), Edward
(10 st, 2 lbs) and Lucy (7 st). Also included in the dinner party was
Richmond's niece Georgina Lennox with whom the twenty-two-year-
old Edward was passionately in love.

Edward FitzGerald was the darling of the family: the twelfth of
Emily's twenty-two children, he was doted on by his mother and siblings. His father, the Duke of Leinster, had died when he was only ten
and his 'Uncle Richmond' had taken him under his wing. Aged sixteen, Richmond had secured him a place in the Sussex Militia, of which
he was colonel. Eager to see action, the following year he went to
America to fight in the War of Independence and proved his mettle.
The summer of the Goodwood dinner party, Richmond had taken
him on a tour of inspection of the Channel Islands followed by study
with a tutor at Goodwood. It was during this time, when he was staying at Stoke (his uncle George's home), that he had fallen in love with
his cousin Georgina. Sadly, it was not to be; although Georgina willingly accepted his proposal, her parents were adamant in their refusal.
So off to Canada he went with his regiment where he spent time with
the Iroquois and was adopted by them as an Indian chief. On his
return, Richmond secured a promotion for him in the army. The very
next day, much to Richmond's annoyance, he threw it all in for a seat
in the Irish Houses of Parliament in support of his brother, William,
now Duke of Leinster.

Always headstrong and passionate, Edward embarked on an affair
with Richard Brinsley Sheridan's wife, the beautiful singer, Elizabeth
Linley. A baby girl was born, only to die not long afterwards, following

her mother to the grave. Edward then fell in with the republican Thomas Paine, staying with him in revolutionary France and renouncing his title. He was struck off the Army List and was fast becoming an increasing embarrassment to his family. In France, he fell in love with another beauty, Pamela, the illegitimate daughter of Philippe Égalité. He married her, and they returned to Ireland just before The Terror. There, encouraged by Pamela, he signed up with the United Irishmen and plotted Irish independence from Great Britain. He travelled to France to seek support against 'the unjust influence of Great Britain' and became mixed up in plans for an Irish rebellion and invasion from France.[54] For several months, he went into hiding with a £1,000 price tag on his head, but on 19 May 1798, he was discovered and wounded resisting arrest. He died not long afterwards in Dublin's Newgate Prison while awaiting trial on a capital charge of treason.[55] The family were devastated. Louisa had had to beg the Lord Lieutenant, Earl Camden, on her knees to see her dying nephew, only to be refused; it was only through the kindness of the Lord Chancellor, the Earl of Clare, who took her in his own carriage, that she was permitted to see him. As soon as Richmond heard the news, he went at once to fetch Pamela (who was staying in London) in his carriage and brought her and her young children back to Goodwood where they were joined by a grieving Emily and her family. Yet again, Goodwood was a place of refuge. Pamela remained there for a couple of months until she moved to Hamburg, leaving two of her children to be brought up by Emily, and Edward's unmarried sister, Sophia.

*   *   *

High on the South Downs, racegoers cheered as the Prince of Wales's horse, Rebel, galloped flat out in a head-to-head race with Richmond's horse, Cedar. It was the third and final day of the first public race meeting at Goodwood and spirits were high. Watching from his wooden stand with local dignitaries, Richmond felt a glowing sense of pride; horseracing had found a new home at Goodwood. Rebel won the race and, with it, the Prince of Wales pocketed 100 guineas. Richmond was not too bothered as Cedar had won a two-mile sweepstake on the opening day.

Two years previously, in 1800, Richmond had let the officers of the Sussex Militia hold a race meeting on the Harroway, the narrow ridge on the top of the Downs behind Goodwood. The following year, he held a private two-day meeting laying out a new course and pitching several tents for refreshments. In the evening, guests attended the Chichester Theatre on the first night and a ball in the Assembly Rooms on the second. Unfortunately, Richmond was laid low with gout, but it did not dampen his enthusiasm and he threw himself into the preparations for the 1802 meeting. Local interest ran high, and with the success of the 1802 meeting, the Goodwood races became a permanent fixture in the racing calendar.[56]

Standing up on the Downs watching the horseracing, Richmond must have reflected on all that he had achieved on the Goodwood estate. Aside from all of the building works, landscaping and gardening, he had increased his landholdings from around 1,100 acres to 17,000 acres. These included the neighbouring estates of Halnaker and East Dean.[57] The purchase of Halnaker, a much older and more historically important estate than Goodwood, enabled him to divert the main Chichester to Petworth road; it ran just a little too close for comfort so was moved further east passing through Halnaker. On the coast, he built a house and stables at Itchenor where he could exercise his racehorses on the beach and sail his yacht; it was a favourite retreat for his sisters and numerous nieces and nephews.

After enjoying a brief flirtation with Lady Bess Foster, bosom companion of Georgiana, Duchess of Devonshire, Richmond found comfort in the arms of his housekeeper, Mary Blesard, who was more than thirty years his junior. In 1802, he bought Mary, or Mrs Bennett as she became known, a fine house at Earls Court complete with stables and coach house and a small farm attached. They had three daughters – Elizabeth, Caroline and Mary – Mary being born posthumously. As he neared the end of his life, Richmond's sister Sarah remarked that he was enjoying himself like a man of twenty-one, even though he was seventy-one.

Sarah spent the last four months of Richmond's life with him and was by his bedside when he died at Goodwood on 27 December 1806. All those who were dear to him were remembered in his Will, including Henriette, Mrs Bennett and her daughters, and loyal servants. His funeral took place on 5 January in Chichester Cathedral, 'in the most private and least expensive manner', and his body was laid in the family vault alongside those of his father and grandfather. It was now for his nephew, Charles Lennox, to assume the mantle as the fourth Duke of Richmond.

*Rash and impetuous, the fourth Duke of Richmond was involved in
two duels as a young man. Portrait after John Hoppner
(© Trustees of the Goodwood Collection)*

7

Brussels Interlude

'There was a sound of revelry by night,
And Belgium's Capital had gathered then
Her Beauty and her Chivalry – and bright
The lamps shone o'er fair women and brave men;
A thousand hearts beat happily; and when
Music arose with its voluptuous swell,
Soft eyes looked love to eyes which spake again,
And all went merry as a marriage bell;
But hush! hark! a deep sound strikes like a rising knell!'

Lord Byron, *Childe Harold's Pilgrimage* (1812-18)

The summer of 1789 was one of the wettest on record, with May being particularly wet. At dawn, on 26 May, two army officers made their way to Wimbledon Common. Travelling in separate carriages, each was accompanied by a fellow officer. Reaching the common, the carriages drew up at a respectful distance from each other and the accompanying officers exchanged a few words. Glancing up at their respective comrades, they measured out twelve paces and marked the points. The dropping of a handkerchief was then agreed upon by both parties as the signal to fire. The accompanying officers then retreated, and the two opponents took their positions. Moments later, the handkerchief fell and one gentleman fired, grazing a curl of his opponent's hair. Surprisingly, the shot was not returned, and the opponent's comrade said he thought that enough had been done.

At this critical point, a clipped dialogue arose between the two parties – Colonel Charles Lennox (nephew of the third Duke of Richmond) and his second, the Earl of Winchelsea on the one hand; and the Duke of York (second son of George III) and his second, Lord Rawdon on the other. Observing that his opponent had not yet fired, Rawdon stated it was not the duke's intention to fire and that the duke had only come out to give Lennox satisfaction and bore no grudge against him. Lennox, visibly tense, pressed York to fire but again he refused. Winchelsea then went up to York and said he hoped his highness would have no objections in calling Lennox a man of honour and courage. This the duke refused and again said he had only come out to give Lennox satisfaction. If Lennox was not satisfied, then he might fire again. To this, Lennox said he could not possibly fire again on someone who did not mean to fire at him and, leaving it at that, both parties departed having 'behaved with the most perfect coolness and intrepidity'.[1]

The duel had arisen because the Duke of York had accused Lennox of not retaliating to an insult at D'Aubigny's Club. The problem was that the supposed insult had been made at a masquerade and Lennox denied all knowledge of it. When pressed to name the offender, the duke could say no more than that he had heard the insult. Lennox then wrote a circular letter to all the members of the club asking them if anyone remembered hearing anything and, if so, who said it. Eliciting no satisfactory answer, Lennox wrote to the duke asking him to clear his name. Getting no response, he had to conclude that it was York himself who had delivered the insult and therefore reluctantly challenged him to a duel. It was a difficult decision to make as not only was the duke a member of the royal family, but he was also Colonel of the Coldstream Guards, Lennox's own regiment. But the rules of society at that time were quite clear – one must defend one's honour even unto death.

A few days after the duel, the officers of the Coldstream Guards met to discuss the incident and issued a public statement: 'It is the opinion of His Majesty's Coldstream regiment of Guards, that Lieutenant Colonel Lenox, subsequent to the 15th instant, has behaved with *courage*; but, from the peculiarity of the circumstance, not with *judgement*.'[2] Unfortunately, the whole affair was reported in the press.[3] Rumours circulated that it was a deliberate challenge to the Richmond family who were political opponents of York and his elder brother, the Prince of Wales, having taken their father George III's side during the Regency Crisis. As if to rub salt into the wound, just over a week later, the Prince of Wales snubbed Lennox at a court ball held for the king's birthday; again, this was picked up by the press.[4]

There was no doubt that Lennox was of a rash character. Just over a month later, he was involved in another duel against Theophilus Swift, who had slandered his character in a pamphlet. They met near Bayswater and Swift was wounded in the stomach. 'The dispute was then amicably settled, and Mr. Swift was conveyed home without betraying any particular signs of pain.'[5]

Lennox, the only son of George and Louisa, had been brought up at Stoke not far from Goodwood, in the expectation that he would one day inherit the dukedom from his uncle and with it the responsibilities as head of a great English family. For a brief moment it had looked like his uncle might marry the avaricious Bess Foster with the risk that his inheritance might be usurped, but Lennox's wife Charlotte had quickly put a stop to that along with Henriette. Entering the army when twenty-one, his uncle Richmond kept a close eye on his progress as he rose through the ranks. After the duel with the Duke of York, he transferred regiments to the 35th Foot and, having a natural aptitude for soldiering, eventually became a full general in 1814.

Shortly before he died, the third Duke of Richmond poured his heart out in a letter to his nephew. They had often had their differences of opinion, mainly over politics (Lennox was a firm supporter of Pitt) and

Richmond liked to discuss things with him 'in that friendly and candid manner that my inclinations lead me to with you'. But on this occasion, Richmond was hurt at his nephew's 'extreme reserve' to open up to him, writing, 'Towards me you seem to have a regard, and a sense of gratitude for former & present attentions but no wish to make an intimate friend of me . . . such coldness you must be sensible will have its effect on the openness and warmth of my disposition. It is true that the difference in our ages may in general be pleaded as a sufficiently natural bar to such intimacy . . . I never could see any impediment but in your close disposition, and desire to live in more idle Company, to our being on the most friendly and communicative footing together.' Looking to the future, he reflects, 'As I grow old & my time short, what have I to look to for the continuation of my family and the various schemes that one forms its benefit and advantages but you. In you centres my future pride for the family. I am anxious both for your character and happiness as its probable representative. I am not ambitious for you in any way, for I too well know that ambition only leads to vexation. But I wish you to enjoy with credit those advantages which you will fall into by inheritance . . . I wish you to take care of your numerous family which is one of the first duties of a father, and for that purpose to be prudent.' Complimenting his nephew on his 'great patience' and 'good temper', he despairs that he 'suffer[s] foolish passions to interfere with a domestic life . . . You too often seek in wine to forget care, and sometimes in company that does you no credit. Aversion to accounts makes you neglect your affairs which must bring you into great distress & difficulties, while at the same time the education and provision for your numerous children would require the strictest attention to and regularity in your affairs and many privations in you to enable them to live.' He then urges Lennox to economise and start saving or 'the amplest fortune would slip thro' your hands without effectuating the sacred purpose which honour and duty as well as affection calls on you to perform.'

Turning to the management of the Goodwood estate, Richmond tells him, 'There are a thousand particulars in which I should wish to instruct you, and which I may say without vanity no one else can so well instruct you, because no one has had my experience in it.' He would love his nephew to spend more time in Sussex so he could get to know him better, and tempts him with the offer of 'hunting, shooting and the society of some pleasant neighbours' to stave off any boredom. He even goes so far as to suggest that Lennox's wife, Charlotte, would be 'more pleasant' if Lennox 'were inclined to be more domestic'. After chastising him for going racing at Epsom rather than visiting his 'old sick uncle' and seeing his sons who were home from school on holiday, he goes on to question whether he should continue his career in the army given the lack of opportunity for high command and his nephew's want of aptitude in certain areas. Towards the end of the letter, he apologises that he has 'bored you with a very long letter but having my pen in my hand I was glad to open my heart to you. I feel low, and uncomfortable, and neglected, perhaps sowered by perpetual successions of painful disorders which make me the more want the attention of those I love.' He ends, 'My notions may be onerous but I am sure they are dictated by the purest affection for you. Your ever affectionate uncle, Richmond.'[6]

Although most of Richmond's advice was ignored, there were some home truths that were hard to stomach. Lennox did indeed have a large family to support with a wife and fourteen children (seven boys and seven girls). His wife, Charlotte, was a force to be reckoned with. She was the daughter of the fourth Duke of Gordon and his formidable and beautiful wife, Jane. Brought up as the eldest of seven children, she had a domineering character that blew hot and cold depending on her mood. When she was twenty-one, she had married the young Charles Lennox in a secret ceremony at her family home, Gordon Castle, much to her mother's delight who was keen to marry her daughters well. Lennox had just been posted to Edinburgh as colonel of the 35th Foot, in the wake of his duel with the Duke of York.

The third duke's call to economy on the part of his nephew turned out to be hypocritical. When his debts were added up after he had died, they came to a staggering £180,000. Building work at Goodwood was halted, leaving the two new wings incomplete. The offer to Lennox to go overseas to Ireland as Lord Lieutenant was therefore an attractive proposition, enabling him to escape some of his creditors.

The new Duke and Duchess of Richmond departed for Dublin in April 1807, replacing Charlotte's brother-in-law, the Duke of Bedford. As Lord Lieutenant, Richmond enjoyed all the trappings of state, with official residences in Dublin Castle and Phoenix Park. Following the Act of Union in 1800 when the Irish parliament had moved to London, things were a little quieter in Dublin, although no less busy. The fourth Duke of Richmond threw himself into his new role and became very popular, travelling all over Ireland. He was able to indulge in his love of foxhunting and horseracing, and their home in Phoenix Park was always full of friends and family. One regular guest was the young Arthur Wellesley, later Duke of Wellington, who was Chief Secretary for Ireland. Wellesley relished the fun atmosphere of a family home filled with laughter and antics and developed close friendships with the children, particularly Georgiana. After he left in 1809 to lead the campaign in the Spanish peninsula, he kept up a lively correspondence with the children and their mother. Writing to Charlotte in 1811, he looked back fondly to times spent with her family, admitting, 'I have not laughed or enjoyed anything so much since certainly.'[7]

In 1812, the year before their return from Ireland, tragedy was to strike. The Richmonds' third son, Henry, who was a young Midshipman in the Royal Navy, fell from the rigging of his ship, HMS *Blake* and was killed. He was only fourteen. A lock of his blond hair, a naval button from his hat and his gold ring were sent home to his grieving mother who carefully stowed them away in a little velvet and gold-thread purse he had given her. His family sent a notice of his death to their friends, lamenting the loss of their son and eulogising on his character: 'Quick discernment, gentleness of temper, kindness of disposition, and a rare generosity of heart, were the characteristics of this noble Youth!'

Despite this setback, the Richmonds' time in Ireland was largely a happy chapter in their lives, particularly for the children, who enjoyed going to the theatre, shooting expeditions, sightseeing and visiting Ireland's beauty spots. At one point, Richmond overstepped the mark and, much to his wife's fury, became enamoured of Augusta Somerset, an acknowledged beauty who was already married. The two of them rode out together regularly and, on one unfortunate occasion, a note from Augusta to Richmond ended up in his wife's hands. After asking Richmond to ride with her and dine together that evening, it ended: 'What fine fun we shall have! The old Puss will burst with jealousy.' Charlotte was livid but, when she confronted her husband, he calmly reprimanded her for opening his post, told her to ignore the contents and insisted that Augusta should continue to dine with them. It caused a minor kerfuffle in Dublin society.[8]

*   *   *

A glistening open-top carriage swept through the lodge gates at Goodwood on an overcast summer's day in June 1814. Its two occupants smiled benevolently at the gatekeeper who bowed low while his wife curtsied. The carriage was escorted by a troop of cavalry and in its wake followed more carriages, some with coachmen resplendent in the royal livery. As it made its way through the park, the wheels crunching on the newly metalled drive, its passengers admired the tall cedars of Lebanon and the venerable chestnuts with which the grounds were studded. Gradually, the house came into view, the grand stable block giving way to the pristine stone- and flint-work of the new entrance front. Pulling into the turning circle, the carriage came to a standstill beside the great double-storeyed portico. A postilion jumped down, opened the carriage door, bowed his head and held out his arm as a support. Standing in the portico waiting to greet the visitors were Charles, fourth Duke of Richmond, his wife Charlotte with their children, and the senior household servants. Their guests were Alexander, Emperor of Russia, and his sister, Catherine, Duchess of Oldenburgh.

Alexander and Catherine had arrived in England on 6 June, along with the King of Prussia, Field Marshall Blücher, and a host of princes, dignitaries and courtiers, to celebrate Napoleon's defeat and subsequent exile to Elba. The Treaty of Paris had just been signed by the four great powers of Austria, Prussia, Russia and Great Britain and the allied sovereigns' visit was to be a huge celebration of peace in Europe prior to the Congress of Vienna later in the year. There had been an exhausting round of entertainments, parades and ceremonies, including racing at Ascot and a naval review. On the morning of their visit to Goodwood, Alexander and Catherine had left Portsmouth at eleven o'clock, stopping on their way to review 7,000 troops on Portsdown Hill, accompanied by the Prince Regent and the King of Prussia. Changing horses in Chichester, the Prince Regent and King of Prussia went on to Petworth, while the Tsar stopped off at Goodwood where extensive preparations had been under way for three days prior.

Richmond led his royal guests into the Front Hall, newly finished with its screen of Guernsey granite columns across the rear and pair of chimneypieces covered in antique bronzes and sculptures. They then proceeded into the Egyptian Dining-Room, the late duke's pride and joy that had been completed only ten years earlier. The third duke had inherited a love of all things Egyptian from his father. Following Napoleon's disastrous Egyptian campaign, the artists he had taken with him had published their drawings and everyone in Europe had become Egyptian fanatics. The third duke had eagerly snapped up Vivant Denon's *Planches du Voyages dans la Basse et la Haute Egypte pendant les Campagnes de Bonaparte* (1802) and asked Wyatt to design his new dining-room in the Egyptian style. The result was one of the most exotic rooms in England, with scagliola walls resembling sienna marble and Egyptian ornament on the doors, cornice and mantelpiece; even the chairs had Egyptian crocodiles on them. Down the centre of the table stood four magnificent ormolu candelabra with Egyptian figures and hieroglyphics. Their majesties then sat down to breakfast (a formal meal like a wedding breakfast) and 'expressed themselves highly delighted with the splendid hospitality with which they were received by their noble Host and Hostess, as well as with the beauties of the place'. They then continued their journey, joining the rest of the party at Petworth as guests of the Earl of Egremont.[9] Two days later, having said their goodbyes to the Prince Regent at his Pavilion in Brighton, they departed from Dover.

Less than a month later, Goodwood was playing host to an entirely different group of people. A large crowd had gathered in the park to watch one of most important cricket matches of the year, organised by Richmond for a purse of one thousand guineas. Some of the best players in the kingdom opposed each other as Lord Frederick Beauclerk's eleven battled it out against George Osbaldeston's eleven. Richmond umpired and the match, scheduled for three days, was over in two. The result, widely reported in the press at the time, was a victory for Osbaldeston's team by seventeen runs.

The fourth Duke of Richmond was something of a cricket celebrity himself. Naturally tall and athletic, he was a fine batsman and wicket-keeper and played whenever he could. A founding member of the Marylebone Cricket Club, both he and the Earl of Winchilsea persuaded Thomas Lord to start a new cricket ground in Dorset Fields, guaranteeing him against any financial losses. Lord's, as it came to be known, was opened in 1787 and remained in Dorset Fields (now Dorset Square) until 1811. Never one to turn down an opportunity of playing, Richmond played with his brother-in-law, the Marquis of Huntly, in the Gordon Castle team a month after his wedding. The match was against the 55th Regiment and he scored 136 not out, the first known century in Scotland.[10]

When he returned from Ireland in 1813, he resurrected the Goodwood Cricket Club with a new set of rules; the first rule was that the members would meet twice a week in the park to practise and Mr Gilbert would pitch a marquee and provide refreshments. Gilbert was the landlord of the Duke of Richmond's Arms, the inn that had been built by the third duke at the entrance to the park, next door to the tennis court and kitchen garden. The members of the club even had their own dress – white flannel jacket trimmed with blue silk and white trousers.[11]

The summer of the allied sovereigns' visit was to be the last one Richmond enjoyed at Goodwood. The expense of living in England in a style suitable for someone of his rank, combined with the burden of a large family and a wife who had a weakness for gambling, was just too great. He needed to retrench and therefore made the decision to move abroad and live in Brussels 'with all his Family for a year on an Economical Plan'.[12]

*   *   *

Charlotte Richmond was not amused. Having spent two days reaching Dover from London, they then had to wait another five days for the weather to improve before crossing the English Channel. Leaving at midday on board HMS *Redpole*, they eventually arrived at Boulogne at half-past eight in the evening. It was pitch black and the tide was out, so when they disembarked from the three boats that carried them from the ship, they had to walk a mile and a half up the beach. Cold and wet, with tired and hungry children at her heels, Charlotte was furious when she discovered that the inn where they were to stay the night was full. A kind gentleman gave up his room, and two-thirds of the party went elsewhere. The following day, the party made their way to Calais to pick up their carriages before travelling via Dunkirk and Bruges to Brussels, arriving on 14 October, sixteen days after leaving London.[13]

Richmond himself had taken an advance party with his two eldest daughters, leaving his wife to bring the rest of the family. The latter comprised seventeen people, which included Spencer Madan, a young gentleman who had just been employed as tutor to the younger boys. Madan, the son of a clergyman, was a sensitive, bright and earnest young man of sound judgement. Well connected, he was also an old school fellow of the eldest son, the Earl of March, at Westminster. However, nothing could have prepared him for the wild behaviour of his charges and the demanding character of his mistress. His letters to his family reveal the constant social dilemmas he was faced with on a daily basis, often arising from the duchess's whims. He often bore the brunt of her fierce temper, calling her 'one of the sourest, most ill-tempered personages I ever came across in my life' and complaining of her 'haughty and disagreeable behaviour . . . & her constant & ill-judged interference with regard to the boys'.[14] In reality, as the mother of thirteen children, she was probably stretched to her limit managing household affairs, her family and settling into an alien city with ongoing financial worries, not to mention her penchant for gambling. The duke, on the other hand, was kinder to him. Madan described him as being 'a man of some talent, of sound understanding and judgement, and . . . of the most polished manners and the strictest honour'.[15]

Together with the Low Countries, Belgium had been occupied for twenty years by France under Napoleon's rule. Brussels, a largely Catholic city, had been freed from French power by the allies on 1 February 1814. In April, Napoleon had abdicated and, at the Treaty of Paris, the whole area had been formed into a new state known as the Netherlands. To maintain stability, the British left an army contingent in the former Austrian Netherlands, commanded by the Hereditary Prince of Orange. The Duke of Wellington was Commander-in-Chief of the whole Anglo-Netherlands Army and, following the Congress of Vienna, the Prince of Orange's father, the Sovereign Prince of Orange, became King of the Netherlands.

The Richmonds had chosen Brussels as there was a much lower cost of living than in Britain, where overseas trade restrictions had inflated prices. It was therefore seen as an attractive alternative for English people wishing to save money, particularly upper-class families like the Capels and the Grevilles who could maintain a standard of living that was beyond their reach in England. The endless round of balls and dinners kept everyone amused in the evenings, while picnics, horseracing and hunting were among the entertainments laid on during the day. The presence of an English garrison formed another attraction, particularly for any matchmaking mothers anxious to marry their daughters off to a string of eligible officers ripe for the picking. At the heart of the Brussels social scene was the dashing and charming Prince of Orange, nicknamed 'Slender Billy'. He was a great anglophile, having been educated at Oxford University and having served in the British army as aide-de-camp (ADC) to Wellington.

Rather than living in the most fashionable part of Brussels, centred around the Parc de Bruxelles, the Richmonds rented a large red-brick house in the Rue de la Blanchisserie. The street had been so named because a laundry business had been established there in the seventeenth century. Wellington referred jokingly to it as 'The Wash House', much to Charlotte's annoyance. The house had been built only twenty years earlier by a coachbuilder, so the smart three-storey residence was flanked by two barn-like wings that had been used for the coach-building business. The wing that had been used as a showroom was converted into a schoolroom and playroom for the younger children where they played battledore and shuttlecock on wet days. The property abutted the old city ramparts and there was a large garden for the children to run around in as well as plenty of stabling for their horses.

All thirteen of the Richmonds' children were in Brussels with them. The eldest three sons were in the army. Captain the Earl of March – an 'excellent young man' according to Madan – had fought in the Peninsula with the 13th Light Dragoons before becoming assistant military secretary and ADC to the Duke of Wellington. After acting as a volunteer in the storming party at the Siege of Ciudad Rodrigo, he exchanged into the 52nd Foot and was with them at the Battle of Orthez (27 February 1814) where he was hit by a bullet in his chest. The bullet remained in him for the rest of his life, 'from the Effects of which he has not recovered, but Faints at the least transition from heat to cold', as Maria Capel told her grandmother.[16] March was then appointed extra ADC to the Prince of Orange, his erstwhile fellow ADC from the siege of Ciudad Rodrigo. He had his own small house within the grounds of 'The Wash House'. George, the second son, was a lieutenant in the 9th Light Dragoons and had been an ADC to Wellington for some time. His younger brother, William, had been an ADC to Wellington at the Congress of Vienna, and rode back from there to Brussels with him. However, Wellington decided on a policy of only having Peninsula War veterans, so William was moved to be ADC to Major General Peregrine Maitland, who would eventually become his brother-in-law when he eloped with William's sister Sarah.

The younger boys – Frederick, Sussex and Arthur – were under the tutelage of Madan and were described by their mother as 'the most headstrong untoward little pickles she ever knew'.[17] Certainly, they tested Madan's patience to the full. The seven daughters – Mary, Sarah, Georgiana, Jane, Louisa, Charlotte and Sophia – ranged in age from twenty-three to just five. Madan said of the four eldest daughters, 'They are the most good-humoured, unaffected girls I ever met with, exceedingly highbred but without an atom of pride,' adding, 'They do not deserve to be coupled with the D'ss, whom they resemble but in name.'[18]

Once the Richmonds were settled in Brussels, the duke indulged in his passions for horseracing, cricket and hunting. He was a steward of the Brussels races where, according to Madan, 'the horses being for the most part chargers, and the riders gentlemen of the Guards'.[19] Both Richmond and March entered horses in a race meeting on 10 October 1814 and William had a serious riding accident in a race at Enghien the following year where he 'was taken up for dead, but has experienced a most wonderful recovery', as Madan reported.[20]

Nothing could keep Richmond from playing cricket. On 13 June 1815, Madan told his father: 'The family are at present gone to Enghien to a cricket match amongst the *gentlemen of the guards*, in which the Duke takes a part. You have of course heard of his fame as a cricketer; he was, I believe, considered to be one of the two best in England, the other is Ld. F. Beauclerc.'[21]

As for hunting, Richmond again took the lead, as Maria Capel wrote: 'On Saturday next there is a Grand Wolf Hunting to take place in the Forest of Ardennes about 50 Miles from here. It is to last a *fortnight* – Papa & The Duke of Richmond are Prime Movers &, as it carries them & *The Cream of our Society* off, we think it is a great Bore.'[22]

As the Richmonds enjoyed themselves in Brussels and its environs, the political situation in Europe was hotting up. On 26 February 1815,

Napoleon gave his captors the slip and escaped from the island of Elba with a small force, landing on the French mainland six days later. Troops sent to intercept him threw down their arms and joined the cause, so that by 20 March when he entered Paris, he had an army behind him. Meanwhile, the armies of Britain, Russia, Austria and Prussia were mobilising a combined force of 150,000 men on France's eastern borders. Some of the foreigners in Brussels fled as soon as there was a whiff of danger, but the Richmonds, Grevilles and Capels stoically remained. When Wellington entered Brussels on 4 April, accompanied by young William Lennox, he immediately set about preparing the army to meet its formidable opponent, particularly calling for those who had served with him in the Peninsula.

Nobody quite knew what Napoleon intended, although the likelihood was that either he would strike towards Brussels or that the allied armies would invade France. Despite the rumours and panic that were rife in Brussels, the parties continued unabated. Lady Caroline Capel joked, 'Balls are going on here as if we had had none for a year.'[23] Wellington gave a ball on 3 June, the British ambassador on 5 June and Wellington again on 7 June with another one planned for 21 June, the anniversary of his Peninsula victory at Vittoria. He did not escape Caroline's criticism: 'The Duke of W- has not improved the *Morality* of our Society, as he has given several things & makes a point of asking all the Ladies of Loose Character.'[24] Despite his flirtations, Wellington was playing his cards close to his chest with regard to military matters. 'Nobody can guess Lord Wellington's intentions, & I dare say Nobody will know he is going till he is actually gone. In the meantime, he amuses himself with Humbugging the Ladies, particularly the Duchess of Richmond,' wrote Caroline.[25]

On 12 June, Napoleon left Paris, heading north-east. Charlotte Richmond had planned to give a ball on 15 June, but she was understandably unsure whether it could take place, so she asked Wellington, 'Duke, I do not wish to pry into your secrets, nor do I ask what your intentions may be: I wish to give a ball, and all I ask is – May I give my ball? If you say, "Duchess, don't give your ball," it is quite sufficient – I ask no reasons.' Wellington replied, 'Duchess, you may give your ball with the greatest safety, without fear of interruption.'[26] His words were to prove fatally flawed.

*   *   *

The gravel crunched beneath Wellington's black evening shoes as he paced backwards and forwards in the Parc, deep in thought. Several groups of officers were standing nearby, some in grave conversation, others anxiously observing the Iron Duke. Every now and then he paused; an officer ran up to him, took orders and swiftly departed. It was five o'clock in the afternoon of 15 June and the Parc looked just as it did on any other summer's day. Tall trees cast their shadows over neat lawns and fashionable people could be seen strolling along its paths, winding their way through thick shrubberies. Charlotte Waldie, newly arrived in Brussels, described how it was 'crowded with officers, in every variety of military uniform, with elegant women, and with lively parties and gay groups of British and Belgic people, loitering, walking, talking, and sitting under the trees! There could not be a more animated, a more holiday scene; everything looked gay and festive, and everything spoke of hope, confidence and busy expectation.'[27] However, beyond the confines of the prim park railings and the pretty pastel-coloured houses overlooking the Parc, things were far from calm.

Earlier that morning, Wellington had had reports of French movements near the border but had carried on as normal with routine work. Everyone expected that nothing would happen until early July when the combined allied armies would advance into France. Dinner parties had been held from the usual hour of 3-5 p.m., and the Prince of Orange had dined with Wellington. During dinner, Wellington had received news that Napoleon was on the move, so he had decided to get some fresh air in the Parc while issuing orders at the same time. He was expecting to march the following morning and declared his intention of going to the Duchess of Richmond's ball; he hoped that other officers would do the same. Then, hearing that the French had attacked Prussian outposts and had seized Charleroi, he ordered the troops to assemble at their headquarters. By late afternoon, the distant sound of gunfire could be heard in the city, causing concern among the foreigners, some of whom were already making preparations to flee.

The clatter of hooves on cobbles could be heard from 10 p.m. as guests started to arrive for the ball at the Richmonds' residence in the Rue de la Blanchisserie. The Richmond family were all present, as well as the boys' tutor, Madan. As the ball was a private party, hosted by Charlotte Richmond, the two hundred or so guests were made up of her friends, relations and acquaintances, about half of whom were army officers. Other guests were British civilians, Belgian and Dutch aristocrats, individuals of various nationalities and diplomats. Senior officers included the Prince of Orange, the Duke of Brunswick and the Earl of Uxbridge (commander of the Anglo-Netherlands cavalry); Richmond's relations included his nephews, Lord Apsley and his brother Seymour Bathurst, and the Duchess's cousins, Colonels John and Alexander Woodford. Also present were Lieutenant Charles FitzRoy and General Maitland, both of whom were destined to marry two of the Richmond daughters.[28]

Everyone eagerly anticipated the arrival of Wellington, who unbeknown to most of the guests was busy making preparations for action the following day. Away from the glamour of the ball, bugles and drums began to sound the 'assembly' in Brussels at about 10.30 p.m. Accompanied by Müffling, the Prussian liaison officer, Wellington arrived very late at the ball. One of Richmond's daughters, Georgiana, immediately rushed up to him to ask whether the rumours of the French advance were correct. His reply was blunt: 'Yes, they are true; we are off tomorrow.'[29] He put on a brave face and tried to appear calm and collected but it was noticed that he was discreetly issuing orders to officers.

After supper, there was a spirited display of Highland dancing by four sergeants from the 92nd Regiment of Foot (later known as the Gordon Highlanders); it was a regiment that was particularly close to Charlotte's heart as it had been raised by her parents and present in

Dublin when her husband was Lord Lieutenant. The sergeants were accompanied by the legendary pipe-major Alexander Cameron and they treated their audience to a Highland reel and a sword dance, an individual dance over two crossed swords. The latter was an ancient Scottish dance and one of the origins of the Highland reels that had been developed in the eighteenth century. As the daughter of the chief of Clan Gordon, it was highly appropriate that Charlotte's ball should have a Scottish flavour. Her daughter Louisa recalled: 'I well remember the Gordon Highlanders dancing reels at the ball; my mother thought it would interest the foreigners to see them, which it did . . . there was quite a crowd to look at the Scotch dancers.'[30]

Apart from the Highland dancing, there was almost certainly waltzing. Being cut off from the continent for so long, English dancing had remained stodgily rooted in the eighteenth century. However, across the Channel fashions had moved on and the waltz, which had first become fashionable in Austria, was all the rage. At first, Richmond frowned on it – as Maria Capel told her grandmother – and would 'not let His daughters Waltz. But as hardly anything else is danced here he must soon give up the Point.'[31] By the time of his wife's ball, his daughters were probably gaily waltzing around the room.

Just as the guests were finishing their supper, Lieutenant Henry Webster arrived, spattered with mud and bearing an important message. Webster, one of the Prince of Orange's ADCs, had just galloped ten miles from Braine-le-Comte, only stopping to change horses once. The gate-porter asked him to wait for five minutes while the guests rose from supper, sensibly realising that the appearance of this young officer would cause panic among the ladies. Out of breath and peeping through the door, Webster could see Charlotte Richmond on the Prince of Orange's arm and Lady Charlotte Greville on Wellington's as they made their way back to the ballroom. Dashing into the room, he handed the despatch to the prince, who passed it unopened to Wellington. Wellington discreetly slipped it into his coat pocket. Webster then waited anxiously outside in the hall until Wellington had had an opportunity to read the message. In a low voice, Wellington then asked Webster to summon the prince's carriage for him to return to his headquarters at Braine-le-Comte. Very quickly, the news spread that the French were advancing, and the officers gradually started to slip away. The band halted mid-bar at the sudden exodus from the dance floor. Madan wrote, 'A sad gloom overspread the entertainment, and a trying scene of leave-taking followed.'[32]

The Duke of Brunswick assured Georgiana Lennox that his Brunswickers would be sure to distinguish themselves, as she had done them the honour of accompanying Wellington to their review several weeks earlier. She said a tender farewell to the handsome Lord Hay, a young ensign, who surprised her by his excitement at the impending action.[33]

Meanwhile, Charlotte Richmond stood at the door imploring the officers to 'wait one little hour more' and 'not spoil her ball' while Wellington asked her husband for a map.[34] Richmond took him aside into his dressing room and spread out a map on the bed, assisted by his young daughter, Louisa. Studying it, Wellington snorted, 'Napoleon has *humbugged* me by God, he has gained twenty-four hours march on me.' Asked by Richmond what he intended to do, he replied, 'I have ordered the army to concentrate at Quatre Bras, but we shall not stop him there and, if so, I must fight him *here*,' placing his thumbnail on Waterloo.[35] Then, with a quick 'adieu', he left the house by a side door. The other guests left just after 2 a.m. and made their way home through streets alive with soldiers who were given orders to depart at about 4 a.m. Lady De Lancey stood at her window, watching them march through the city gate, 'and saw the whole army go out. Regiment after regiment passed through and melted away in the mist of the morning.'[36]

The following day, the dashing Lord Hay, heart-throb of the ladies and idol of his peers, was killed in action, along with two other former guests – the Duke of Brunswick and Colonel John Cameron, commander of the 92nd Foot.[37] The fighting had been fierce at Quatre Bras, an important crossroads linking communications from Nivelles and Brussels with those from Blücher's position at Ligny. From his stand at Charleroi, Napoleon had ordered Marshal Ney to take possession of Quatre Bras. However, the overall result of the day was indeterminate with heavy casualties on both sides.

As Wellington established his position at Mont St Jean, just south of the village of Waterloo, the wounded began to arrive in Brussels. Madan wrote to his father: 'On Saturday morning, the attention of us and the Bruxellois was taken up with the wounded who arrived by hundreds. I never saw so dismal a sight. Poor fellows some without an arm, some without a leg, covered with blood and dust, worn with fatigue and hunger, some fainting, others raving with pain, were brought crowded upon carts and waggons under a burning sun.'[38]

On Sunday 18 June, the day of the great battle, Wellington's aim was to keep Napoleon at bay until the arrival of the Prussians. That morning back in Brussels, Richmond gave orders that his family should be ready to depart at a quarter of an hour's notice and rode out to the battlefield to ask Wellington's opinion on whether to leave the city. At two o'clock, the inhabitants of Brussels heard the cannonading begin, as described by Madan: 'The doubt and anxiety visible in every countenance as we walked upon the ramparts listening to each *coup de cannon* was extreme and, at home, the poor D'ss harassed by the thoughts of the Duke being absent, of her 10 children with her, and her 3 sons in the action was a pitiable object.'[39]

Richmond, ever the man of action, insisted on watching the battle, riding round the battlefield with his fifteen-year-old son William who was still recovering from his riding accident. The historian William Siborne recounts: 'Just as the Enniskillings were on the point of advancing across the Wavre road to charge, an individual in plain clothes on their left called out, "Now's your time!" This was the late Duke of Richmond . . .'[40] Richmond's blood must have been running very high as two of his sons were involved in the fighting – March was ADC to the Prince of Orange and George was ADC to the Duke of Wellington. After the Prince of Orange was wounded, March whipped the Orange cockade out of the prince's hat lest he be recognised – an action that the prince said probably saved his life.[41] March then joined Wellington as an extra ADC for the rest of the battle.

By late afternoon, Richmond felt able to leave the battlefield: 'At 4 the Duke came home, and reported that all looked favourable, but we must still be ready to start,' wrote Madan. 'About seven just as we were sitting [down] to dinner came a messenger to say that Wellington had gained his battle, and that the French were retiring. Wounded officers came in at intervals but knowing nothing. About ten arrived 8,000 prisoners with 2 eagles and stands of colours and soon after a note from an ADC of the Duke of Wellington to say that the victory had been complete.'[42]

The devastation of the battle was felt by everyone, none more so than by the inhabitants of Brussels who tended the many wounded streaming into the city. Thousands of soldiers were killed on both sides – Wellington alone lost 3,500 from his army, with another 3,300 missing and 10,200 wounded.[43] Of those guests who had attended the Duchess of Richmond's ball, eight were killed at Waterloo and two died later of wounds. Thirty-five of the guests were wounded, including the Earl of Uxbridge, who had commanded the cavalry until his leg was blown off, prompting him to exclaim to Wellington, 'By Gad, I've lost my leg,' to which Wellington coolly replied, 'By Gad, so you have.'[44]

The day after Waterloo, Richmond and his daughter Georgiana took a turn in the Parc with Wellington. Georgiana observed how sad he looked and, when they congratulated him, he said, 'It is a dearly bought victory. We have lost so many fine fellows.'[45] Later that day, Richmond and his two sons, March and George, drove around the battlefield in their coach. Peter Soar, the duke's coachman, said it presented such a sight as he hoped never again to witness. He picked up a large number of trophies and curiosities and took in a forlorn terrier lying upon the body of its master.[46] On the Tuesday, Richmond's son William rode over the battlefield with his father and, even though the wounded had been removed, he was appalled by the sight: 'There lay heaped together dead men and horses . . .'[47]

Nearly seven weeks after the battle, Richmond took the Capel daughters to see the battlefield, including the farm where their uncle, Lord Uxbridge, had had his leg amputated. Georgiana reported back to her grandmother, 'From the house we went into her [the owner's] pretty neat little garden in the *centre* of which his leg is interred, it was overgrown *with weeds, which we cleared away.'*[48]

As the English basked in the glory of victory, the Richmonds' sangfroid in the face of the enemy advancing did not go unrewarded. For their loyalty of staying in Brussels and keeping going as if nothing was happening, Wellington presented them with Napoleon's campaign chair. He also gave them a 'Champ de Mai' banner that had been given to him by Louis XVIII. Charlotte Richmond was presented with Napoleon's silver breakfast plate last used at the Ferme de Caillou on the morning of the battle. Two years later, the grateful people of Brussels presented her with a china tea and coffee service painted with views of all the main battle sites and uniforms of the different soldiers. Her ball was to go down in history as one of the most famous there has ever been.

*   *   *

The Richmond family were besotted with their dogs. The fourth duke was particularly devoted to his spaniel Blücher, named after the Prussian general whose arrival at Waterloo with the Prussian army had saved the day. In the summer of 1819, Richmond took his daughters Mary and Louisa with him on a tour of Upper Canada; Blücher came, too. The previous year, Richmond had been made Governor-in-Chief of British North America, taking some of the children with him while Charlotte stayed behind to look after the younger ones. Sarah came, too, but as the wife of General Maitland, who had been appointed Lieutenant Governor. The family had narrowly avoided a society scandal when Sarah had eloped with Maitland not long after Waterloo and Wellington had had to intervene; now things were more harmonious.

Richmond was proving to be a very able governor-general, actively engaged in the strengthening of forts, opening up river navigation and digging canals. He also found time to indulge in sport, enjoying his favourite pastimes of shooting, cricket and tennis. In the July of their summer tour, they stayed at Government House at Sorel in Quebec and, while there, a pet fox belonging to a soldier had attacked Blücher. Leaping to his dog's defence, Richmond was bitten on his hand by the fox while trying to separate them. He wrapped a handkerchief around his hand and thought nothing more of it. The party then continued their journey visiting Montreal, Kingston and Toronto and inspecting garrisons along the way. When they returned to Kingston, travelling at one point in canoes, Richmond said goodbye to his children and left them to make their own way to Montreal, while he continued on his tour, visiting settlements on the Rideau river.

Towards the end of August, Richmond complained of a pain in his shoulder that was preventing him from sleeping well. Two days later, he refused to be shaved by his valet and when they were walking through the swamps, experienced spasms whenever he saw someone make contact with water. Arriving later that morning at Richmond, a settlement that had been named after him, he asked for some paper so he could write a long letter to his daughter Mary sharing his concerns for his health. Later that day, he had more spasms whenever he was near water – even for drinking – and sank into a depression with premonitions of his own death.

The following day, the party was due to continue by canoe. With great fortitude, Richmond boarded the boat but, as soon as he was seated, panicked, leapt out on to the shore and ran into the wood. His companions, greatly alarmed, then accompanied him to a nearby farm where he sought refuge in a barn rather than the house as it was further away from the water. There, suffering deeply from violent spasms, he resigned himself to his fate. He made his peace with God, forgave his enemies, and dictated final messages to his family and close friends. In the evening, he was moved inside the farmhouse and, the following morning at 8 a.m. on 28 August, he died, the victim of rabies caught from the pet fox.[49]

Everyone was deeply shocked. He had been due to arrive in Montreal to great celebrations. Instead, the well-wishers were greeted by a coffin. He was buried in the Cathedral of the Holy Trinity in

Quebec City where a marble monument was erected to his memory. It is carved in low relief with a classical woman, bowed in grief, mourning the death of her soldier husband.

From an inauspicious start as a hot-headed youth, Richmond had become a paragon of duty and honour. His dying words for his son and heir, March, were: 'I know he will regret being Duke of Richmond but [tell him] that I am satisfied I leave my Titles and Estates to one of the best and most honourable Men in England. Tell him I know he will take care of his brother and sisters . . . I die in charity with all the World and in perfect confidence of mercy from the Almighty . . . I give Blücher to Mary – she will cry at first but turn him in when she is alone and shut the door.'

*The young Prince and Princess of Wales are among the guests sitting
on the steps outside the Large Library for raceweek in August 1866
(© Trustees of the Goodwood Collection)*

8

Glorious Goodwood

*'The Goodwood week is, as it were, sui generis [unique]; a great
nobleman, sincerely taking to heart the true interests of the turf,
and, anxious to offer a good example, did not hesitate to throw
open his park to all comers, and any visitor to the course will have
noticed the quietness pervading the whole scene. With magnificent
scenery, first-rate racing, and good society to select from, a man
would indeed be fastidious who did not consider the Goodwood
course the perfection of all our race-grounds.'* [1]

Memoir of Charles Gordon Lennox,
Fifth Duke of Richmond, 1862

At the end of February 1839, Charles, fifth Duke of Richmond and
his wife Caroline threw an enormous party to celebrate the
coming of age of their eldest son and heir, the Earl of March. There
was a whole day of festivities. In the morning, a stag hunt took place
in the park at Goodwood, followed by an enormous banquet for three
hundred gentlemen, hosted by Richmond's younger brother, George,
who was MP for West Sussex. It was held in the 'royal' tennis court,
which had been decorated for the occasion with flags, banners, laurel

wreaths and swathes of flowers. As the daylight dwindled, thousands of coloured lamps were lit and, when March entered with his father, a rapturous applause went up. High up on the South Downs, flames leapt into the night sky from a huge bonfire on the summit of the Trundle, the highest point for miles around and, at the entrance to the park, the lodges were illuminated for the arrival of the guests to the evening's entertainment.

Seven hundred people attended the ball in the evening. The guest list read like a *Who's Who* of Sussex sprinkled with a few celebrities, such as the Marquess of Anglesey, father of Caroline Richmond and hero of Waterloo (when he was still Lord Uxbridge). The carriages drew up at the end of a temporary avenue, stretching one hundred feet from the garden steps of the Large Library window, across the lawn and down to the drive. Bedecked with flowers and laurels, the avenue twinkled in the cold winter night with hundreds of coloured lanterns. Charles and Caroline Richmond received their guests in the Front Hall – converted into a drawing room for the occasion – while guests sat down to dinner in the Egyptian Dining-Room, Long Hall, Tapestry Drawing Room and Old Dining-Room. After dinner and with full dance cards, the assembled guests proceeded to the newly finished Ballroom and danced into the early hours of the morning. There was a flutter of alarm when some of the decorations in the vast conservatory opening off the Ballroom caught light, but order was soon restored.

The gentry were not alone in being entertained. Two days later, Richmond welcomed nearly two hundred of his tenants to dinner in the Ballroom and, on the following Saturday, seven hundred children from the school in Boxgrove and Westhampnett Union feasted in the park. To top it all, every employee was given a bonus.[2]

These acts of generosity and bonhomie were not mere ducal gestures; they came from the heart. Richmond cared deeply, not only for his family, but also for those he employed and who were under his care. He took his duty seriously and tried to set a good example to his ten children, maintaining a delicate balance between discipline and genuine affection.

The lavish entertainments for his son's twenty-first birthday also marked the completion of Goodwood House, started by the third duke at the end of the eighteenth century. It had taken almost forty years to finish the two new wings. Eight years after his father's death, the fifth duke had completed what became known as the Yellow Drawing Room, the principal reception room leading off the Front Hall. This magnificent room, fifty-five feet long, was richly upholstered with amber-coloured striped silk. The walls, curtains, pelmets, sofas, ottomans, couches and chairs all shimmered in the candlelight, the silk trimmed with expensive *passementerie* (decorative tassels, braid and trimmings). Huge giltwood mirrors and pier tables added to the richness, with pieces of the third duke's Sèvres china displayed on the tables. A vast Axminster carpet, richly woven with swirls of flowers in blues, greens, pinks and golds, covered the oak parquetry flooring and above hung two great ormolu chandeliers.[3] The whole ensemble was in the fashionable French Revival style, made popular by George IV at Windsor. It was also a nod to the family's French ancestry and their Aubigny inheritance. At the end of the Drawing Room there was an apse with a fitted banquette, flanked by doors on either side: one leading to the Duchess's boudoir – a circular room – the other into the new Ballroom.

When the third duke had died, the Ballroom was unfinished with neither floor nor ceiling in place. Originally planned by him as a picture gallery, by the time of its completion in 1838 it had become a ballroom. The money to finish it – and indeed to lay on such grand entertainment for March's coming of age – had come from the Gordon inheritance in 1836. It was only by sheer luck that this had happened. Charlotte Richmond's father, the fourth Duke of Gordon, had entailed the Gordon estates on his grandson (the fifth Duke of Richmond), realising that it was unlikely that his son, George, Marquess of Huntly, would have any children. When George duly died leaving no legitimate offspring, the entire Gordon inheritance landed in Richmond's lap.[4] The Gordon landholding in Scotland was vast – 269,000 acres in the north-east of the country centred around Gordon Castle in Morayshire but also including a large London house. In recognition of his inheritance, Richmond added Gordon to his surname Lennox.

The new Ballroom was designed by the architect John Elliott of Chichester, also in the French Revival manner. Measuring nearly ninety feet long, the far end was ornamented with a minstrels' gallery. Daylight poured in from five large windows on one side, the three central ones recessed behind four towering Guernsey granite columns. The windows were hung with rich drapery supplied by the London upholsterers Miles and Edwards, while four huge mirrors adorned the walls, one reputedly having the largest plate in the kingdom at the time.[5] A heavy gilt cornice ran around the entire room and three great ormolu chandeliers hung from the ceiling. A supper room for eating in adjoined the Ballroom, with arched windows looking out on to the garden.

Just as Richmond gained Gordon Castle, he lost the Aubigny estate in France. A lawsuit brought by one of Emily's children and her husband called the *Code Napoléon* into play, resulting in the sale of Aubigny in 1842. The proceeds were divided between the numerous descendants of the second Duke of Richmond; the only people who benefited from the lengthy litigation were the French lawyers and King Louis Phillippe who shared in the spoils.[6]

The loss of Aubigny was a blow to Richmond, particularly as it came in the wake of a family tragedy. The previous year, his second son Fitzroy had begun the journey home from Canada where he had been posted with the army. Proceeding to New York, he boarded the steamship *President*, the largest passenger ship in the world, en route to Liverpool. She was seen the following day battling against the elements in a violent storm that lasted for two days but then disappeared. Back home, his anxious family waited for news. As the months passed by, hopes of his survival petered out. Eventually, they had to accept that their beloved son and brother had been lost at sea, drowned with all one hundred and thirty-six souls on board.[7]

*   *   *

As the harvest was being cut in 1836, a mysterious vehicle lumbered out of the park at Goodwood, drawn by six horses. It resembled a cross between a gypsy caravan and a cattle cart, with the wheels tucked underneath making it very high. As it made its way north, pedestrians gawped in amazement and passing coachmen and passengers looked on incredulously; they had never seen anything like it in their lives. Some speculated that a dangerous wild beast was locked up inside; others that it contained a notorious criminal. In fact, its occupants were two racehorses secretly making their way to Doncaster for the St Leger Stakes – Elis and his companion, The Drummer. Their owner, Lord George Bentinck, had already staked £1,000 on Elis to win and had secured long odds at 12/1. When Elis had been seen at Goodwood a few days before the race meeting, the bookies dismissed his chances, knowing it took fifteen or sixteen days for a horse to walk the 250 miles between Goodwood and Doncaster (at the time, the only way of getting a horse to a course was by carefully walking them there). What they did not know was that Lord George had had a horsebox constructed in secret by Mr Herring, a coachbuilder in Long Acre, London, complete with padded sides and a hard-stuffed mattress on the floor to prevent any hurt should the horses fall down. Even Herring was kept in the dark as to its purpose.

The horsebox trundled on, covering eighty miles per day, changing post-horses as it went and stopping at Lichfield racecourse en route to exercise the occupants. Lord George even insisted that the horses were fed only hay or corn from Goodwood. When they arrived at Doncaster, to everyone's amazement, Elis was as fresh as a daisy. Two days later, he stormed home to victory in the St Leger and Lord George pocketed his handsome winnings – the world's very first horsebox had done the trick. From then on, horseboxes enabled horses to be taken to racecourses all over the country and the opportunity to enter horses in many more races than previously possible revolutionised horseracing in Britain.[8]

Lord George was a great friend of the fifth duke and a key figure in the development of the racecourse at Goodwood. Like Richmond, he was passionate about horseracing. His love-affair with horseracing had begun at Goodwood when, aged twenty-two, he had won the eccentric-named Cocked Hat Stakes (so called because the riders had to start and finish wearing a three-cornered hat). From that time onwards, he absorbed himself in the turf with relentless energy and single-mindedness. Richmond, who was ten years his senior, was a willing accomplice – and sometimes tool – in Lord George's schemes, many of which were first introduced at Goodwood. These included the pre-race parade of horses and public saddling, designed to hinder the skulduggery that went on behind the scenes and with which the sport was rife. In 1829, great earthworks were undertaken to extend the Goodwood racecourse to the foot of the Trundle and a new stand was built to seat three thousand people.

Racegoers hailed from all levels of society, thrown together by their shared love of the sport. For much of its early history, racing at Goodwood took place over three consecutive days (Wednesday, Thursday and Friday) with five or six races every afternoon. A list of the runners, riders and owners was printed on pocket-sized race cards and sold to racegoers. The racing was accompanied by much eating and drinking and the inevitable betting. Bookmakers – or 'legs' as they were known – had first appeared around 1800 and were as much a part of the scene as the booths and marquees set up on the course.[9]

Despite these improvements and the general acclaim, throughout the 1830s, Richmond was running the racecourse at a loss.[10] Lord George may well have been propping him up, but both were driven by a desire to create the finest racecourse in the country. Richmond was also on a roll with his horses – in 1827, he won the Oaks with Gulnare and, two years later, won all seven open races at Ascot. He took on a trainer, John Kent, who more than proved his mettle. Soon, other racehorse owners were sending their horses to Goodwood to be trained by Kent, including the Earl of Chesterfield who sent Priam, one of the greatest horses of all time.

In 1841, Lord George moved all of his horses to Goodwood to be trained by Kent and the Goodwood stable became one of the most successful in the country with as many as 120 horses in training. Kent was assisted ably by his son John who eventually took over as trainer, having learnt the trade from his father. At vast expense, the Halnaker Gallops were laid to enable the horses to be exercised whatever the weather, and more stables were built. When Lord George pushed for more stabling, Richmond put his foot down and laughingly replied, 'If you had Chichester barracks, you would fill all the stalls!'[11]

Richmond had his best year as an owner in 1845, winning the Oaks with Refraction and the One Thousand Guineas with Pic Nic. That same year, the Jockey Club passed a resolution: 'That the unanimous thanks of the Jockey Club be rendered to his Grace the Duke of Richmond, for his Grace's indefatigable exertions and eminent services in the House of Lords, whereby many obsolete statutes which threatened destruction to the best interests of the Turf, have been repealed, and the remaining laws in regard to horseracing put upon a safe and satisfactory footing.' Between them, Richmond and Lord George had been responsible for the 'cleaning up' of horseracing – particularly betting – and introducing measures at Goodwood that had been adopted elsewhere and form the basis of horseracing today. These included a system of flags for the start (instead of shouting) and tidiness for the jockeys (who should wear 'a silk, velvet or satin jacket, and in boots and breeches').[12] There is no doubt that most of these innovations were the brainchild of Lord George but he needed the support of Richmond both at Goodwood and in the House of Lords to push them through.

In many ways, Richmond and Lord George were very different. Richmond never laid a bet while Lord George gambled thousands of pounds. In 1845, Kent estimated that Lord George's winnings that year alone were nearly £100,000, a huge amount of money when a family in good society could live comfortably on about £1,000 a year.[13] There was the added complication that Lord George was in love with Caroline Richmond. Although it was almost certainly a case of unrequited love – Lord George admitting so to his cousin, the diarist Charles Greville – he was rumoured to be the father of the Richmonds' tenth and last child, Cecilia.[14]

Every year, Lord George would be among the guests staying at Goodwood for raceweek. The Richmonds usually arrived from London the week before and, on the Saturday prior to the meeting, they would be joined by a few intimate friends and relatives. On the Monday, everyone else would arrive to be greeted by their hostess at the front of the house where a marquee was always erected, and guests relaxed under the portico. Dinner was served in the Ballroom where a long table was laid down the middle of the room, decorated with gold and silver trophies and handsome pieces of plate. After dinner, there was dancing in the Egyptian Dining-Room for the younger guests, while whist and billiards kept the elder generation amused. One of the Goodwood customs that often surprised foreigners (such as the King of Holland) was the reading of the following day's racing entries after the ladies had left the room. Bets followed and, on Goodwood Cup day, the health of the duke was proposed, to which Richmond briefly responded.[15]

It was at one of these dinners after the third day's racing in 1846 that Lord George dropped a bombshell. The ladies had left the room and the conversation had turned to the gargantuan scale of Lord George's racing establishment. Appearing to be nodding off, Lord George suddenly looked up and asked, 'Will any of you give me £10,000 for all my lot, beginning with old Bay Middleton and ending with little Kitchener [his jockey], and take them with all their engagements and responsibilities off my hands?' Quick as anything and realising it was a bargain, George Payne asked to be given until noon the following day to make up his mind. 'Agreed,' replied Lord George quietly and, with those words, his racing career came to an end.

As it so happened, it was Edward Mostyn who ended up buying the stud – all 208 thoroughbreds – and he promptly sold most of them on.[16] Two years later, Surplice, probably Lord George's best horse, won the Derby, the one race that had always eluded him. Surplice then went on to win the St Leger and, despite Lord George's parliamentary pressures (which had been the main reason he had sold all his horses), he spoke to Kent about getting back into racing. It was not to be. One week later, while walking to dinner across the fields at home, he dropped down dead of a heart attack; he was forty-six.

*   *   *

> *'We took advantage of an open piece of grass near the house at Goodwood, and descended soon after 8 p.m. Mr. Coxwell, after throwing a rope to a cricketer, landed us so gently that we would not have crushed a daisy. We were afterwards drawn by a rope to the front of the house for the benefit of a few gazers. I had hoped that Mr. Coxwell would here tether his balloon and continue our journey next day, but it was Sunday and so he resolved to pack it up, otherwise the upper current being again north our wishes might this day have been happily accomplished. Our thanks are due to Captain Valintine and other good people there assembled for the assistance they gave us in packing up.'*
>
> (West Sussex Gazette, July 1863)

The landing of a hot air balloon in the park at Goodwood, while a cricket match was taking place, caused something of a stir in the summer of 1863. The balloon had ascended from Crystal Palace earlier that afternoon with four passengers, including Henry Coxwell, a well-known balloonist, and James Glaisher, a meteorologist. They had drifted past Croydon and Epsom before passing over Horsham in the hope of making it to the Isle of Wight. But the weather conditions were against them, so they floated over the South Downs and came to rest at Goodwood where they were put up for the night by Captain Valintine, the agent.

For both Richmond and his son, March, cricket was a pleasant diversion from more serious matters, particularly politics. When he was only twenty-four, March was made president of the Marylebone Cricket Club, the club that his grandfather, the fourth duke, had helped set up. The association with the family was still very strong – the club's 'egg and bacon' colours are traditionally thought to have been based on Richmond's racing colours (yellow shirt with scarlet cap). But more often than not, it was others who enjoyed playing and watching cricket in the pleasant surroundings of Goodwood while their noble host beavered away in London.

From 1812 until his father's untimely death, the fifth duke was Tory MP for Chichester – a job he combined with his military duties. He then moved to the Upper House and was at one point tipped as a possible successor to Wellington as Prime Minister. Charles Greville, the political diarist, gave the rough with the smooth in his assessment of Richmond, who was one of his good friends: 'He happens to have his wits, such as they are, about him, and has been quick and neat in one or two little speeches, though he spoke too often, and particularly in his attack on the Bishop of Oxford the other night . . . he lives in the country, is well versed in rural affairs and the business of the quarter sessions, has a certain calibre of understanding, is prejudiced, narrow-minded, illiterate, and ignorant, good-looking, good-humoured, and unaffected, tedious, prolix [long-winded], unassuming, and a duke. There would not have been so much to say about him if they had not excited an idea in the minds of some people of making him Prime Minister . . .'[17]

Richmond was a hard-line Tory who was opposed to Catholic emancipation and free trade, vigorously resisting the repeal of the Corn Laws. For four years he was Postmaster General, diligently serving in the cabinet of Earl Grey's Whig government (he moved to the Whigs having refused to side with Wellington against the Reform Act). It was while he was a cabinet minister that Greville wrote acerbically in his diary: 'He is utterly incapable, entirely ignorant, and his pert smartness, saying sharp things, cheering offensively, have greatly exasperated many people against him in the House of Commons . . . He has, in fact, that weight which a man can derive from being positive, obstinate, pertinacious, and busy, but his understanding lies in a nutshell, and his information in a pin's head. He is, however, good-humoured, a good fellow, and personally liked . . .'[18] Fortunately for them both and the sake of their friendship, Greville's diaries were only published after both their deaths.

Throughout his life, Richmond kept up an exhaustive correspondence embracing many different subject matters. In this, he was aided by his personal secretaries, in particular Dr Archibald Hair, his life-long friend and companion who had saved his life after the Battle of Orthez when he was hit by a musket ball in the chest.[19] Richmond would scribble a few words at the top of each letter received to show how he had responded – 'need not answer' or 'must be mad' – and Hair would file them.[20] Richmond was renowned for the brevity of his replies. On one occasion, Rusbridger, his agent, received a two-word letter from him. Rusbridger then made a bet with John Kent senior that he would produce the shortest letter in existence. Kent accepted the bet and promptly won it – he drew out of his pocket a reply he had just had from Richmond that read: 'Kent – Yes. Richmond'.[21]

One area of constant correspondence was agriculture. In 1832, he was elected vice-president of the Smithfield Club, founded in 1798 to encourage the breeding of cattle and sheep, and still in existence today. Richmond's own passion was his flock of Southdown sheep, which consistently won awards and of which he was very proud. He was also involved with the Royal Agricultural Society, which sprung out of the Smithfield Club in 1837. When its president, Earl Spencer, died in 1845, Richmond was chosen to replace him.

Although he had left the army in 1816, Richmond always regarded himself as a soldier. Four years after leaving, he was made colonel of the Sussex militia and took his duties very seriously. He was always ready to help war veterans, in particular those whom he had served alongside. Following Waterloo, anyone who had fought had been awarded a medal – the first time a medal had been given to all ranks. Those who for various reasons were not present at the battle but had taken part in the Peninsula wars, felt aggrieved at having nothing to show for their service (many of them had been shipped straight from France to fight in North America in 1814). Wellington took a strong stance against them, arguing that his soldiers should fight for honour rather than medals. Richmond took the opposite view and became the champion for the Military Service Medal as it became known. There

was a long and drawn-out public campaign, plastered all over the press
and debated in Parliament but, eventually, Queen Victoria agreed to
award the medal, although it only went to surviving veterans. As a
thank-you to Richmond, a subscription was raised for a 'testimonial'
from all of the former soldiers. This took the form of a massive silver
centrepiece that was presented to him at a banquet in London on 21
June 1851 (the anniversary of Vittoria), at which some two hundred and
fifty veterans were present. The sculptural centrepiece, made by Hunt
and Roskell, depicts Richmond standing on a column in his peer's
robes, directing Britannia to give the medal to Mars and Neptune.
Military trophies are propped against the column, on which are listed
the naval and military battles, while four groups of soldiers and sailors
stand on the plinth. The plinth itself is adorned with low-relief battle
scenes of Trafalgar, the Nile, Vittoria and Orthez. To display it at
Goodwood, a circular table with rotating marble top was commissioned, complete with a pull-out scroll describing it. The trophy was a
fitting tribute to Richmond's efforts and a lasting memorial to all of
those battles that preceded Waterloo.

*   *   *

A photograph of the raceweek house party in 1866 shows a young
Prince and Princess of Wales sitting on the steps of the Large
Library. The guests are carefully arranged in a seemingly informal
grouping with the gentlemen at the rear and the ladies in front,
their dresses billowing around them. The prince, in an early
instance of the sartorial elegance for which he would later become
famous, wears a cream-coloured suit, distinguishing him from the
other men who are all dressed in black. Behind him sits the young
Earl of March, near contemporary of the prince, with March's sister,
Caroline nearby. It was less than a month since Caroline had carried
the train of Princess Helena, Queen Victoria's third daughter, at her
marriage to Prince Christian of Schleswig-Holstein in the Chapel at
Windsor Castle.

The Waleses had journeyed to Goodwood from Osborne House on the Isle of Wight. Crossing the Solent in the royal yacht *Alberta*, they had travelled by train from Portsmouth to Goodwood.[22] The invention of the steam engine – and the ensuing network of railways that had spread across the country – had transformed travel in Britain. Journeys that had previously taken days now took hours. No longer were travellers subjected to bouncing and jolting along in a carriage or stage coach; trains offered a smooth ride with pleasant views of the countryside rushing past. With the new ease in travel, country house guests could stay for much shorter periods of time and, in the grander houses, house parties were given added impetus by the presence of the Prince of Wales, or Bertie, as he was known. He was at the epicentre of a fast group known as the Marlborough House Set (named after Bertie's London residence) where blue-blooded aristocrats rubbed shoulders with *nouveau riche* bankers and industrialists.

The railways also transformed Goodwood during raceweek, which become known as 'Glorious Goodwood', an epithet coined by the Victorian press. 'All the difficulties that heretofore existed in reaching this delightful locality have been removed,' reported *The Times* in 1843, 'and the vicissitudes of road travelling, so frequently experienced by persons of the highest rank, altogether obviated.'[23] Visitors flocked to Goodwood and every spare bed in Chichester was taken. The presence of royalty at Glorious Goodwood added to its allure. George IV, a keen patron of the turf, had loved coming to Goodwood to the extent that when he was on his deathbed, he arranged for a relay of post boys to convey the results to him at Windsor. William IV inherited his brother's impressive stable of horses. Naively entering them all in the 1830 Goodwood Cup, he took home first, second and third prizes.

After Bentinck's death, the racecourse had taken a hit and attendance dropped as Richmond's health and energy declined.[24] By 1860, he was in a wheelchair suffering acute pain from gout and unable to attend the races. Later that autumn, he returned from Gordon Castle to his London house in Portland Place and died there attended by his faithful friend, Dr Hair.[25] He left instructions that he should have a very private funeral with no ceremony, and gave permission for a surgeon to ascertain the direction of the musket ball that had lodged itself in his body all those years ago at the battle of Orthez.[26] A beautiful stained-glass window was erected in his memory above the altar in Boxgrove Priory by the Goodwood tenantry.

Although Queen Victoria never came to Goodwood, her son Bertie took up racing with gusto and was a regular guest at Goodwood from the early 1860s until he died. Bertie was among the many guests who allowed themselves to be weighed. When he came in 1864 as a young buck of twenty-two, he weighed a modest 12 st 6 lbs. Unlike his wife (who weighed a discreet 8 st 7 lbs in 1881), he only ever allowed himself to be weighed once again by which time he had shot up to 15 st (1875). Bertie's weight paled into insignificance when compared to Prince Edward of Saxe-Weimar, husband of the fifth duke's daughter, Augusta. On 27 January 1884, he weighed 19 st 4 lbs 'before dinner'. By the end of the year, he had increased to 19 st 11 lbs. On several occasions, the delicate parquetry flooring in the Yellow Drawing Room caved in under his weight.

The Goodwood house party was not the only aristocratic gathering in the neighbourhood. At various times during the Victorian and Edwardian eras, other house parties were hosted at Stansted, Uppark, West Dean, Cowdray, Petworth, Slindon and Arundel.[27] The *West Sussex Gazette* reported on the 1866 races: 'This year we found either more aristocratic ladies, whose gay and fashionable attire formed an extra embellishment to the brilliant equipage, or that they more frequently went to the course. This, perhaps, was induced by the visit of the Prince and Princess of Wales, who, as is well known, honoured His Grace the Duke of Richmond by becoming his guests.' Many people stayed in Bognor, then a fashionable seaside resort, including the Dukes of Beaufort and Hamilton. The former was known as 'The Blue Duke' (after the colours of the Badminton Hunt) and became one of the best-known sporting figures in England.

The Lawn at Goodwood, painted twenty years later, depicting some of the fashionable crowd during raceweek, is filled with leading figures of the day, including the composers Gilbert and Sullivan. At the centre of the painting, Bertie can be seen chatting to the Duchess of Montrose, a celebrated racehorse owner who was known in racing circles as 'Mr Manton' (ladies were not allowed to own or train horses). Other members of the royal family watch from the balcony of the grandstand while the sixth Duke of Richmond gives a lady a hand up the steep bank.

Although his real love was field sports, the sixth duke enjoyed his horseracing. Aged twenty, he was elected a member of the Jockey Club and rode several winners at Goodwood over the next four years. Like his father before him, he served as aide-de-camp to Wellington when he was a young officer in the Royal Regiment of Horse Guards. It was probably through Wellington that he met his future wife, Frances Harriet Greville. Her father, Algernon, was Wellington's private secretary and her grandmother, Charlotte, had glided from supper to the dance floor on Wellington's arm at the famous Duchess of Richmond's ball in Brussels. Frances was a model Victorian wife; a formal photograph taken of her in her forties shows a demure-looking lady doing her needlework, seemingly weighed down by anxieties in contrast to the frilly white dress cascading around her legs, propped-up parasol and flower-decked bonnet lying beside her on the ground.

Not long after her father-in-law's death, Frances was the recipient of two additions to the Goodwood family: Guh and Meh. They were two of the first ever Pekingese dogs in England. In 1860, when the Old Summer Palace in Peking was destroyed by British troops during the Second Opium War, five Pekingese dogs were discovered. One was presented to Queen Victoria, a pair was given to the second Duke and Duchess of Wellington, and the remaining pair to Frances, who had recently become Duchess of Richmond. The dogs made their home at Goodwood and, well into the twentieth century, Frances's second son and daughter-in-law, Algernon and Blanche, continued the tradition by establishing the Goodwood Kennel and breeding champion dogs.[28]

*   *   *

The fifth of November 1883 marked a momentous day in the annals of Goodwood history – the opening meet of the Goodwood Hunt. It had been seventy years since hounds had been kennelled at Goodwood, when the fourth duke had given them to the Prince Regent. The hunt servants were resplendent in their yellow coats with scarlet collars and cuffs, while the subscribers wore Charlton blue with gilt buttons. The Earl of March, who was the Master, was accompanied by his wife and sister-in-law; gathered around them was a large field of mounted followers, pedestrians and spectators in carriages, including several family members. The meet was held in front of Wyatt's Kennels, which had been converted into accommodation for the hunt servants. New Kennels had been built on the other side of the road to house the pack that had come, to a large extent, from the Earl of Radnor in Wiltshire. The aptly named stud groom, Fox, had charge of forty-five horses, and George Champion, for many years huntsman of the Southdown Hounds, had come to take charge at Goodwood.

Under a bright sky, the hunt moved off to Valdoe Coppice where fox and hounds were hampered by the huge number of foot followers. After finally killing a fox that had made a dash into the carpenter's workshop, the hunt then trotted off to Boxgrove Common to seek some action.[29]

March had thrown himself into this new venture. He had spent almost a year trying to reclaim the historic Charlton hunting country, and the new kennels – modelled on those at Petworth – had been a considerable financial investment. Without fail, he recorded every day's hunting activity in his hunting diary, singling out 'red-letter' days by writing in red ink. But the dream was to be short-lived.

The agricultural depression of the 1880s hit landed estates hard. Rents at Goodwood had been reduced from as early as 1879 and, by 1894, rental income had fallen by almost a quarter.[30] Ever since its revival, the sixth duke had been maintaining the hunt at his own expense. He had tried unsuccessfully to introduce subscription, so it was against this economic backdrop that the tough decision was made to disband the hunt.

The final meet was held on 13 April 1895 at Molecomb, March's home on the Goodwood estate. Seventy mounted followers turned up and it was widely covered in the press, including *The Field*. After the final kill, *The Field*, reported: 'There was a long pause, and someone said, in a hushed voice, "This is the funeral." Everyone seemed reluctant to move from the spot; but five was the hour, and at length, slowly and sadly, by twos and by threes, the members of the Hunt melted from the sad field.'[31]

A shooting party at Blackwater Lodge on the Glenfiddich estate in 1885.
The future seventh Duke of Richmond stands on the left with his sons, Set, Esmé and
Bernard; General Baillie and John Balfour stand in the doorway, with John's brother,
Edward standing on the right. A Goodwood Pekingese sits at Bernard's feet
(© Trustees of the Goodwood Collection)

Scottish Interlude

'I . . . never experienced such delightful sensations as when I
first saw the dear hills and met each gale loaded with perfume,
the children were skipping about amidst the heather like fauns
of which there were millions. Before night, I was upon the
top of every hill and went to every favourite spot as if I had
expected to find a beloved friend there. Indeed, this summer
has yielded me nothing but delight . . .'

The Duchess of Gordon to Dr James Beattie,
12 August 1784.[1]

A fine grey horse pawed the ground, attentive to its female rider.
Mounted side-saddle, she was elegantly dressed in a regimental
jacket with flowing tartan skirt and black-feather bonnet. The feathers quivered as she leant down and whispered a few words into the
ear of an eager-looking young Highlander. After a brief exchange, he
nodded to the lady and she dismounted. Taking a coin from her
purse, she placed it between her teeth. Beaming with delight, the
Highlander leant forward as if to kiss her and took the coin in his
teeth. When he had done so, she congratulated him, shook his hand

and an officer standing close by started writing down his details. For ever after, the Highlander could boast that he had kissed a duchess.[2] The coin itself was a golden guinea, nicknamed 'the king's shilling', which signalled the young man's agreement to join the 100th Regiment. Later known as the Gordon Highlanders, the regiment was raised in 1794 by the duchess's husband, the fourth Duke of Gordon, to help fight the French.

This is one of the many legendary stories concerning Jane, Duchess of Gordon, the mother of Charlotte Richmond and, along with Louise de Keroualle, the most illustrious ancestress of the Dukes of Richmond. Born Jane Maxwell, she was a famous beauty who was celebrated in song as 'The Flower of Galloway'.[3] Her early years were in stark contrast to her later life. As a child, growing up in genteel poverty in the heart of the Old Town in Edinburgh, she and her sister used to ride down the Royal Mile on the backs of pigs being driven to market.[4] Another lark of theirs was to leap from travelling cart to cart, in the process of which she lost a finger. As a teenager, the philosopher Henry Home, later Lord Kames, took her under his wing. Kames was a leading figure in the Scottish Enlightenment and he found in Jane an intelligent pupil, who loved literature and had a quickness of mind. When she was seventeen, she married Alexander, Duke of Gordon, head of one of Scotland's most illustrious families, and became a sparkling hostess 'who was the life of all circles she entered'.[5]

Jane created a storm in Edinburgh with her lavish entertaining and soirées. Up-and-coming artists were swept up in her wake, including the poet Robert Burns. When she moved to London, she became the leading Tory hostess, arch-rival to Georgiana, Duchess of Devonshire. She threw herself into the 1784 elections, campaigning for William Pitt the Younger, who dubbed her 'the first whipper-in of the Tories'.[6] Dressed from head to foot in Black Watch tartan taffeta for a ball, she set a new trend in fashion that had the Spitalfields weavers working overtime. At the same time, she introduced Scottish reels to London's ballrooms, which soon became all the rage in even the highest circles.

But just as Jane was hailed by her admirers, she was vilified by her enemies, particularly over her matchmaking for her daughters. Nathaniel Wraxall summed it up: 'In her daughters centred principally her ambitious cares. For their elevation, no sacrifices appeared to her to be too great, no exertions too laborious, no renunciations too severe. It would indeed be vain to seek for any other instance in our history of a woman who has allied three of her five daughters in marriage to English dukes, and the fourth to a Marquis.'[7] She even had William Pitt in her sights for Charlotte before settling on Charles Lennox, heir to the Duke of Richmond.

As an antidote to high-society life – particularly as her marriage fell apart – Jane found solace in the wilds of the Highlands. Although the main family seat was Gordon Castle in Morayshire, it was at Glenfiddich Lodge, a hunting-box built between 1772 and 1774 by Jane's husband, Alexander, that she fully relaxed. The single-storey dwelling was tucked into the hills in a sheltered position overlooking the Fiddich, a tributary of the Spey. Large sash windows embraced extensive views of the surrounding countryside – its construction coinciding with the rise of the Picturesque movement (Scotland's landscape had increasingly come to be seen as an embodiment of the Romantic Movement, in particular satisfying Picturesque ideals).[8] Here, the children ran freely among the hills enjoying the fresh air and swimming in the river and burns. Jane called it 'this dear romantic Glen' and wrote of its 'rural delights . . . You cannot think how delightful it is, the stillness, the fragrance, after the tiresomeness of a London life . . . it is in the most beautiful part of the mountains, woods, lakes and rivers.'[9]

By the early 1790s, Jane and her husband were living apart. She could no longer tolerate living under the same roof as her husband and his mistress, Jean Christie, who was to bear him several children. Although she would occasionally put on a brave face and stay at Gordon Castle, she spent the summer and autumn months at Kinrara, a thatched farmhouse overlooking the Spey in the heart of Badenoch, surrounded by the majestic hills of the Cairngorms. Despite its rustic simplicity, her friends and relations continued to come and stay with her: 'Half the London world of fashion, all the clever people that could be hunted out from all parts . . . flocked to this encampment in the wilderness during the fine autumns to enjoy the free life, the pure air, and the wit and fun the Duchess brought with her to the mountains.'[10] In the early 1800s, Jane built a new house a mile upstream. Guests came and went, and she carried out Picturesque improvements to the garden and surrounding landscape.[11]

Having recklessly spent money earlier in her married life, she involved herself in philanthropic endeavours. She was keen to improve the lives of the poor around her, whether it be their health, morals or education.[12] When she died in 1812, she was buried on the banks of the Spey at Kinrara. A granite pyramid stands over her final resting place inscribed with the names of all of her descendants and recording for posterity their aristocratic alliances. But her greatest legacy was her rich and varied life and her ability to make people feel at ease whatever their station in life.

*   *   *

For Jane's descendants, Glenfiddich always held a special place in their hearts, and the sweet smell of peat fires burning in its grates evoked happy memories of holidays in the Scottish hills. Not long after the Richmonds inherited the ancestral Gordon estates, Queen Victoria and Prince Albert also fell in love with the Highlands. After Albert's death in 1861, Victoria's love affair with Scotland grew even stronger as she sought solace visiting the country that brought back so many happy memories. On one of these Scottish holidays, just six years after Albert had died, she visited Glenfiddich as a guest of the sixth Duke of Richmond. The expedition was not without its mishaps.[13]

Sending an advance party of maids and luggage, the queen, Princess Louise and Jane Churchill set off from Balmoral in a carriage driven by the Highlander John Brown. It was a bright September morning with a howling gale. They soon caught up with the luggage cart, which had got stuck trying to go up a steep hill and needed four cart horses to get it moving again. A wrong turning by the postilions delayed them further, and when they reached the bottom of a very steep incline, Louise and Jane had to get out and walk. They passed over the Lecht – not far from iron mines belonging to Richmond – before stopping for lunch perched in the heather, just outside Tomintoul. There they were joined by Richmond's keeper, Lindsay, who accompanied them through Glenlivet to Tomnavoulin, where they met up with Sir Thomas Biddulph, a courtier, who had brought on their ponies. The idea had been to ride the rest of the way to Glenfiddich, but the wind was such that they carried on in their carriage. The last leg of their journey took them through pretty countryside with rolling hills against the backdrop of the Cairngorms. At teatime, the rain set in and continued as they drove through Dufftown. A few miles later, they finally reached the gates of Glenfiddich and wound their way up the narrow glen, overlooked by deer on the hilltops with the Fiddich river babbling below. It was getting dark and the party were tired.

Unfortunately, the message of their imminent arrival had not reached Richmond, so he was not there to greet them. In his absence, they were given tea in the drawing room and shown to their rooms – all in a row off a long passage carpeted in Gordon tartan. Victoria was relieved that the maids had arrived but was not amused when she discovered that the luggage had not: 'We waited and waited till dinnertime, but nothing came. So we ladies . . . had to go to dinner in our riding-skirts, and just as we were.'[14] Richmond and Biddulph joined the ladies for dinner before taking their leave. Jane then read *Pride and Prejudice* to the queen until eleven o'clock, while still waiting for their luggage. Desperate to change, Victoria held out until two o'clock in the morning before going to bed. As she wrote in her journal, 'I . . . had very little sleep at first; finally, fatigue got the better of discomfort, and after three I fell asleep.'[15]

The following morning – Wednesday – was wet, so Victoria occupied herself with reading and writing in the drawing room. This light-filled room had been given over to her for the duration of her stay. It had full-length windows on three sides under a deep coved ceiling. Around the tops of the walls, rows of antlers were hung, decoratively arranged to lend an air of rusticity. A matching antler mirror and chandelier completed the look. The chairs and sofas were covered in simple, white loose covers, the same fabric being used for the curtains and pelmets. Victoria liked Glenfiddich: 'The house in itself is really a good one, the rooms so well sized and so conveniently placed, all close to each other.'[16]

When the weather cheered up, Victoria went for a ride on Sultan around the grounds. At the stables, she met an old underkeeper, Stewart, who had fought at Waterloo with the fifth duke. During lunch, Richmond's piper played the bagpipes for the queen outside her window and then, afterwards, she went for another ride with Louise. This time, they were accompanied on foot by Richmond and his forester who walked 'so fast that Brown led me on at his full speed, and we distanced the others entirely'.[17] The afternoon's excursion took in a view of the ruined Auchindoun Castle and they did not return until seven o'clock, the queen admitting, 'I was very tired; I am no longer equal to much fatigue.'[18]

On Thursday, Richmond accompanied the queen on a visit to the 'Elf House', a little cave in the hills. Here, Victoria and Louise tried sketching without much success. After a picnic lunch, they set off again riding over the moors where Victoria was mesmerised by the sight of eight stags. 'Oh! Had dearest Albert been here with his rifle!' she exclaimed in her journal.[19] On their way back to the lodge, Victoria tried sketching again but was defeated by a cloud of midges which bit her mercilessly. Later that evening, Jane finished reading *Pride and Prejudice* to them.

Victoria sketched some more the following morning before taking leave of her host and departing for Balmoral. In her closing remarks, she wrote: 'The cuisine, though very simple, was excellent, and the meat etc. the very best – only a female cook. The Duke was very kind.'[20] When she returned to Windsor, she sent Richmond a dinner service that she had had made specially for 'use at Glenfiddich as a memorial of her visit to you there in September last'.[21]

The sixth Duke of Richmond was particularly fond of Glenfiddich. As his granddaughter later wrote, 'Here a great landowner might become a simple gentleman and, escaping the burden of his heavy responsibilities, might sink himself not only in the memories of his care-free childhood, but in the happiness of true friendships . . .'[22] Richmond was eighteen when his father inherited the Gordon estates and, for the rest of his life, he visited Scotland for several months every year. Although Goodwood was his principal residence, his love of field sports meant that Scotland had an added allure. He was a true sportsman who was never happier than when he was striding across the open moor with a gun, often on his own. From the age of twenty-one he kept a game book, meticulously recording the bag whether it be shooting, stalking or fishing. Through these game books – some of which are pocket-sized – it is possible to catch glimpses of his character, otherwise hidden by a duty-driven exterior. 'Shot <u>very badly</u> with new guns – birds very wild but numerous,' he wrote on the Glorious Twelfth, 1886. He went back to his old guns the next day and 'shot very well'. The following year – presumably after Purdey had refitted the offending guns – he wrote, 'Shot very well with new guns'.[23] Elsewhere, a few pen-and-ink sketches of shooting and stalking fill the margins. One also sees how much time he spent shooting; in 1865 alone, he had twelve days grouse shooting, forty-eight days shooting other game (e.g. pheasant and duck) and seven days stalking. The pattern of the year was usually shooting and fishing in Scotland from August to the end of November, followed by shooting at Goodwood until the end of the season (January). Alongside his game books sit the records of who the game was sent to: grandees like the Duke of Portland and Earl Cawdor; numerous relations, including his sons at school; servants such as the kitchen maids and house maids; and acquaintances like the station master at Huntly and the matron at the Infirmary in Chichester. Kippers were clearly a delicacy liked by the aristocracy, as they were only sent to the highest in the land, including the Dukes of Cambridge and Beaufort and Leopold de Rothschild.[24] A highly efficient system was in place to deliver all of this fresh game via the new network of railways that covered the country.

Rail travel made getting to Scotland much easier and Richmond could do the journey from London in a day. On several occasions, he dashed back to London to the House of Lords before coming straight back. This did not pass unnoticed and led a future historian to write of him: 'A man of little calibre ..., an aristocratic amateur of the old type, whose main concern seems to have been to get the business of the session over and depart to the Scottish moors with that other hammer of the grouse, Lord Cairns.'[25] There was certainly tension in the sixth duke's life between his love of sport – particularly field sports – and his career as a politician.

Richmond had a relatively successful career in Parliament. He was elected Conservative MP for West Sussex in 1841 and held on to his seat until his father died and he moved to the Upper House. Over his years in both Houses of Parliament, he gained a reputation as an authority on agriculture, becoming president of the Smithfield Club and a trustee of the Royal Agricultural Society. Like his father, he loved his Southdown sheep and kept a famous herd of Shorthorn cattle at Gordon Castle. As a high-ranking peer in the House of Lords who had proved his loyalty to the Conservative party, he held several senior positions. In 1867, he became president of the Board of Trade under the Earl of Derby's premiership. After Derby's death, he was chosen as leader of the opposition in the House of Lords. When the Conservatives got back into power under Benjamin Disraeli, he was also made lord president of the council. With this role came control of the education department and he helped steer the 1876 Education Bill through the Lords. There was gossip in certain quarters that Richmond might replace Disraeli as prime minister, although the Marquess of Salisbury felt he was 'unfit for the post' and 'that his appointment would justify the title of the "stupid party"'.[26]

When Disraeli moved to the upper house as Earl of Beaconsfield, Richmond stepped down as Conservative leader and focused on agricultural issues; he was dubbed 'the farmers' friend' by the Prince of Wales at a meeting of the Royal Agricultural Society in 1883. His final government appointment was as the first secretary of state for Scotland, in Salisbury's cabinet. Although he lasted only six months (the Conservatives were defeated in the general election of November and December 1885), he was conscientious in his responsibilities and got the department off to a good start.[27]

Queen Victoria held Richmond in high regard (a feeling that was mutual) and, as a consolation prize for stepping down as leader in the House of Lords, in 1876 she made him Duke of Gordon, the title that had died out in 1836. Victoria felt that it was not right 'that when these great possessions pass into English hands, they should be treated as a secondary possession and, in some cases, like Lord Aveland, who has Drummond Castle, or who will have it when his mother dies, probably be treated like a shooting place. By conferring this great title on the D of Richmond it will at once do away with this, and have the very best effect.'[28]

Ironically, Gordon Castle and its associated estates *were* treated by Richmond as 'a shooting place', although for Richmond they meant much more. He maintained an almost paternalistic attitude towards his tenants and the local community, akin to a great Scottish chieftain. In the local town of Fochabers, he introduced a free water supply, a sewerage system and public baths; on his estates, he built and improved cottages and farm buildings and spent huge sums on drainage. When the agricultural depression threated to overwhelm his tenants, he lowered their rents considerably. A royal commission was set up to enquire into its causes and to find remedies, with Richmond as chairman. At a later inquiry into the same subject, he was one of the most important witnesses, giving details of his vast estates. At the time of the hearing (1894), Richmond was the fourth-largest landowner in the country, with a combined total of 289,000 acres, mostly in Scotland (Goodwood was 19,716 acres).[29] On the arable land in Scotland alone, he had 882 tenants. All of the improvements in Scotland had cost him nearly £200,000 and, over the same period, he had lost approximately

£400,000 in rent reductions. His annual income was estimated at around £80,000 – a huge figure when compared to the annual rents of his arable tenants, nearly half of whom were paying less than £10 per annum.[30]

Running estates in both Scotland and Sussex inevitably meant more work for Richmond, and his absence from one or other for long periods of time. However, this did not mean that Richmond took his eye off the ball – quite the contrary. At Goodwood, Richmond had spent nearly £30,000 on building new cottages and repairing old ones, so the estate now held just over four hundred cottages. The new ones were named Duchess Cottages in honour of his wife, Frances. By the time of the second inquiry, Richmond was a widower. After forty-three years of marriage, Frances had died on her birthday, aged sixty-three. She had been a devoted wife and mother of their six children, quietly performing her duty as hostess at Goodwood, Gordon Castle and Belgrave Square (their London home), as well as supporting her husband in all of his other responsibilities. Queen Victoria, who had never recovered fully from Albert's death, wrote to Richmond on the day of Frances's death:

'Windsor Castle
'March 8, 1887

'The Queen can hardly find words to express her warm & true sympathy with the Duke of Richmond in this his hour of terrible grief & bereavement, which has seemed to come so suddenly upon him and his family. The Queen not having heard for some time was in hopes that the Duchess had entirely recovered her severe accident last Nov: & was therefore greatly surprised & shocked when she heard on Wednesday last in London of her alarming illness.

'The Queen does not attempt to offer any comfort to the Duke for there is none to give in a grief so great & a loss so irreparable as the one the Duke has now to endure – no loss can equal that of *the partner of your life – the sharer of all your joys, trials and sorrows! The Queen knows too well what this is & she prays God to support the Duke & give him strength to bear this terrible blow. She would ask him to express her sympathy to his children & accept the sincere condolences of Princess Beatrice & Prince Henry.*

'*The Duchess looked so strong & well always, that it is difficult to realise the sad truth.*

'*The Duke has always been so kind to the Queen & so ready to help her on all occasions, that she feels doubly for him in his affliction.*'[31]

Victoria's letter was followed the next day by one from her son, Bertie, again expressing his deep sadness at the duchess's death. He writes: 'We have on so many occasions received such kindness & hospitality from you & the Duchess . . . May He who does all for the best give you strength to bear this heavy blow.'[32] The Richmond family were to remain close to the royal family over the next two generations.

*　　　*　　　*

The side tables in the dining-room of Gordon Castle groaned with food. Bread rolls were piled high and cold meats and game stood waiting to be carved. After a hearty breakfast, the house party guests relished making their own packed lunch for a day on the river. Grouse, ham, beef, venison – whatever was in season – would be carved, sliced or pulled apart and stuffed into the rolls, along with generous helpings of chutney and mayonnaise. One of the guests, Arthur Coventry, was heard to mutter to himself as he wielded the carving knife, 'Now, Coventry, my pretty boy, what is your choice?'[33] Jammy buns formed the second course, prepared by neatly cutting off the top crust, scooping out the middle, and then filling it back up with jam or honey, before popping the top back on again. The lunches were then shoved into bulging fishing bags that were left in rows on the carpet, waiting to be taken to 'the Shankery'. After the last guest had left, the dining-room looked in a sorry state with food debris strewn everywhere.[34]

Making one's packed lunch was just one of the many rituals for a fishing house-party at Gordon Castle. Each year, after raceweek had finished, the entire Goodwood household would make its annual pilgrimage to the Highlands. A special train would be hired to take them from Euston Station in London to Scotland. Trunks, suitcases, bicycles, shooting equipment and fishing paraphernalia – even pets – were piled on board with children and servants, and the summer holidays began. Meanwhile, Goodwood was left shuttered up, run by a skeleton staff.

The house party at Gordon Castle was usually made up of a mixture of extended family and close friends, invited for their shared love of fishing. While Glenfiddich – and its satellite Blackwater Lodge – offered exceptional grouse shooting and deer stalking, Gordon Castle was famed for its salmon fishing on the Spey. The inheritance of the Gordon estates and the subsequent enjoyment they gave coincided with the Victorian romance with the Scottish Highlands. Despite the hardships endured by much of its native population, the north of Scotland became a tourist destination and playground for the rich.[35] The historical novels and poems of Sir Walter Scott helped fuel the romantic vision of the Highlands. Travel became easier, as railways were added to the web of roads, harbours and canals constructed during the Scottish Enlightenment. From the late 1840s, Thomas Cook developed package tours that opened up Scotland to a wider audience. Victoria and Albert's purchase of Balmoral and their Celtic enthusiasms (Victoria was a great fan of Walter Scott) helped turn the Highlands into a cult. Scottish history was idealised and was reflected in architecture, 'clancestry' and tartan.[36] Artists such as Sir Edwin Landseer and Horatio McCulloch stirred people's imagination with their emotive paintings.

It was against this background that sport took off. As well as the traditional pursuits of stalking, shooting and fishing, people also embraced healthy outdoor activities like rambling, mountaineering and yachting. Sporting estates sprung up all over the Highlands and it became a part of the social calendar to holiday in Scotland from August to October. The fashion reached its peak in the 1880s and lasted until the outbreak of the First World War.

The Gordons played their part in this romanticised view of Scottish history. After the battle of Bannockburn (1314), Robert the Bruce granted lands in the north-east of Scotland to Sir Adam Gordon from Berwickshire. Later that century, they settled in their new lands and established themselves as one of the most powerful clans in Scotland, initially based at Huntly Castle in Aberdeenshire. In 1479, the second Earl of Huntly built the ancient tower-house of Bog-of-Gight (windy bog), later known as Gordon Castle. It rose tall and slender above the marshes and could only be reached by a causeway and drawbridge. At the close of the sixteenth century, the fifth earl was made Marquess of Huntly by James VI of Scotland. His son lost his head supporting James's son, Charles I, in the Civil War but, at the Restoration, their estates were restored, and Charles II elevated the fourth marquess to become Duke of Gordon. The second duke carried out a wave of improvements at Gordon Castle following his travels in Italy and filled the castle with classical sculpture. It was his grandson, Alexander, fourth Duke of Gordon, who married Jane Maxwell and, between them, they transformed the higgledy-piggledy Renaissance castle with the assistance of a young architect called John Baxter.

It was Baxter's castle that the Richmonds now enjoyed. Built on a gargantuan scale, Baxter's design subsumed the old castle, including the original tower-house, to present a well-ordered symmetrical façade with flanking wings. The whole ensemble, with crenellated roofline, measured 568 feet long. The principal reception rooms were on the first floor: dining-room, drawing room, billiard room and library, all decorated in the neo-classical style. Only in the ground-floor entrance hall, where it was carpeted wall to wall in Gordon tartan with claymores and regimental standards decorating the walls, did you get any sense that you were in Scotland.[37] It was just outside the hall, on the front doorstep, that Landseer painted a portrait of Cecilia Lennox

as a little girl, looking charmingly demure with her skipping rope. In
her childhood innocence, Cecilia would have been blissfully unaware
that Landseer was passionately in love with her great aunt, Georgina,
Duchess of Bedford (Charlotte Richmond's younger sister). Indeed,
their love affair was partly played out in the wilds of the Scottish
Highlands and Landseer was thought to have been the father of
Georgina's youngest daughter, Rachel.[38]

Children always played a part in the Gordon Castle fishing parties.
Several generations of Gordon Lennox children had very happy memories of summers spent in Scotland. On one occasion, the chaos of
nursery tea was interrupted by a visit from the Prince of Wales, the
future King George V. Muriel, one of the sixth duke's granddaughters,
sat in silent amazement as he picked up a covered dish to discover toasted
buns. He then proceeded to eat one, much to the children's delight.[39]

George V loved nothing more than coming to Gordon Castle for a
week's fishing on the Spey. After one such visit in September 1899, he
wrote almost immediately to Richmond, from the Station Hotel in
Perth, to thank him for his hospitality:

> 'My dear Duke
>
> 'We arrived here last night quite safely at 10 after a very
> comfortable journey. I take this first opportunity this morning
> before starting for Drumlanrig to send you a few lines to tell you
> how charmed we both were with our visit to Gordon Castle. Our
> weather was certainly not all that could have been desired; but I
> enjoyed my week's fishing more than I can say, I suppose I was
> rather unlucky at first, but my last two days made up for it all &
> yesterday when I got four fish was the best day I have ever had.
> Thanks for your telegram telling me the result of the day's fishing,
> I am very glad Berkeley Paget got one of 34 lbs. I shall never forget
> the great kindness that you, Lady Caroline, & all your sons
> showed us during our visit & I can assure you that it was much
> appreciated by us. I shall miss Geordie Shanks very much as I was
> out with him every day, it was so kind of you letting him come

with me, as I know he generally goes with you. With many kind
messages to Lady Caroline & all your family & hoping you will
have very good sport, with renewed thanks for all your kindness.
  'Believe me my dear Duke most sincerely yours,
  'George'[40]

Geordie Shanks was Richmond's devoted head gillie. Always dressed in estate tweed and bowler hat, he oversaw as many as twelve other gillies who invariably spent much of their working day wearing waders. Shanks taught many of Richmond's family to fish, including the young Muriel who was only eleven when she killed her first salmon (salmon are traditionally 'killed' rather than 'caught'). Fishing was his life and he even had a room named after him: the 'Shankery'. Here, gillies and fishermen congregated, waders were dried, flies sorted, and reels oiled. On days when there was no fishing – and despondency reigned supreme – Shanks would console Richmond's grandchildren by making toffee with them over the fire in the Shankery.[41]

The fishing on the Spey at Gordon Castle was some of the best in Scotland and the names of its pools were music to the ears of those lucky enough to fish there: Rock, Otter's Cave, Chapel, Aultdearg, Lennox Water, Cruive Dyke, Dipple, Lilley's, Bulwark, Bridge, Quarry, Stynie, Braehead, Dallachy, Eskil and Railway Arch. On one exceptional day in October 1886, the thirteen rods killed between them a total of seventy-four fish. Richmond himself killed eight fish that day, while his two unmarried daughters, Caroline and Florence (who fished Dipple alternately) killed four and three respectively.

If luncheon was a private affair, either seated on the river bank or gently rocking in a boat, dinner was much more formal. Richmond disliked any form of ostentation, so the Goodwood tradition of recording one's weight in the weighing book helped jolly the evening along. During his 1899 stay, George V had happily noted 'kilt before dinner' as if the trappings of Highland regalia might make him appear heavy – in fact, he weighed only 10 st 10 lbs.[42] Dinner was taken in the dining-room, where full-length portraits of former Dukes of Gordon surveyed the guests seated below Baxter's delicate neo-classical ceiling. During pudding, the rousing sound of bagpipes rose up from the gravel path in the garden below, as Pipe-Major Mackenzie strode backwards and forwards and the guests fell silent. After ten minutes, he entered the dining-room and gave a stirring march around the table before everyone rose and stood still while he played a Highland reel. Finally, the guests departed to the tune of 'The Muchin' o' Geordie's Byre', Richmond's personal favourite. Muriel, who spent much of her childhood at Gordon Castle, wrote emotively of the pipes: 'The weird wailing sound is full of "longings", of a nostalgia that belongs to the land of mists. The song of the pipes has in it the hush of the wind in the pine trees, eternal, distant, and strangely moving. At moments this nostalgia, in a few broken bars, changes, and there comes into the skirl the anger of the northern storms, wild and enchanting, pregnant with the rush of the sea and the fierceness which belongs to the ancient legends of the North, then again it settles down into the dominating and arresting quality of wistfulness, a quality which gives you a clutch in your throat and quickens the beating of your heart.'[43]

Every morning, the household was awoken to the sound of Pipe-Major Mackenzie playing 'Hey, Johnnie Cope', a quick march that heralded the dawn as he paraded around the castle. On Sundays, after breakfast, the whole house party would congregate in the hall before proceeding together to church on foot. Their route took them down the broad walk, between neatly clipped boxed laurels and flower-filled urns, up the balustraded stone steps and through the vast kitchen garden to the Scottish Episcopal Church. Situated on the edge of the park, with its twin-towered façade facing towards the square in Fochabers, the church had been built by the redoubtable Elizabeth, widow of the last Duke of Gordon, who had sold some of her jewellery to pay for it. The church was on the raised ground floor (with a school beneath) and, under Richmond's tenure, had been remodelled, including the insertion of exquisite stained-glass windows designed by Edward Burne-Jones and made by Morris & Co. Richmond's late wife, Frances, was commemorated in a window depicting St Ursula visiting the sick.[44] Touchingly, her window overlooked the 'castle pew', the front two rows reserved for the Gordon Lennox family.

* * *

On the stroke of one on Friday, 1 October 1903, the front door of Gordon Castle was opened solemnly, and the sixth Duke of Richmond's coffin was carried out. It was attended by the male members of his family, all wearing full Highland dress. The female members of his family could be glimpsed watching from the windows, their pale faces betraying their grief. In deep silence save for the crunch of gravel beneath thousands of feet, the cortège moved off down the main avenue. It was a calm, still day with a faint chill in the air. From across the park, the slow tolling of the church bell could be heard. Nearly three thousand people had gathered from the far reaches of the Highlands to pay their last respects to 'the farmer's friend'. Staff, tenants, crofters, farmers, fishermen, gamekeepers and dignitaries spread like a great black veil over the gardens. The coffin was borne to the station in Fochabers, where the female members of the family had gathered to watch it being placed into a carriage carpeted in Gordon tartan. At 2.20 p.m., the train slowly pulled out of the station, shrouding the family in a puff of steam, and bound for Chichester.[45] The funeral and interment was to take place the following day in Chichester Cathedral.

Just over two months earlier, Richmond had arrived in Scotland for his annual stay. Already frail, the house parties that year were quieter than normal, mainly made up of family. In September, concerns were such that his London medical adviser, Mr Venning, was called for. When Venning returned to London, it seemed to outsiders that Richmond had rallied, and he was even spotted in Fochabers accompanied by his daughter, Caroline. However, in the last week of September, he had a relapse and, over the course of four days, sank lower and lower until he died just after midnight, on Sunday 27 September, surrounded by his family, the Fochabers doctor and his faithful servant, Osborn.[46]

Richmond had been duke for forty-three years and had never once swayed from doing his duty. The press, in the typically sycophantic style of the day, eulogised his life: 'Born to one of the highest positions in the country, he adorned it by his courtly grace, and in his leading positions in the State he provided to all of exalted station a noble ideal.' His immense landholdings, he 'held inviolate and cherished', and 'maintained the bountiful hospitality' at both Goodwood and Gordon Castle.[47]

As the flags at Goodwood and Gordon Castle fluttered at half-mast it did indeed seem the end of an era. Seismic changes loomed on the horizon and world events would soon shatter the traditional status quo. No longer would the aristocracy wield such power in national life; a new class of politician was emerging. During Richmond's lifetime, he had served his country selflessly and diligently; but the positions he had attained were very much part and parcel of his station in life as a landed aristocrat. Over the next one hundred years, it was to be the sport that would continue unscathed. At Goodwood, the annual raceweek fixture was now an integral part of the summer social season, traditionally marking its end before the yearly exodus to Scotland or the Isle of Wight (for Cowes Regatta). But 'Glorious Goodwood' was not just an exclusive horseracing meeting for those of noble birth; anyone could attend the races no matter what their background. It was this generosity of sharing their mutual love of sport that Richmond passed on to his descendants. Although the inheritance of the Scottish estates had meant more sports for the Richmonds to enjoy (grouse shooting, fishing and stalking), these were predominately private affairs for the family and their close friends. But at Goodwood, perfect strangers were welcome to come and enjoy the thrills of horseracing up on the South Downs and the more sedate – but no less exciting – sport of cricket in the park.

Champion golfer James Braid at the opening of the Goodwood golf
course in 1914; Braid was the designer of the new Downs course
(© Trustees of the Goodwood Collection)

10

Widowerhood

*'Considering our own early influences, first and foremost I
must place my father, for he was not only the kindest and
wisest of counsellors, but the most devoted father, and
certainly the simplest and most unassuming of men.'*

Lady Muriel Beckwith, daughter of the seventh
Duke of Richmond[1]

Society guests gathered at St Paul's Church, Knightsbridge, at midday on 10 November 1868 for the marriage of the Earl of March, son and heir of the sixth Duke of Richmond, to Miss Amy Ricardo. St Paul's had only been founded in 1834, a great Gothic edifice built to champion the ideals of the Oxford Movement in the Anglo-Catholic tradition. It was up the aisle of this hallowed building that the twenty-one-year-old bride walked on the arm of her father, Percy, wearing a white satin dress trimmed with Brussels lace. Her matching veil was held in place by a diamond tiara in the shape of delicate fern leaves and her rich auburn hair was adorned with orange blossoms. She was attended by five bridesmaids whose white satin dresses were embroidered with ivy, the badge of the Gordon family, and tied with

Gordon tartan bows; white tulle veils covered their heads. March's best man was his close friend, Captain Chaplin. After the ceremony, the wedding party proceeded to Prince's Gardens for the wedding breakfast where the bride and groom were welcomed by the band of the Grenadier Guards playing Mendelssohn's 'Wedding March'. At half-past three, the newlyweds departed for their honeymoon in Eastbourne.[2]

Amy was to become a much-loved figure in the family, winning everyone over by her kindness and gentleness. Unlike previous Richmond spouses, Amy was not from an aristocratic background. The Ricardos were originally Sephardi Jews from Portugal who established themselves as bankers in Holland by way of Ireland. At the time of the Napoleonic Wars, they settled in England, converted to Christianity and were chiefly involved in finance, the most famous member of their family being David Ricardo, the political economist.[3] Amy's parents lived at Bramley Park in Surrey, a large Italianate mansion that was once the childhood home of Gertrude Jekyll. It is not clear how March and Amy met, but it may well have been through mutual acquaintances in the Grenadier Guards (both of Amy's brothers were to become officers in the Grenadiers). Unlike her husband, Amy's interests were more intellectual and artistic; she was content to read a book on the river bank or while away the hours filling her photograph album. She was also a talented musician and played the piano and organ. But her greatest legacy is her catalogue of the picture collections at both Goodwood and Gordon Castle, a labour of love that she dedicated to her husband.

Despite their differences, March and Amy seem to have been very happily married. They had five children: Charles, Evelyn, Violet, Esmé and Bernard. A charming clutch of letters written by Amy to 'Charlie' when he was very young survive and show her tender nature. Holidaying in the spa town of Homburg in Germany, a popular destination for Victorians wanting to take the waters, she writes: 'I have got all your photographs in the room too, and am trying to make it look as much like home as possible: I wish you all were here too, and not only your dear little faces in the pictures!' A few days later, she tells him: 'I have just got a letter from Nanny and am very sorry to hear you have all got colds: you must make haste and get well before I come home! . . . I am going to try and draw you a German postman on this envelope to shew you what funny sort of caps they wear . . . Now for today Goodbye with love and kisses to you all – It won't be long now before we meet again I hope . . . Bless you all – Your loving mother Amy March'. They must have been in Homburg for March's health as Amy explains: 'Papa has got the gout in his toe again, and has to drive about in a carriage instead of walking.' After chatting about the horses and dogs she sees in the streets, she tells him, 'I have to go twice a day to drink water at the wells: the water is very nasty indeed and tastes like a bad egg in fizzy water with a rusty nail in it and it smells like a bad drain! I also have a bath of the fizzy water, and that is very nice indeed, so cool and refreshing, and I am sorry when the time comes to get out again.'

The children were being looked after by their nanny and reports on their progress were clearly flying backwards and forwards between various members of the family. In a letter dated just 'Monday', Amy writes to Charlie: 'So I hear from Aunt Lina [March's unmarried sister] that both your top teeth have come out! Are the new ones to be seen yet? I hope they will soon appear!' Amy fills the letters with snippets of information that would have delighted a five- or six-year-old boy: '. . . we played at lawn tennis all the afternoon, and I won a great many games: the German officer came again and played with Papa, and once he tumbled down flat on his face! A little girl has just gone by, riding on a very smart donkey with a red saddle: I think she was rather afraid of tumbling off, for she was holding on tight with both hands – I wonder if you have tumbled off Crocus yet?'

Amy always wrote to her children whenever they were separated. Staying with their friends the Balfours at Balbirnie in Fife, she tells Charlie: 'This is our wedding day: ten years ago this day, Papa & I were married in that very church where you go in London, St Pauls.' After thanking and praising him for his letter written in French, she signs off, 'Lots of Kisses and blessings to each of my bairns from your loving Mother'. It may have been that Amy was already suffering from the illness that would eventually bring her to an early grave. She admitted to Charlie that she had been so ill at Balbirnie that she could not write, and the doctor had made her stay in bed for two days.

Only three more letters from Amy to her children survive and they date from the following year, 1879. Confined to her bedroom, away from Goodwood, she writes: 'Isn't this disappointing, my being kept here so long, & now they say I must not move till Saturday: these naughty doctors! If one didn't know that they do it all for our good, I think one w'd feel rather inclined to disobey them! If it w'd only be fine weather! I am longing to hear all about you and all your doings . . .' The last two letters are written faintly in pencil because she was worried she might spill ink on the sheets in her weak state. Addressed to Charlie, they are full of questions about what he and his siblings have been getting up to. Clearly in great pain, she makes light of her illness: 'You w'd laugh if you c'd see my 2 poor legs! The swollen one is all done up in cotton wool, & sits on a pillow! The other poor one has got so thin, from having all the work to do, that you w'd never think they were a pair.' Charlie, otherwise known as 'Set' in the family (his courtesy title was Lord Settrington), has written the date 'April 1879' at the top of one of the letters. Tragically, she died later that summer, on 23 August, aged thirty-two; her son Bernard was only one year old. A report of her death says that she had breast cancer, another mentions phlebitis (inflamed vein) in the leg.[4] A newspaper cutting kept by Charlie spoke of 'the terrible nature of her malady' which had 'for a long time precluded all hopes of recovery . . . To know her was to love her. Sweet-tempered and gentle, her beautiful face was only the reflection of a still more lovely nature, and the dreadful sufferings which accompanied her last illness were borne with angelic patience and heroic fortitude.'[5] Her body was laid to rest in the family vault beneath the Lady Chapel in Chichester Cathedral, following a simple funeral service.

*   *   *

A stained-glass window depicting St Cecilia, patron saint of musicians, was erected in Amy's memory in the Scottish Episcopal Church in Fochabers (or Gordon Chapel as it was known). Like the window commemorating Frances, it was designed by Edward Burne-Jones. In the upper section, St Cecilia stands embracing a small pipe organ, as her heart sings to God – Amy would often play the organ herself during services when the family were in Scotland. The lower scene shows St Cecilia, her husband Valerian (a Roman nobleman who became a Christian), and an angel of the Lord who stood watch over her.[6]

With the death of Amy, the joy went out of March's life. Photographs of him as a young man often show him smiling with a twinkle in his eye but, after his wife's death, it is as if someone has turned out the lights and his face takes on a stern expression. His sister, Caroline, or 'Aunt Lina' as she was known, took on the role of mother to his five young children while he buried his grief – undealt with – beneath a typical English stiff upper lip.

Three years later, in 1882, March remarried. His bride was the nineteen-year-old Isabel Sophie, the daughter of William and Mary Craven, and a descendant of the first Duke of Richmond.[7] This time, the summer wedding took place at the Savoy Chapel, which was filled with the cream of society. Isabel was an undoubted beauty with a tall slender figure and minute waist but, in his heart, March still grieved for Amy. Isabel gave birth to two daughters, Muriel and Helen, who joined their half-siblings in the nursery and, to outward appearances, everything looked fine.

But the marriage was doomed. Nobody could replace Amy in March or his children's hearts and, to make matters worse, Isabel did not enjoy blood sports, which made the annual trips to Scotland unbearable. According to the family butler, Compton, one autumn Isabel finally had enough and walked out on March, leaving him behind at Gordon Castle.[8] Shortly afterwards, she contracted typhoid and died in London aged twenty-four. March was by her side.

Aunt Lina's role as mother-figure to seven children was now more important than ever, especially as the twice-widowed March became even more emotionally shut up. Freddie, the ninth Duke of Richmond, wrote of his great aunt: 'Aunt Lina was . . . a true Victorian spinster superbly erect in shape and mind . . . Splendidly upright, tight-waisted and festooned with glasses and watch on gold chains, brooches and other tinkling pendants she naturally became a mother in need especially to the two little daughters of Isabel who were only babies when she died.'[9] Lina's role as surrogate mother was not her only responsibility; after her own mother had died earlier that year, she had become de facto hostess at Goodwood and Gordon Castle for her father. That role continued when her brother succeeded to the dukedom.

* * *

On 17 March 1900, Set wrote to his grandfather, the sixth duke, from Bloemfontein in South Africa:

> 'My dear Grandpapa,
>
> 'I have also written to Papa by this mail so you will doubtless see his letter. We got in here with no trouble to speak of, all the fighting was over at Driefontein where we had a very sharp tussle. The Buffs and Welsh Regiment did most gallant service there & lost heavily in driving the Boers from their position with the bayonet. The place next morning was a very unpleasant sight. We are in clover here, living in Steyn's house which is the "Presidency" & most palatial. Bernard is wonderfully fit; the Guards Brigade are the admiration of all from the splendid endurance they have shown all through this very trying 5 weeks. He has grown a beard but is otherwise not much changed, though of course very thin & in splendid condition . . . It is a very healthy climate, hot by day & deliciously cool in early morning & at night. I am very fit indeed although not by any means corpulent; we have had some stiffish days lately.

'. . . We are certain I think to be here for at least 3 weeks. The "romance" of war loses considerably when one sees the realities. It is not a pleasant sight to see our poor Tommies lying about killed & wounded. I must say it is perfectly wonderful how the wounded men behave, not a murmur, under boiling sun & pouring wet night very often. Every man and boy in the force here has the greatest confidence in Bobs & would go through anything to serve him. We gave him a tremendous ovation the night we entered here, at dinner, & he made a speech that simply made one choke. He wound up by saying that he was the proudest man in the whole of the British army at that moment! I sincerely hope we shall see the Transvaal collapse as quickly as the O-F State; they have, I think, already begun to feel more qualms . . . In great haste, & hoping to be back in time to back Leonard's horses at Goodwood.

'Yours affectionately

'Charlie'[10]

Set, along with his younger brothers Esmé and Bernard, was in South Africa as part of the British forces fighting the Boers. His father and uncle – Algernon, or 'Algy' as they called him – were also involved in the conflict. Set had only recently returned from Ireland where he had been aide-de-camp to the commander-in-chief, Field Marshal Lord Roberts. The Boer War started at the beginning of October 1899 and initially went badly for the British. At the end of December, Lord Roberts was called in and given overall command, forming his staff from far and wide, and asking his former aide-de-camp, Set, to join him. Roberts was mourning the loss of his only son, Frederick, who had been mortally wounded just days earlier fighting the Boers at the battle of Colenso, for which he was awarded a posthumous Victoria Cross. Set's presence would have been some comfort to Roberts as Set was a near contemporary of Frederick's at Eton.

Set's letter was written four days after the British had captured Bloemfontein, the capital of the Orange Free State and the site of failed negotiations to avert the outbreak of war. The Presidency was taken over as accommodation for Roberts – or 'Bobs' as he was known to the soldiers – and his officers. They were joined there later by Lady Roberts, her two daughters and Set's young wife, Hilda. A handful of other letters written by Set were kept by his grandfather, along with some from Esmé and Hilda. In all of them, there is a poignant longing to be back home, especially enjoying the sport in Scotland. Poor Bernard came down with 'a sort of malarial fever from damp' and collapsed causing a great deal of concern.[11] Fortunately, he recovered. Despite the situation they found themselves in, all three seem to have maintained their sense of humour. Writing from Cape Town in April, Esmé jokes that, 'All London seems gathered here and one seems to know everybody.'[12]

In April, Set told his grandfather with great excitement that 'Bobs' had applied to the Marquess of Lansdowne (the war secretary) asking that Set be given a captain's commission in a Guard's regiment.[13] When Roberts – himself an Irishman – was chosen as the first colonel of the newly formed Irish Guards, he promptly ordered Set to transfer, the appointment becoming official on 15 August.[14] Hilda helped out by dying his hat plume a blue-green colour to match the sash of the Order of St Patrick, thereby taking her place in regimental history.[15]

Before the war was over, Set's father, March, came out to South Africa as colonel of the 3rd (Militia) battalion of the Royal Sussex Regiment, arriving in March 1901 and remained there until the end of hostilities in May the following year. A keen amateur photographer, he compiled two photograph albums recording his time there. As a young man, March had been an officer in the Grenadier Guards but had retired in 1869 when he became Member of Parliament for West Sussex. When the 3rd battalion was formed in December 1899, March was an obvious choice as colonel being a local grandee and a former guards officer. When the battalion returned home on board SS *Dominion*, they were given a rapturous welcome in Chichester.[16]

The sixth Duke of Richmond took a deep interest in the Boer War. His concern for the wounded led him to convert the Kennels (by then staff accommodation) into a private hospital for wounded soldiers where they could convalesce. There was accommodation for fifty patients and both he and Lina made sure all of the men were comfortable, treating them with game, eggs, pipes and tobacco, and newspapers.[17]

With so many members of the Gordon Lennox family fighting in the Boer War, there was huge relief when they all returned home safely. A photograph appeared in the press of Richmond sitting on a chair in front of his three grandsons, Set, Esmé and Bernard, towering over him in their bearskins and representing three guards regiments: the Irish Guards, Scots Guards and Grenadier Guards respectively. Another Burne-Jones window was commissioned for Gordon Chapel, this time depicting St Raphael, patron saint of travellers, above a scene of St Raphael safely leading Tobias on his journey. Beneath is the inscription: 'To the glory of God in thanksgiving for the safe return from the War in South Africa (1900-1902) of Charles Henry Earl of March, Algernon Charles Gordon Lennox, Charles Henry Lord Settrington, Esmé Charles Gordon Lennox, Bernard Charles Gordon Lennox.'[18] As a memento of their time in South Africa, Set and his brothers presented their grandfather with the Boer flag taken from the Volksraad (Parliament) in Pretoria when it was captured by the British. He proudly hung it up at Gordon Castle beside the other flags and standards.

*   *   *

The house party guests sauntered into the newly decorated dining-room after morning prayers in the Long Hall. Breakfast during raceweek was always informal, particularly as the royal family breakfasted alone in their private suite of rooms. In anticipation of a full day ahead, there was plenty of food: bacon, grilled kidneys on toast, fish, kedgeree and eggs in every form were the hot options; devilled bones, chicken and game, game pies, York hams, pickled fish and potted game were the cold choices if you desired a second course.[19] The muffled clink of coffee and teacups accompanied the lively chatter about the upcoming racing.

The dining-room had been given a facelift when March had succeeded to the dukedom in 1903 and moved into Goodwood House. Using the excuse that Edward VII did not like it, the old Egyptian Dining-Room had been swept away and replaced with a tasteful classical room hung with tiers of eighteenth-century family portraits – even the crocodile mounts on the backs of the dining chairs had been removed. The room was completed in time for the 1906 raceweek house party, along with works carried out in the royal apartments.[20] The royal apartments were in the north wing and included the Tapestry Drawing Room and Tapestry Bedroom. To mark the internal revamp, all of the state rooms were photographed by James Russell of Baker Street, London, whose father had been a local Chichester photographer. The rooms were filled in the typical Edwardian manner with cluttered groups of furniture interspersed with billowing palms and vases of chrysanthemums.

After breakfast, the guests drifted into the front hall to read the newspaper, study the day's form or continue their conversations. The hall was comfortably arranged with sofas and chairs and, on hot days, the guests spilled out on to the portico to recline in wicker seats. Some guests strolled to the stables to have a sneak-peek at the favourites, while others went back to their bedrooms to catch up on their correspondence. Edward VII often used this part of the day to call a Privy Council meeting in the Tapestry Drawing Room, making the most of the many Privy Counsellors in the house party. Goodwood raceweek reached its zenith during the Edwardian period, with the king present at every meeting and the house filled with the élite of society, many of whom were responsible for leading the country.

Later that morning, all the guests were requested to take their place for a formal photograph on the lawn outside the ballroom. James Russell was the official photographer, a particular favourite of Edward VII, who had talent-spotted him over forty years earlier with the result that Russell had gone on to photograph many of the crowned heads of Europe.[21] Perhaps surprisingly, the king himself directed where everyone was to sit or stand. The resulting photograph is a snapshot of Edwardian high society. Edward VII is seated in the centre, flanked on his right by Countess Benckendorff, the Russian ambassador's wife, and on his left by Richmond's youngest daughter, Helen, who had taken over the role of hostess at Goodwood from Aunt Lina. Behind them stands Richmond in between the Prince of Wales and the Marquis de Soveral. Soveral was a Portuguese diplomat whose nickname was the Blue Monkey. He was an intimate friend of Edward VII and was adored by the ladies for his wit and charm. Other society figures include Alice Keppel, Edward VII's long-term mistress, and the Marchioness of Londonderry. The latter was a leading political hostess whose affair with the dashing Harry Cust led her husband to stop speaking to her in private, only communicating with her through a third party.[22] The circles within which most of the guests moved were very small. Many of them regularly attended house parties at stately homes all over the country and a handful were part of Edward VII's racy Marlborough House set. Despite Edward VII's friendships with Jewish bankers (such as the Rothschilds) or *nouveau riche* plutocrats, Richmond maintained a staunchly traditional guest list. The Goodwood guests were mostly members of the English aristocracy, many of whom were connected by marriage.

Edward VII's presence at 'Glorious Goodwood' gave it a huge boost in prestige and he dubbed it 'a garden party with racing tacked on'. His personal interest in it even stretched to the dress code. Worried that it was becoming more of a fashion show than a serious race meeting, he suggested that the Turf Club members wear 'pot hats' or straw hats. Unfortunately, they failed to respond, so he took matters into his own hands and, in 1904, he wore a white silk top hat instead of the regulation black one, knowing that the gentlemen would follow his lead. The fashionistas desperately tried to get their own 'royal model' hat for the remaining days' racing, sending their valets dashing up to London to their hatters.[23]

The house party photographed in 1906 captures the moment when Edward relaxed the dress code still further by wearing a lounge suit (instead of a morning suit) and a grey bowler hat. Other gentlemen

– including Richmond – are wearing a homburg hat and a few wear straw boaters. The ladies, meanwhile, are resplendent in all their Edwardian finery of long summer dresses and hats brimming with flowers and feathers. The whole photograph is given a relaxed air by the gentlemen seated cross-legged in the front row. It was this relaxed atmosphere that pervaded the whole meeting and helped make it such a popular occasion at the end of the summer season.

Having been photographed, the guests gathered on the lawn in front of the house and, as the stable clock struck twelve, the carriages and cars appeared from the stables, drew up by the portico for the guests to climb into, before sweeping off again bound for the racecourse. There, they entered the new grandstand that had opened in 1904. It had a royal pavilion at the paddock end for Edward VII and a ladies' box at the other end for Queen Alexandra with an underground passage linking the two. No expense had been spared – the king's lavatory was made of monogrammed marble and the fittings were silver-plated.[24]

The racing that week was blessed with four days of sunshine. Despite grumblings by the sporting press that the quality of racing was not what it had been in former days, *The Morning Post* hailed it a 'highly successful meeting'.[25] Although the king had no runners himself that year, he did have the pleasure of watching the progeny of his champion racehorse Persimmon take home first and second place in the Goodwood Cup – the big race of the week – as well as winning the Halnaker Plate. Named Plum Tree, Plum Centre and Plum Blossom respectively, there was much witty commentary in the papers the following day.[26]

With regard to the relaxing of the dress code, in a tongue-in-cheek round-up of the week, *The Sporting Times* cheekily remarked: 'Goodwood in flannels this year seemed too much of an innovation to some gentlemen to be possible . . . Perhaps the greatest thrill of the meeting was the appearance of M de Soveral in silk trousers.'[27] Even the press had their fair share of the action – every year there was a cricket match between Jockeys and Press.[28]

After the horseracing, the house party guests came back to Goodwood House and played tennis or croquet on the tapestry lawn, or watched from deckchairs in the shade of the great cedars of Lebanon. Edward VII was very fond of croquet and, on one occasion, partnered Richmond's young daughter Muriel. Unsurprisingly, she was very nervous and, even when she played badly, was buoyed by his encouraging remarks, such as, 'Well tried!'[29] After the game had finished, the king had tea on the veranda with Richmond serving him and his fox terrier, Caesar, sitting on his lap.

As in the Victorian era, dinner took place in the ballroom with full pomp and circumstance. Seated around an enormous table overflowing with flowers, pineapples and plate, the guests waded their way through course after course of rich fare. One delicacy served up by Albert Rousseau, the French chef, was turtle soup, a favourite of Edward VII.

After dinner, the ladies withdrew to the yellow drawing room while the gentlemen passed round the port and blew smoke rings into the air from their cigars. Later, when they rejoined them in the drawing room, smaller groups broke off to play cards or billiards before retiring for bed. Writing in her diary at the end of the evening, Viscountess Chelsea wrote: 'A lovely day. Played at croquet with His Majesty and Mr Keppel. Played bridge in the evening and ended having won £14.' This was the equivalent of an annual agricultural wage at the time.[30]

Goodwood was not without its fair share of bedrooms to accommodate guests for large house parties. Apart from the bachelors' bedrooms – which were numbered just one to five – every bedroom had its own name, more often than not relating to its decoration: Orange Flower Bedroom, China Bedroom, Scarlet Bedroom, White Bedroom, Ivy Leaf Bedroom, Chinese Bedroom, Rosebud Bedroom, Blue Bedroom, Royal or Tapestry Bedroom and Oak Bedroom. Most of these had dressing rooms attached. As might have been expected, there were plenty of servants' bedrooms, some of which were more like dormitories – the twelve-bedded room and the nineteen-bedded room.

House parties could never have taken place without a considerable number of servants working hard behind the scenes. There were two teams that operated inside the house on a day-to-day basis – the males headed by the house steward and the females under the housekeeper. Another team operated outside, which included those working in the stables, gardens, gate lodges and laundry. Within each team, there was a strict hierarchy. The most important staff were known as the 'Upper Ten' and the others as the 'Lower Five', although these figures bore no relation to the actual numbers of servants in the house. When guests stayed, they brought their own valet or lady's maid with them, who automatically assumed the name of their master or mistress and were seated in the servants' hall according to their employer's rank.

The 1901 census gives us a good glimpse of life at Goodwood 'below stairs'. The household consisted of thirty-three people, which included Aunt Lina and two of her nieces, Muriel and Helen. The house steward was John Cheeseman, described by Muriel as 'dignified and awe-inspiring, he moved about with authority, even the children treating him with due respect'. Cheeseman was responsible for paying wages and bills, ordering household supplies, organising travel arrangements and keeping accounts. According to Muriel, even his room 'had a strange and wonderful odour which assailed the nostrils not unpleasantly as soon as one opened the door. This was not a singular smell, the nature of which could be quickly recognised, but rather a veritable pot-pourri of scents, mysterious to many, though the discerning nose could easily diagnose the blend emanating from bottles tilted hospitably and glasses that had just been emptied, leaving a fresh and spirituous aroma of glasses about to be emptied.'[31]

Henry Thatcher was the groom of the chambers. His tasks included ringing the bell for morning prayers and making sure everything was in order in the house, both upstairs and down, with particular attention to the fires, writing desks, lamps and candles, as well as the general security of the house. Next in the pecking order came John Osborne, the duke's valet. Every morning he woke up Richmond, bringing hot water for shaving and laying out his clothes for the day. He also packed and unpacked for him, bought tickets, arranged transport, and only retired to bed after his master. William Twigg was the under butler, responsible for wine, silver, proper conduct of meals, checking the fires in the main rooms, sorting the mail, ironing the paper and receiving visitors.

The housekeeper was Susan Washington, vividly recalled by Muriel: 'Mrs Washington, the housekeeper – or Washy, as we called her – was a great character, and had extraordinary knowledge of the family history . . . She was a wonderful show-woman, and it was one of her duties to pilot people around the house. Washy never missed an opportunity of glorifying the family.'[32] Washy was the keeper of the keys to the storerooms and meticulously recorded all housekeeping expenses. She also engaged all female staff. Beneath Washy was Annie Hayes, the lady's maid who looked after Aunt Lina, travelling with her mistress when needed.

Entertaining the royal family meant the food had to be top notch, so Richmond employed a French chef, Albert Rousseau, who was given the nickname 'Monsieur Jean Jacques' after the famous French philosopher. Together, these characters comprised the Upper Ten, while the Lower Five was made up of the male contingent of three footmen, an usher, a steward's aide, a baker and three gardeners; the female contingent comprised five housemaids, a still room maid, three kitchen maids, a scullery maid, a schoolroom maid and a needlewoman. Philip Eldridge – known as 'Flip Flops' behind his back – was the usher. He was 'absolute monarch of the servants' hall . . . a rigid disciplinarian, he had strict views regarding deportment and manners to which he made all his satellites conform.'[33] As if there were not enough staff, every Friday morning an army of charwomen arrived to scrub the stone stairs and passageways. On Friday evenings, everyone let their hair down with a dance in the servants' hall after supper, with one of the stablemen playing the concertina accompanied by someone else on the fiddle.[34]

Separate to the strict servant hierarchy was the governess, Katharine Moffat, dearly loved by Muriel and Helen. Known as 'Moffy', she won the hearts of everyone, including guests, who often would be found in the schoolroom chatting to her.[35] Moffy, being well bred herself, occupied a hinterland – neither servant nor family member, she had her own special place in the complicated social order of Edwardian England.

Life at Goodwood in the Edwardian era was pretty much self-sufficient: milk and meat came from the Home Farm; game from the shoots; venison from Scotland; fish from the Spey and Fiddich; fruit and vegetables from the walled kitchen garden and hot-houses, as well as herbs and cut flowers; and freshly baked bread from the baker. The estate was in its heyday. Everyone knew their place and it functioned like a well-oiled machine, embracing modern technology as it was developed, from the Home Farm to the Stables, from the service wings to the potting sheds. Servants were, on the whole, loyal and content, and enjoyed summers in Scotland when they accompanied the family to Gordon Castle and Glenfiddich. But this seemingly invincible hierarchy and tradition would soon be shattered and, within a decade, the old order would seem a remote and distant dream.

*   *   *

'THE WAKE OF THE WHITE BALL, GOODWOOD'S LATEST GLORY' was the headline in the *South of England Advertiser* on 4 June 1914.[36] The article gave a report of the opening of the new golf course at Goodwood on the previous Saturday, an event attended by over six hundred people.[37] To mark the occasion, Open Champions James Braid and Ted Ray played an exhibition match in the morning and partnered with Captain Cecil Hutchison and Martin Smith respectively in the afternoon for a four-ball match. There was great amusement among the spectators when the commentator, Major Jellicorse, dubbed the pairs 'England' (Ray and Smith) and 'Scotland' (Braid and Hutchison) and the afternoon turned into a struggle between the nations. In the end, 'England' was victorious, which meant another win for Ray who had beaten Braid that morning. Watching the players from the sidelines were various members of the Gordon Lennox family, including Richmond himself and four of his children, all keen golfers. The Bishop of Chichester and his wife were also among the throng of spectators.

Golf had been played at Goodwood since 1901 when the Chichester Golf Club moved on to the estate from North Mundham (where it had been founded in 1892). Using part of the Kennels as their clubhouse, a new 18-hole golf course was laid out on the Downs by estate employees. Members were entitled to wear the club colours of a red coat with dark blue collar and, of the sixty members, fifteen were ladies.

Golf had been increasing rapidly in popularity from the 1880s and was taken up with gusto by several of Richmond's children. The sixth duke had laid out a nine-hole course in the park at Gordon Castle towards the end of his life and the seventh duke actively encouraged the sport, becoming president of the Chichester Golf Club in 1906. Three years later, he asked them to take over the maintenance of the course and, in 1913, it was rechristened the Goodwood Golf Club.

Richmond's younger sons, Bernard and Esmé, were both enthusiastic golfers. In 1912, Bernard suggested that a new course be designed and offered to invite James Braid down to Goodwood 'free of expense to the club' to have a look. Braid's subsequent scheme was promptly approved, and work began on the new course in the autumn of that year. Bernard was elected captain in 1913 and the membership mushroomed.[38] When the course was opened on 30 May 1914, everything seemed perfect: 'The day was beautifully fine; in fact, it could not have been better for golf . . . It was "Glorious Goodwood" indeed; the surroundings were beautiful, and the golf was excellent.'[39]

Less than a month later, Archduke Franz Ferdinand was assassinated in Sarajevo and the horrors of the First World War were set in train. The Great War, as it became known, was to have a devastating effect on the Gordon Lennox family that would see their lives changed for ever.

Charlie, the beloved eldest son of Set and Hilda, who would have become ninth Duke of Richmond had he not been killed tragically at Archangel in northern Russia in 1919
(© Trustees of the Goodwood Collection)

11

The Great War

'One after another, the flower of youth, of the best and most brilliant of England's sons, had crossed the Border Line, never to return – and yet another was added to that legion of mothers who had given all they had, and whose courage in their grief was heroic.'

Elisalex de Baillet Latour, 1937[1]

On 26 July 1914, George V wrote from Buckingham Palace:

'My dear March

'I very much regret to say that I find it is quite impossible for me to leave London tomorrow to pay you my promised visit at Goodwood which I had been so much looking forward to. The political crisis is so acute with regard to the Irish question & now the probability of a general European war necessitates my remaining in London for the present & I much fear I should not be able to leave until the end of the week, if then. I am sure you will understand how disappointed I am. I hope you will have fine weather & that the racing will [be] good.

Believe me very sincerely yours

'George R.I.'[2]

Raceweek went ahead as usual but there was a cloud hanging over it. On the first day of racing (28 July), Austria-Hungary declared war on Serbia. The following day, three of the gentlemen from the Molecomb house party (home of Set and Hilda) had to return to London. The day after raceweek ended, Germany declared war on Russia and, two days later, declared war on France. The next day (4 August), Britain declared war on Germany.

Thinking the war would be over by Christmas, volunteers joined up in their thousands. The patriotic fervour was particularly strong among the aristocracy and landed gentry, many of whom were already serving in the army or navy. By 1914, Set had retired from the army, but both Bernard and Esmé were still serving officers.

On 12 August – the Glorious Twelfth – instead of walking the heather-clad mountains shooting grouse at Glenfiddich, Bernard left England as part of the British Expeditionary Force, 'to help the brave Frenchmen and Belgians' as he noted optimistically in his diary. He was commanding No. 2 Company of the 2nd Battalion Grenadier Guards. The glamour of war quickly faded away as the full horrors of trench warfare took hold. Bernard's diary entries bring home the ghastliness of it all: 'The moment the Dutchmen tried to advance, a deadly fire was poured into them and each time they were mown down, their dead bodies were lying feet deep . . . Apparently no one knew how close the Germans were as we were hardly out of our trenches before they began shelling us hard . . . I ran down the road like hell, and had only just time to get into the ditch until a shower of bullets churned up the dust, the Company were not following . . . I had 103 lined up and, after the explosion, I had 44 left . . . how it missed Jeffreys, Powell, Pike and self will forever remain a mystery.'

Bernard took part in the exhausting retreat from Mons and the battle of the Aisne, before being deployed to Ypres. There, he was in the thick of intensive fighting made worse by the terrible weather conditions. On 10 November, he was hit in the head by a piece of shrapnel. He had the wound bandaged and then ordered his men to 'hang on to the trenches, like grim death until I return'. But he never returned. Having proceeded only thirty yards, a shell burst close to him, sending a piece of shrapnel straight into his body just under his heart and killing him instantly. He left behind a young widow, Evelyn, and two small sons, Geordie and Sandy. Letters of condolence poured in, highlighting his kindness and natural leadership abilities. One of the men in his Company wrote: '. . . he has led the Company into action many times. His men would follow him anywhere. His men would come first, and he would frequently visit each man in their trench. For those killed he could do nothing, but for those wounded he would help bandage up and with comforting words.' Another wrote: 'He was a brave soldier and a Gentleman. All his soldiers worshipped him for he was so good-hearted to us all. He led us to safety many times. He would share in the trench digging and be the first to set an example.'[3] Like so many of his class, duty to one's country was paramount, and he gave the ultimate sacrifice.

The family were devastated. Richmond provided a house for Evelyn and her two sons in Halnaker, next door to Goodwood. He became a father figure to his two grandsons, instilling in them a lifelong love of fishing and shooting just as he had done with their own father. The Goodwood Golf Club, of which Bernard had been so proud, was closed for six days as a mark of respect and, the following year, his younger brother Esmé took on the mantle as club captain.[4]

*   *   *

'Buckingham Palace
'June 22nd, 1915

'My dear March
    'I am so sorry to hear that Geordie Shanks died on the 19th.
He was a charming old man & I spent many a happy day
fishing with him. He will be greatly missed on Spey side. 87 is a
fine old age. Fancy you killed your first salmon with him 55
years ago.

'I heard you had turned Gordon Castle into a hospital, I am sure it is greatly appreciated by these poor wounded fellows, who are all so cheerful & grateful for anything that is done for them, at least that is my experience after seeing many thousands of them. I trust that Esmé has now recovered from his serious wound.

'These are indeed very anxious times but we must not be down-hearted.

'Believe me very sincerely yours

'George R.I.'[5]

The death of Shanks marked the end of an era for Richmond (whom the king still affectionately called March). A widower now for twenty-seven years, Bernard's death the previous November was still raw. With a sense of foreboding at the end of 1913, he had written his wishes for his own funeral and burial. He asked for a 'very simple and inexpensive' funeral and instructed that his body be placed beside his first wife, Amy, noting 'a place has been kept for that purpose'. Even after all this time, Amy was still the love of his life. He also requested that 'a small cairn about 6 feet high to be put up to my memory' at Glenfiddich.[6]

Although he was unable to fight in the war, Richmond did all he could to support the war effort. As Lord Lieutenant of both Banffshire and Moray, much of his focus was in Scotland where he helped recruit soldiers, many of whom he knew personally. Like his father before him, he took a paternalistic approach to his tenants and those who worked on his estates. The war only served to increase this approach to life, especially as he felt an obligation towards those he was recruiting. His daughter Muriel recalled: 'My father's instinct was always to throw open his estates to the public that they might benefit them. He wanted all he enjoyed to be enjoyed by those living about him . . . It was this instinct for sharing his possessions with others that prompted him during the Great War to turn the Castle into a hospital for soldiers.'[7]

Like many country houses up and down the country, Gordon Castle became a military hospital. It opened its doors on 26 November 1914 – just over a fortnight after Bernard's death – with thirty beds. With the desperate rise in casualties, it soon increased its capacity to one hundred beds. Richmond, assisted by his youngest daughter, Helen, took a great personal interest in the hospital. It was run by the Red Cross Society with many of the nurses coming from the Voluntary Aid Detachment. Helen was already a leading light in the Red Cross and also oversaw the hospital at Syon House, one of her husband's family seats. The Red Cross had valiantly risen to the challenge of caring for the thousands of broken, wounded and battle-stricken men coming back from the Front. The whole country was behind them, with a contemporary writing: 'This great crusade of mercy was the silver lining of the sombre war cloud.'⁸

Around forty rooms were given over to the hospital – about half the castle – including the entire west wing. Fifteen wards were created, as well as a men's recreation room and a surgery that was fully equipped by Richmond and Helen. The great dome, decorated with hundreds of antlers of deer killed at Glenfiddich, now looked down upon convalescing soldiers instead of blue-blooded sportsmen. Patients usually stayed for a month and there was plenty to keep them occupied: billiards, bagatelle, cards, draughts, chess, concerts and even dances kept them indoors. Outside, invigorated by the fresh Scottish air and beautiful surroundings, the men could enjoy golf, cricket, football, quoits, croquet, boating and hockey. As the lake froze over in the winter, everyone donned their skates for ice-skating.

Richmond liked to go around the wards visiting the patients and offering them words of encouragement or sympathy. He provided newspapers and magazines for everyone, as well as an endless supply of writing paper. Instead of feeding large numbers of house party guests, the produce from the enormous walled kitchen garden, together with game, venison and fish, all went to the hospital kitchen. As a treat, Richmond would take keen anglers fishing on the Spey, allowing them to send their catch home to their loved ones. One salmon killed by a Lovat Scout – a regiment recruited originally from gamekeepers on Highland estates – was sent to George V with a label attached to it saying that it had been captured by a wounded soldier from the Gordon Castle hospital. Often, Richmond would give departing soldiers a set of antlers as a reminder of their time at the castle.

In the summer, everyone threw themselves into fundraising for the numerous war charities that became more and more crucial as the war dragged on. In the autumn of 1916, a great fête was held in the grounds of the castle in aid of the Gordon and Seaforth Highlanders regiments. Sporting prowess was tested, along with Highland dancing. Bands played, stalls overflowed with donated goods and refreshments were served liberally. In a large marquee, an exhibition of war relics included treasures from the Gordon Castle armoury sitting alongside modern weapons of destruction.[9]

It was to this hive of activity at Gordon Castle that Esmé dashed back when he was on leave from France in February 1917. Esmé had been serving with the Scots Guards when he had been badly wounded by shell fire at Zandvoorde during the first battle of Ypres in October 1914, not long before Bernard was killed. By 1917, he had seen further action in the battle of Loos and was by now commanding the 95th Infantry Brigade.[10] Back at home, all he wanted to do was escape to the river bank and fish the Spey. Over five days, he killed a salmon each day, recording their weights and the river and weather conditions in his fishing book, just as he had done in peacetime.[11] In April the following year, he was wounded again by an explosion when the farmhouse he was staying in near Bois Moyen in France took a direct hit.[12]

Back at Goodwood, the house was largely shut up. By 1917, the number of servants had dwindled to twelve, having been twenty just before the start of the war.[13] As on other landed estates, many of the men who worked at Goodwood joined up to fight in defence of their country. They had valuable skills that were welcome in the army, such as shooting, using special tools, looking after horses and driving motor vehicles. When conscription was introduced for all men aged eighteen

Caroline, Duchess of Richmond, in a bravura portrait by Sir Thomas Lawrence, hanging above an eighteenth-century giltwood table possibly from Richmond House. *(Photograph: James Fennell)*

Glenfiddich Lodge, the rustic Highland retreat created by Jane, Duchess of Gordon, in a watercolour by her granddaughter Lady Louisa Tighe. *(© Trustees of the Goodwood Collection)*

Gordon Castle, the vast seat of the Dukes of Gordon, inherited by the fifth Duke of Richmond in 1836. Watercolour by J. Cassie. *(© Trustees of the Goodwood Collection)*

The Lawn at Goodwood by Walter Wilson and Frank Walton, 1886, depicting an array of high society including Edward VII and Gilbert and Sullivan. St Roche's Hill (known as the Trundle) is in the background. *(© Trustees of the Goodwood Collection)*

Frances Harriet Greville, the dutiful wife of the sixth Duke of Richmond, after whom many cottages at Goodwood were named. *(© Trustees of the Goodwood Collection)*

Lady Cecilia Lennox, youngest daughter of the fifth Duke and Duchess of Richmond, depicted at Gordon Castle by Sir Edwin Landseer. *(© Trustees of the Goodwood Collection)*

The raceweek house party in 1906 with Edward VII seated in the centre, relaxing the dress code by wearing a lounge suit and bowler hat. The seventh Duke of Richmond stands behind the king and Alice Keppel is seated on the far left. *(© Trustees of the Goodwood Collection)*

The Ballroom laid up for a banquet during raceweek, circa 1906. The table decoration includes racing trophies won by the fifth Duke of Richmond. *(© Trustees of the Goodwood Collection)*

A farm on the Goodwood estate was flattened to make way for RAF Westhampnett, an important fighter-pilot station during the Second World War. *(© Tangmere Museum)*

Freddie March, later ninth Duke of Richmond, winning the Brooklands Double-Twelve in 1931 with his co-driver, Chris Staniland. *(© Trustees of the Goodwood Collection)*

Cedars of Lebanon, planted by the third Duke of Richmond in 1761, tower over the Goodwood cricket ground. *(© Trustees of the Goodwood Collection)*

The Goodwood Revival Meeting taking place at the Goodwood Motor Circuit in 2012. It was first run in 1998, exactly fifty years after the circuit was originally opened by the ninth Duke of Richmond. *(Photograph: Alex Shore © Trustees of the Goodwood Collection)*

A Goodwood Cessna flies over Goodwood House. The racecourse can be glimpsed on the horizon.
Photograph: James Martin © Trustees of the Goodwood Collection)

oodwood Racecourse during the Qatar Goodwood Festival in 2015.
hotograph: Christopher Ison © Trustees of the Goodwood Collection)

Jubilee moment at the Festival of Speed in 2012. The sculpture by Jerry Judah contains six historic Lotus Formula 1 cars. *(Photograph: Mike Caldwell © Trustees of the Goodwood Collection)*

The Kennels designed by James Wyatt for the third Duke of Richmond's foxhounds and now a private members' club for all the sports on the estate. *(© Trustees of the Goodwood Collection)*

to forty-one, even more left for the Western Front. The roll call of those killed from the surrounding parishes reveals the extent of the sacrifice paid by men as young as eighteen. Many of them had grown up on the Goodwood estate.

The horseracing, which had taken place every year since 1801, was cancelled for the duration of the war. The golf club carried on through the war years, although it was run by a much-reduced staff aided by voluntary help from the members. They were mourning the loss of Bernard.

As the war raged on overseas, another war was raging closer to home. Its combatants were Richmond and his daughter-in-law, Hilda.

*   *   *

On 15 August 1895, Hilda gave birth prematurely to a son and heir, Charles. Three weeks later, the baby died and was buried in a tiny grave by the door of Boxgrove parish church. Distraught with grief, Hilda blamed her father-in-law, claiming the premature birth had been caused by a row she had had with him over Set's career. Hilda, a strong-willed, capable lady, had engineered Set's appointment as aide-de-camp to Lord Roberts, thinking he needed a proper job. Her father-in-law took her interference in his son's career as a huge personal affront and swore it was a 'rotten sort of job'. Neither Hilda nor Richmond backed down and their relationship never fully recovered.

Hilda was from a family of strong men and women. Her grandfather was the railway pioneer, Thomas Brassey, who became one of the wealthiest self-made Victorians, supported by his indomitable wife, Maria. Rather than continue in trade, their three surviving sons set themselves up as English gentlemen, made advantageous marriages and, by Hilda's generation, the Brasseys had become gentrified. Hilda's father, Henry, was a Member of Parliament for Sandwich and lived at Preston Hall in Kent, a huge Victorian 'Jacobethan'-style mansion that his father had bought for him. While her brothers were sent away to school, Hilda was educated at home by governesses. Sadly, her home-schooling was somewhat poor and Hilda, who was undoubtedly bright, always regretted not having had a better education. She did, however, excel at playing the piano and, when she married Set, brought her Bechstein grand piano to their future home at Molecomb.[14]

Hilda was one of twelve children and much of their childhood was spent on the back of a horse. Many of the Brasseys were keen foxhunters, including her uncle Albert who lived in great splendour at Heythrop Hall in Oxfordshire where he was master of the famous hunt of the same name. Hilda's father had a hunting-box at Lower Slaughter in the Cotswolds and she was able to enjoy a couple of seasons with the Goodwood Hunt before it was disbanded. Hilda's other great sporting love was cricket. As a child, she played on the cricket ground at Preston Hall and, when she married, she joined her sisters-in-law playing at Goodwood. Like golf, it had become fashionable in the late nineteenth century for women to play cricket. Hilda herself played for the White Heather Club, the first ladies' cricket club formed in 1887.

Set had first met Hilda when he was an undergraduate at Oxford. He was a close friend of Hilda's brother, Leonard, who was also at Oxford, and the two friends married each other's sisters (Leonard marrying Violet). Hilda was the complete opposite of Set's mother, Amy. Since her death, Amy had assumed a saint-like persona in the family memory – the ideal of a perfect wife – and Richmond found it hard not to compare Amy's gentle, quiet, bookish ways with Hilda's gung-ho approach to life. On top of that, Hilda's family were in trade, albeit two generations ago, and the Brasseys were not considered smart enough for a future duke. With these thoughts spinning around Richmond's head, it was little surprise that relations between Richmond and Hilda were tense. After the sixth Duke's death, Set and Hilda lived at Molecomb while Richmond lived in Goodwood House with his daughter, Helen, acting as hostess when needed. Having a 'rival' hostess at both Goodwood and Gordon Castle was yet another cause of friction.

Hilda eventually gave birth to another son in January 1899, a brother for their two daughters, Amy and Doris. In the family tradition,

he was also christened Charles and known by the courtesy title Lord
Settrington. Five years later, Frederick was born, named after Frederick
Roberts, Lord Roberts' son, who had been killed fighting in the Boer
War in South Africa. Like former generations of the family, Charlie –
as he was known – kept a game book where he not only recorded the
bag but also pasted in photographs. On 10 September 1910, while
staying at Gordon Castle, he proudly wrote: 'My first salmon'. It
weighed a very respectable 20 lbs and was killed in the Upper Bulwark
pool where Doris had also killed one earlier in the day. The following
year, again while staying at Gordon Castle, he shot his first partridge.
The next season he shot his first grouse while he and his father were
staying at Blackwater Lodge at Glenfiddich. Finally, in September 1913,
he shot his first stag, noting: 'I shot it about 5.30 p.m. after stalking it
since 10 a.m. with Father & Jimmie Anderson.' Sometimes, he was
accompanied by his mother, Hilda, who also enjoyed rough shooting.[15]

Before the Great War, large shooting parties were held at
Goodwood. The terrain lent itself to partridge and pheasant shooting
with steep-sided valleys tucked under the Downs. The keepers, all
decked out in brown velvet coats, were led by Mr Long, a diminutive
man not more than five feet tall. Set held a low opinion of the stumpy
Mr Long whom, he said, was quite capable of driving the pheasants
away from the guns instead of over them. For one season, the shoot
was under Set's control as his father had gone on a cruise to the West
Indies. In those pre-war days, they regularly shot over three hundred
birds. Guests included Berkeley Paget, a crack shot who still used
cartridges with brass cases, something of an anachronism at that time.
Other guests were John Trefusis, Lord John Hamilton and Set's brother
Bernard, all of whom were to lose their lives in the war.

Set's son, Freddie, recalled later in life the army of beaters: 'Those
stalwarts were all estate workers seconded to beating for the day.
Swarthy and thick-set Sussex Anglo-Saxon stock, they paraded in great
white smocks, leather gaiters, boots like boats and bowler hats. At the
lunch break they would produce from a large handkerchief chunks of
bread and "puddin'" which they carved off and thrust into their great

mouths all in one sort of movement, knife in hand all the time, "puddin'" stuffed in with back of thumb. This was washed down by dark brown fluid from great quart bottles presumably kept in some equally great pocket beneath the smock. This drink was either cold tea or beer. Thereafter, the gunfire was scarcely audible for the Stentorian belching that echoed through the coverts as they rattled and rustled up the birds for the gentry to shoot.'[16]

The beater's lunch was in stark contrast to the guns. They sat down to a delicious Irish stew, accompanied by baked potatoes and all the trimmings, with mince pies for pudding. It was prepared in the kitchen at Goodwood House and brought in immense wicker hampers to one of the keeper's cottages where it was laid out by Compton, the butler. The Rev'd Dick Wells, sporting parson of Boxgrove, would rub his hands with glee at the announcement of lunch and declare, 'Well – this is by no means the worst part of the day!'[17]

*   *   *

Although Set had retired from the army in 1910, he was still in the Territorial Army and, by 1915, was in command of the Sussex Yeomanry. In the autumn of that year, the regiment was stationed just outside Canterbury prior to leaving for Gallipoli. Hilda went down to Canterbury to spend a last weekend with him and they were lent the Dean's house in the cloisters of Canterbury Cathedral. On their first evening together, Set became very emotional in a way that slightly alarmed Hilda as he was normally so reserved. A few hours after they had gone to bed, he became extremely ill, unable to move and with a raging fever. Hilda was desperate. Alone in a strange house, late at night, and with no knowledge of the city's medical arrangements, she managed to summon the regimental doctor. As Set hung between life and death, he was diagnosed with polio, which had been brought over to England by some Canadian troops stationed nearby. The fever raged for several days and, when it eventually subsided, the terrible reality of the situation became apparent – he was paralysed from the waist downwards.

Set was moved to one of the Brasseys' houses in London to convalesce. Leg supports were made for him that were jointed at the knees and, with crutches, he was able to move around. Eventually, Hilda managed to persuade him to go outside in a Bath chair, accompanied by his teenage son, Freddie. It was a daunting time for him; Set was a sensitive man, who had inherited many of his mother's characteristics, including a love of books. He was an accomplished author, who had written two books based on archival material at Goodwood: *Records of the Old Charlton Hunt* which was published in 1910, and *A Duke and His Friends, The Life and Letters of the Second Duke of Richmond*, which had come out the following year. Now his whole life stretched ahead of him with the grim reality that he was unable to participate in the sports he so loved and for which Goodwood was famous. Added to that was the frustration and distress of not being with his regiment who, some months later, were thrust into the thick of the fighting against the Turks in the Dardanelles. As he sat helpless at home, news of friends being killed and maimed trickled back home.

Soon after the outbreak of war, Set's young boys, Charlie and Freddie, ceremoniously took their two best 'Made in Germany' battleships, filled them with paraffin, set them on fire, and launched them into the middle of the pond at Molecomb. There, among the water lilies, the ships dissolved into molten wrecks and sank into the murky depths witnessed only by the two boys on the bank and the tench fish below.[18] Freddie worshipped his elder brother who was every bit his hero. Good-looking, athletic and with the wavy auburn hair that so distinguished his grandmother Amy, Charlie went straight from Eton to Sandhurst. They both shared a love of all things mechanical and Charlie would send Freddie *The Motor Cycle* magazine at school. For a young boy like Freddie, Charlie was undoubtedly 'cool'. Roaring around on his Douglas motorbike with Freddie riding as pillion, girls fell for him like 'leaves in autumn', as Freddie put it.

Much of their childhood escapades involved making sure their mother, Hilda, did not find out. Hilda adored Charlie, but their personalities also clashed, as one incident shows. Hilda had bribed

Charlie to the tune of one hundred pounds not to smoke until he was twenty-one. One evening, on leave from Sandhurst, he appeared in the drawing room looking resplendent in uniform, nonchalantly smoking a cigarette. As Freddie recalled, 'Almost instantly mother struck an attitude of despair and somewhat hysterically said, "Oh, no! You've broken my heart, darling!" to which the naughty chap replied, "I dare say, but just think of the money I've saved you."'[19]

After passing out from Sandhurst, Charlie joined the Irish Guards who were stationed at Warley Barracks in Essex. Being the proud owner of a Morgan three-wheeler motorcar, he was able to drive up to London for the evening and enjoy some of the nightlife. The lure of the pretty chorus girls on the stage proved irresistible and Charlie would often enlist the help of the liftman at the relevant theatre. His girlfriends included Joyce Barbour and Faith Celli who both became well-known actresses. Freddie remembered Charlie smuggling Faith into his parents' London house late at night, after the theatre, with only his sister Doris in the know. Had Hilda found out, she would have been horrified, as it was frowned upon for members of the upper class to step out with actresses. On one occasion, when Freddie expressed horror that Charlie and Faith were caught in the capital during a Zeppelin raid, Charlie remarked, 'Not at all – it was lovely. Faith clung so beautifully!'[20]

The fun was not to last. In the spring of 1918, the nineteen-year-old Charlie went off to war and had hardly been in France for two weeks before his company took the full brunt of the German Spring Offensive. When a gap was left in the Allied line, a brigade of guards – which included Charlie's company – was despatched to fill it. However, they were totally outnumbered, and thick fog made it impossible to get their bearings. Charlie fought bravely on until only about six of them were left alive. When they lost touch with each other, Charlie was completely cut off, and all he could do was to keep saying to himself, 'I don't want to die.' Realising some Germans were firing at him from the top window of a nearby farmhouse, he drew out his Webley & Scott automatic pistol and emptied its magazine into the window, stopping the fire. Groping around in the fog, semi-dazed, he desperately tried to find his comrades. But all was in vain, for more Germans appeared and he was taken prisoner.

When Charlie was searched, his pistol was discovered. Realising it was not standard army issue (he had brought it with him from home), he was immediately labelled a sniper, for which the punishment was summary execution. The German soldier then set off with Charlie to find an officer who could authorise his execution. By this point, Charlie was rigid with fear and overwhelmed with exhaustion. Just when all seemed hopeless, a shell launched by the retreating British landed almost on top of them both, throwing them to the ground. When Charlie recovered his senses, he realised to his immense relief that the German had been blown to smithereens along with the incriminating pistol. Any sense of elation, though, was quickly replaced by despair when he was captured for the second time and made a prisoner of war.

Back at Molecomb, the family were fraught. A telegram had informed them that Charlie was 'missing', leaving them without even knowing whether he was alive or dead. They had to endure the dreadful uncertainty for about three weeks before news finally reached them that he was alive and a prisoner of war at Karlsruhe in Germany. The relief was palpable.[21]

After the Armistice, Charlie returned home to a hero's welcome in time for Christmas 1918. All the Molecomb staff lined up to greet him, including old George Wackford, the gardener, who caused great amusement in the family when he proceeded to tell Charlie of his ailments.

On Christmas morning, the plan was that everyone would attend the 8 a.m. Holy Communion service at Boxgrove. Unfortunately, Charlie overslept and missed his lift with Doris in the family Swift. Grabbing one of the housemaid's bicycles, he pedalled furiously along a back route until his way was blocked by some heavily padlocked doors in the wall at the Home Farm. Throwing the bicycle over the wall, he made swift work of climbing over, only to discover that he had buckled the front wheel. Realising there was not enough time to make his Divine appointment, he returned home defeated. Missing church was the least of his worries; how would he explain his absence to Hilda, who was looking forward to showing off her hero son to the entire congregation? 'Darling!' she exclaimed in a funereal tone, 'you have broken my heart.'

To which, he replied, 'Well, I don't know about your heart, but I've certainly broken the housemaid's bicycle.'[22]

Peacetime life in the army did not suit Charlie. He was bored and toyed with the idea of joining the newly formed Royal Air Force. Shortly after his Christmas leave, he was seconded from the Irish Guards to do a course in Wireless Telegraphy at the Army Signals School at Dunstable, where he did very well. On one occasion, he visited the ageing Sir Henry Royce in nearby West Wittering with a view to getting a job at Rolls-Royce, but nothing came of it.[23] Always, at the back of his mind, was a nagging sense of guilt that he had done nothing in the war and had somehow failed by being taken prisoner. Finally, a chance meeting with an ex-army pal at the Bachelors' Club in London set his career off in a new direction. He heard that the army were looking for a new brigade signals officer to accompany the Royal Fusiliers to the remote Russian city of Archangel. They were to be part of the Allied Intervention in Russia, supporting the White Russians in their fight against the Bolsheviks. Charlie leapt at the opportunity.

In late May 1919, Freddie was allowed out of school to see his elder brother off from the London home of his brother-in-law, James Coats. The memory of that departure was to remain for ever in Freddie's memory: 'I last saw brother Charles, serenely happy in the open back of a Landaulet taxi leaving that entrance eating strawberries from a punnet we had bought off a street seller. Exit my hero, my guide.'[24]

*   *   *

Under intense fire, Charlie was running for his life with his platoon through the marshy swamps of the Sheika river. It was 10 August, the day that the 45th Battalion of the Royal Fusiliers had arrived at the

Dvina front in northern Russia. The battalion were there to relieve the original 1918 expeditionary force and that day launched an attack to aid their final evacuation. During the attack, Charlie's platoon – who had been fighting a rearguard action – had become cut off. Now they were desperately trying to make their way back to the British lines. As they ran full tilt dodging bullets, they came to a precarious bridge of planks across the swamp. There was no alternative but to cross it, leaving them even more vulnerable to the constant gunfire. In less than no time, Charlie and three others fell into the deep swamp, either hit or trying to avoid being hit.

Not wasting a second, Corporal Arthur Sullivan dived in after them. Despite the incessant gunfire, he hauled Charlie to safety and then did the same thing for the three others, thereby saving their lives. Charlie had been badly wounded in the stomach by machine-gun fire and half of his right hand had been shot off.

Only days before, Charlie had written to his father jokily telling him that 'I have at last discovered a swamp possessing some duck. Unfortunately, any systematic shooting over it is only interfered with by the fact that it is a portion of "No Man's Land". However, we hope to include it among our preserves before long. I wonder where the summer hols are being spent this year – also if you have any prospects of Scotland. I'd give all I have got (Phew!!) to be on the banks of the Blackwater at this moment instead of the Dvina – however, I do see prospects of being back before the leaves are off the trees. Love to all, Charlie.'[25] Now, instead of fishing on the banks of the Blackwater, he was dying on the banks of Sheika, thousands of miles away.

Charlie was rushed to a hospital ship where he was put under the care of chief attendant Albert Pearce-Davies who was instructed to give him twenty-four-hour attention. Despite his wound, Charlie was able to play chess and dictate letters. He told Albert all about his family, including his sisters and younger brother 'who he loved very much'. But there were times when the pain became unbearable and, after some days, he sank into a coma from which he never recovered.[26] On 24 August, Charlie died. He was only twenty years old.

Albert accompanied Charlie's body to Archangel where he was given a military funeral and buried in the Allied Cemetery, according to his family's wishes. On 26 September, Corporal Sullivan, an Australian by birth, was awarded the Victoria Cross for his actions on that fateful August day.

Back at Molecomb, Charlie's family were still recovering from raceweek when a telegram arrived informing them that Charlie had been seriously wounded. Arriving only two days after he had been shot, they were plunged again into the abyss of the unknown. What had happened? How serious were his injuries? Was he going to die? A nervous tension hung over the house; Hilda was trying to control her hysterical temperament, while Set was still coming to terms with his own disability. Doris and Freddie, at home together, made trips to the beach in the two-seater Swift, drawing closer to one another as they tried to process what was happening.

Five days later, the family departed on the train for Scotland to join the seventh Duke of Richmond at Gordon Castle for their annual sporting foray. Richmond was due to be presented with his portrait by the entire Scottish tenantry at a day of celebrations on 26 August. On the eve of the gathering, while Freddie was playing billiards, his mother walked into the room 'ashen, distraught and scarcely conscious'. A telegram had arrived to tell them of Charlie's death. Freddie, stunned from the news, went into his father's room. There, he found him 'pathetically sitting in his wheelchair, staring into space. Shocked. We said nothing. He put out a hand, pulled me nearer and kissing me on the forehead said, "Well, Fred, it's only you and me now."'[27]

Set, Hilda, Doris and Freddie were too shattered to attend the gathering the next day. But Richmond – in a supreme show of fortitude – went through with the occasion. A huge marquee had been erected on the lawn in front of the castle, with a stage draped in Gordon tartan, in the middle of which stood an enormous frame with a pair of curtains concealing the portrait. Most of the guests, many of whom had travelled huge distances to be there, only heard the news about

Charlie when they arrived. Richmond was visibly moved as he stepped on to the stage where his grandsons Geordie and Sandy were seated among their grandfather's factors and senior tenantry. Wearing Highland dress, Richmond looked every inch the Scottish laird as he took his seat.

The activities that had been planned for the afternoon were curtailed in the light of the circumstances, including the cancellation of the bands. The meeting was opened by the oldest tenant, Mr Thomson, who read out a message of sympathy from all of the organising committee before reading a letter of apology from Hilda for her family's absence. In it, her resilience in the face of adversity shines through: 'Our loss is so great that for the moment we feel stunned, but we shall soon pull ourselves together and come out amongst everybody again.'[28] After an address by the committee praising Richmond for his war effort and his benevolence in freezing rents when times were tough, he was presented with an album signed by all of the subscribers to the portrait, 'from every part of your wide estates, from the Laich of Moray to the high-lying countries where the Tap o' Noth and the Buck of Cabrach keep their guardian watch, and further afield to where the willows of lonely Kinrara are watered by the infant Spey'.[29] Mr Merson of Craigwillie, an octogenarian tenant, then rose to unveil the portrait. As the curtains drew apart, the full-length figure of Richmond was revealed, dressed just as he appeared in real life, in Highland dress complete with badger-mask sporran and standing on the banks of the Spey. It was by Sir Arthur Stockdale Cope, a well-known portraitist who had painted Richmond and his sons some years before dressed in their military uniforms.

Richmond now rose to respond, amidst rounds of cheering. Remembering those who had gone forth to fight in the war from the local area, he then went on to deplore the current agitators in the trade unions, warning against their tyranny should they get out of control. Thanking everyone for the portrait, he also said how grateful he was for their forbearance during the war when only essential repairs could be made. His final words were to reassure everyone that, as long as he was alive, there would be no sales of the Gordon estates, despite the heavy tax burden falling on his shoulders. As far as he was concerned, the existing landlord-tenant system was far better and more productive than the owner-occupier alternative, and he urged them to embrace modern advances in farming. He ended by saying that the gathering that afternoon was in his mind a happy family party, before sitting down amid much cheering.[30] Everyone then enjoyed a stroll in the gardens before tea was served in the marquee.

The speeches were widely reported in the local press. When Set and Freddie read Richmond's comments about there being no sales, they raised their eyebrows in silent comment. There had been a steady stream of sales over the previous decade or so. Between 1912 and 1920, Knight, Frank and Rutley claimed to have sold as much as 1.6 million acres in Scotland, equivalent to one-twelfth of the country's land-mass.[31] The agricultural depression, the rise of a newly wealthy élite, political hostility to great landowners and overwhelming increases in taxation, all combined to shake the foundations of the Establishment to the core.[32]

Over the next few weeks, as the family tried to come to terms with their loss, Richmond never uttered a word of encouragement to his grandson, Freddie, who now assumed the mantle of responsibility as eventual heir to the dukedom. Freddie said that, throughout his childhood, it was as if there was a perpetual iron curtain between his grandfather and Set's family. The tragedy was that Richmond was suffering, too, but he had buried the pain from all his losses so deep that he had become almost emotionless to those closest to him. Freddie went through agony trying to decide whether he should become Lord Settrington, the title traditionally used by the Earl of March's eldest son, or whether he should use one of the other lesser titles. In the end, after much discussion with his father – who was extremely sympathetic to his son's concern – they decided that he would be known as Lord Settrington as a memorial to Charlie. So, after the school holidays, Freddie returned to Eton as Lord Settrington.

In the months that followed, Richmond was invited to unveil many memorials to those who had given their lives in the Great War. Meanwhile, the grieving Hilda took up Charlie's game book and had inscribed in it, after the last entry (Goodwood, 6 January 1914), a quote from Thomas Mordaunt's poem 'The Call': 'One Crowded hour of Glorious Life is worth an age without a Name'. On the opposite page, was inscribed: 'Our Beloved Charlie, we see, made no entry in his Game Book after January 1914; From the outbreak of War he felt and repeatedly said, "A book like this meant so little to him now," in consequence he did not enter the few days shooting he had at Glenfiddich in August 1915, Gordon Castle 1916, or Goodwood January 1919. It is for Freddy to carry on this Book from January 1st, 1921. H. M.'

The inaugural race meeting at the Goodwood Motor Circuit on 18 September 1948
with spectators precariously perched on the roofs of wartime huts
(© Trustees of the Goodwood Collection)

12

Horse Power

'From the day I arrived at the first ever meeting in September 1948, I knew that the Goodwood circuit had something special – a particular blend of elements that I never found anywhere else in all my racing experience.'

Stirling Moss, 1999[1]

'February 7th, 1921

'My Lord Duke,

'On behalf of the Agricultural Tenants on your Goodwood Estate, I write to ask Your Grace's acceptance of the Gates which we have recently erected at the Waterbeach entrance to the Park in Memory of Lord Bernard Gordon Lennox and of Lord Settrington.

'While we hope that there may never again arise an occasion for devotion such as theirs, we trust that this visible memorial may in the future inspire those who see it to emulate their example in other fields of service.

'I am, my Lord Duke,

'Your obedient Servant

'Harold W. Drewitt.'[2]

Thirty-one tenants contributed to the new pair of wrought-iron gates beside Park Lodge. They were flanked by smart dressed-flint gate piers, each with a stone tablet on the front and topped by a ball finial. The tablets were mounted with laurel wreaths, surrounding, on the left, the grenade badge of the Grenadier Guards (for Bernard) and, on the right, the star of the Irish Guards (for Charlie), with their respective initials and dates of their deaths (1914 and 1919). It was a poignant reminder of the family's loss in the field of duty.[3]

Nearly three years earlier, the seventh Duke of Richmond had taken the magnanimous decision to give Priory Park, a historic park in the centre of Chichester, to the citizens as a perpetual war memorial. It was gratefully accepted and formally handed over on 30 September 1918, nearly one hundred years after it was first bought by the fifth duke.[4] When Richmond planted a tree in the park to mark the Celebration of Peace in July 1919, little did he realise that he would suffer a further personal loss only one month later.[5] For all his lack of intimacy with his family, Richmond made up for it in his public-spiritedness.

On top of everything else sent to try him, the financial outlook for Richmond was bleak. There had been a huge increase in death duties and income tax (which rose from just under six per cent in 1914 to thirty per cent in 1920).[6] As a result, after the Great War there was a flood of estates coming on to the market. In 1922, Richmond was forced to put the Huntly estate in Aberdeenshire – some 60,000 acres – up for sale, although it failed to find a buyer.[7] Perhaps it was just as well, as it would have meant reneging on his promise to his Scottish tenants. What he and his fellow grandees were witnessing was a territorial transfer of land on a scale rivalled only by those of the Norman Conquest and the Dissolution of the Monasteries.[8]

It was not all gloom and doom at Goodwood, however. After a hiatus of four years, Glorious Goodwood raceweek recommenced in 1919. 'Wars come and go, but Goodwood remains,' declared *The Graphic*, alongside photographs of spectators wearing thick coats to beat the chill that had descended on the racecourse.[9] There were separate house parties at Goodwood House and Molecomb; the former was a 'gentlemen only' affair hosted by Richmond. Among the guests was his close friend Hugh, fifth Earl of Lonsdale. A legend in his own lifetime, he was universally known as the Yellow Earl after the colour of the Lonsdale livery. Hugh was wildly extravagant and had all of his carriages – and latterly cars – painted in bright yellow and always wore a white gardenia in his buttonhole.[10] Each year, he would bring six or seven carriages, along with beautifully conditioned chestnut horses, to convey him and other house guests to the racecourse. He was a great favourite of the gypsies who watched the racing for free from the Trundle overlooking the racecourse.[11] His memory lives on today in the Lonsdale Belt, one of the highest accolades in British boxing.

The seventh Duke of Richmond turned eighty at the end of 1925 and still lived in splendid isolation at Goodwood House, attended by Compton the butler and Washy the housekeeper. Set and his family continued to live at Molecomb, growing increasingly frustrated that Richmond refused to hand over the reins on anything to do with Goodwood or Gordon Castle. Occasionally, they would be invited to tea on a Sunday, walking up the cedar-lined drive of Molecomb and down through High Wood, along a gravel path flanked for its entire length by a blousy Edwardian flower border. Entering through the French windows of the billiard room, they would tiptoe to the Large Library where tea would be ceremoniously laid out by Compton and a footman 'with thumps, bumps, heavy breathing and squeaking shoes'. Freddie vividly recalled the sweet smell of wood – probably cedarwood – that pervaded the rooms and the chiming of all the clocks in unison.[12] There was undeniably a tension in the air, almost as if Set and Hilda were frightened of Richmond and what he might do regarding their inheritance.[13] These visits might have become unbearable had it not been for the regular visits of Set's sister Muriel, who always lightened things up with her wicked sense of humour.[14]

Towards the middle of January 1928, Richmond took a turn for the worse. The family were all called to Goodwood to pay their last respects and, on 18 January, he died in his bedroom overlooking the park. Following his wishes to be buried in the family vault in Chichester Cathedral, Freddie was sent to accompany the undertakers on a recce, the steps being too steep for Set to cope with on his crutches. Freddie found the experience rather eerie, with the coffins of his ancestors stacked on shelves 'in none too orderly a fashion'.[15] When Richmond's coffin was laid beside Amy's on 21 January, he was the last member of his family to be buried in the vault, which was then sealed up for ever.[16]

*   *   *

Freddie woke at the crack of dawn on 25 April 1924. He had butterflies in his stomach and had hardly slept a wink during the night. This was to be his first day's work as a mechanic in the service department of Bentley Motors. Freddie – who was to be known as plain 'Mr Settrington' – rode his motorbike from his sister's house in Regent's Park to Cricklewood in north London. Arriving ten minutes early, he tried to look relaxed as he parked his bike, hoping he was not taking someone else's space. He asked a friendly-looking face where he could find Mr Sparrow, the manager foreman. 'Not 'ere yet,' came the reply. Meanwhile, more workers were arriving, every now and then casting a furtive look in his direction.

As Freddie said, 'First I stood on one leg, then the other, walked out into the yard and back, whistling softly and praying the effect of unconcern was being carried off quite naturally. I returned to the motorbike and performed imaginary actions, turned off the oil which was already off, likewise the petrol, and assumed a puzzled expression over the brake pedal with which there was absolutely nothing wrong. Anything, I thought to myself, to kill these hideous minutes.'

Fortunately, someone soon 'poked a backhanded thumb' and said, 'That's 'im,' and Freddie entered the lion's den, dressed in his blue overalls. He was paired up with Bert Browning, who had been fully appraised of Freddie's real identity, and together they set to work on dismantling a car belonging to Prince George. Bert loyally kept

Freddie's identity secret, to the extent that, four months later, one of the boys in the workshop said to Freddie, 'They say as 'ow there's some bloody lord in this place, Fred – d'ye know which 'e is?' to which Freddie replied that he did not know at all.[17]

The roaring twenties proved to be a rollercoaster ride for Freddie. After Eton, he had been sent to a crammer to prepare him for the Oxford entrance examinations. His tutor was the Rev'd Thomas Hudson, one-time headmaster of St Edward's School, Oxford, who had a genius for bringing out the best in his pupils. On arrival at Hudson's large Georgian rectory in Great Shefford, Berkshire, Freddie had been introduced to Hudson's family, including his two daughters, Molly and Betty. For the first time in his life, Freddie experienced a freedom at the rectory that was in stark contrast to his upbringing at Molecomb. Although Hudson pushed his pupils hard, they had the afternoons free to enjoy themselves, exploring the surrounding countryside, visiting the local town, playing hockey, smoking, going to the cinema or just tinkering about with cars or motorbikes. Among the other half-dozen pupils were Freddie's great school chum, Eddie Somerset, and his cousin Tom Leveson-Gower; the Hudson children – boys and girls – often joined in their antics. It was during his time at Great Shefford that Freddie fell in love with Betty, a vivacious redhead who was a few years older than him.[18]

Hudson's tutoring – and a little bit of cheating – got both Freddie and Eddie through the entrance examinations and they duly went on to Christ Church, Oxford, where they shared the same rooms Set had occupied with Leonard Brassey. Freddie chose to study Agriculture, thinking it would be of some use to him in future life but, in reality, he found it deadly boring. His heart was in mechanics and it was not long before he was completely absorbed in the University Motor Club, racing his newly purchased ABC motorbike. Aside from riding bikes, he became swept up into college rowing where his small size was ideal for a cox. Eventually, when the chance of coxing the university eight presented itself, he was forced to make a decision as to whether to pursue rowing or motorbike racing with his chums. The latter won.[19]

Looking back, Freddie regretted not spending more time on his studies. During his final year at Oxford, he had come to the realisation that he was unlikely to pass his final examinations. Around that time, he had been introduced to Bertie Kensington-Moir, an ex-racing driver who had become Service Department manager at Bentley Motors. Bertie had offered him the Bentley job at nine pence per hour as an 'improver', one up from an apprentice. After gaining his parents' approval – no mean feat – Freddie dropped out of university and became an employee of Bentley Motors. He was helped in his decision by the Dean of Christ Church, who said to him in his end-of-term interview, 'Settrington, from the reports I have you will have to work very hard indeed for your finals in July. I think there has been rather too much motorcycling and not enough agriculture.' [20]

However, parental approval was not to last for long. One morning, while Freddie was staying with his sister Amy and her husband, Jimmy Coats, Hilda appeared. Backed up by Jimmy, she tried to force Freddie to accept a posting as aide-de-camp to the Earl of Lytton, governor of Bengal. As far as Freddie was concerned, it was all part of a plot to separate him from Betty (whom he now wished to marry) and see him settled in a more respectable job. When Freddie protested, in a scene worthy of a soap opera, he witnessed his hysterical mother lying on the floor, clawing the air and screaming at him, 'I cannot see you, I shall die!' Freddie looked on horror-struck, amazed that a stand-off with his mother had come to this. [21]

Hilda had already engineered a meeting between Freddie and their good friend Lord Herbert Scott, chairman of Rolls-Royce. Scott had offered him a job in the newly formed Rolls-Royce service department in New York. Freddie had seen straight through the plot – in which Scott was an innocent party – and politely declined. Secretly, he regarded the Bentley brand as second to none; the Rolls-Royce product seemed to him 'a horseless carriage and a hallmark of wealth rather than sophisticated, modern fast motoring'. [22]

This time, Hilda would not accept 'no' as an answer – and Freddie had to think quickly. Rather than challenge his mother's authority, risking a deeply uncomfortable stand-off and possible heartbreak, Freddie acquiesced, and a telegram was sent to Lord Lytton. When Hilda had calmed down, Freddie dashed off to his job at Bentley Motors, explained what was going on to his boss, and asked for permission to go and see Betty. He then zoomed off in his little Austin Seven to Wendover in Buckinghamshire, where the Hudson family were now living.

After talking the matter over with Betty and her sister Molly, he resolved to stand up to his mother and sent an immediate telegram to Lord Lytton politely to decline the offer, following it up with a contrite letter explaining his actions. Lytton was very gracious and invited Freddie and Betty to come and see him to chat things over. This they did, and he was fully sympathetic to their situation, concluding their meeting by saying, 'Well, good luck to you. I couldn't possibly have encouraged you to join my Indian staff under those circumstances of which, of course, I was totally unaware.'[23]

Thinking things would now quieten down, Freddie was shocked when his two brothers-in-law turned up unannounced on the doorstep of friends he and Betty were lunching with near Wendover. When Freddie appeared, accusations and insults were exchanged between them, embarrassingly in everyone else's earshot. Aside from their verbal abuse, the brothers-in-law had come to tell Freddie that he must meet his father in two days' time at the Connaught Hotel in London where he and Hilda stayed when they were in town. They also let slip that Hilda was still very distressed – to the point of being ill – and that a lawyer would be present.[24] Worried that his actions might be seriously destroying her health, Freddie got Molly to ring up the Coats' family doctor (whom he guessed correctly was treating his mother) and enquire how she was. When the reply came back that she was perfectly well but a little tired, Freddie heaved a sigh of relief and felt a mild smugness in having 'knocked the "mother's health won't stand it" weapon from the arena'.[25] He also arranged for a lawyer friend of the Hudsons, Mr Dunville-Smythe, to accompany him to the Connaught lest things spiral out of control. Dunville-Smythe sweetly took it upon himself to check at Somerset House the sixth duke's Will and was able to report back to Freddie, 'You have nothing to fear; the estate and all the family possessions are fully entailed for generations. No one can disentail without your own agreement.'[26]

Armed with the knowledge that his parents could do no serious harm, Freddie set off for the meeting at the Connaught with Betty, her brother, Tom, and Dunville-Smythe. Leaving the latter downstairs, they went up to Set and Hilda's suite, where the atmosphere was tense. Set was seated forlornly in his wheelchair while Hilda was next door, too ill to see anyone. Set nodded to his lawyer to talk, but the presence of Dunville-Smythe downstairs took the wind out of his sails and he had virtually nothing to say. Freddie repeated that he was adamant that he wished to marry Betty and continue his engineering career and the meeting ended. Afterwards, Jimmy Coats played his hand by evicting Freddie from their London home. The final blow came when Set stopped his allowance, leaving him entirely dependent on his meagre salary.[27]

Fortunately, the following spring (1927), Freddie accepted a job offer as a salesman with a firm of Bentley agents in Hanover Square. He commuted daily from the Hudsons' at Wendover who had taken him in after his eviction. He now wore a suit to work, rather than overalls, although he drew the line at a stuffy bowler hat. Later that summer, his boss, 'KD' (Hugh Kevill-Davies), jumped ship back to Bentley, taking Freddie with him as a junior salesman. With the move came a much-needed pay rise to seven hundred pounds a year. This meant that, finally, Freddie was earning enough money to marry his beloved Betty.[28]

Plans were soon discussed for their marriage and Freddie did well in his new job, including selling a six-cylinder Bentley to the Prince of Wales. There was one glitch – the impasse with his parents. Reluctantly, Freddie wrote to his father at Gordon Castle pointing out 'all the circumstances, known to him so well, and carefully avoiding any reference whatever to the dramas and hysterics of the year before. But in terms of parliamentary negotiation, I "left no room for manoeuvre", and plainly stated that our engagement would appear in *The Times* in two days' time'.[29]

On the eve of the Motor Show at Olympia in October 1927, just as Freddie was about to leave work for the Bentley stand, a letter landed on his desk from his mother, telling him to go and see his father immediately at Richmond's London house in Cadogan Square. With trepidation, Freddie arrived at the gloomy house to be told that his father was being attended by Mr Lorentzen, his Swedish masseur, and would be with him shortly. When he did eventually enter his father's study, all of Freddie's fears melted away as his father 'opened his arms to me with a huge grin and said in as many words that all was now accepted, how soon could he see Betty and, as far as finance was concerned, he was restoring the former arrangement at once. The siege was over. The voice of reason was restored, and I am convinced he was as happy as I was.'[30]

With everyone on speaking terms once again, Freddie spent the last days of his bachelordom at Cadogan Square. He even managed to earn the grudging approval of his aged grandfather Richmond before he died. On 15 December 1927, Freddie and Betty were married at Holy Trinity Church, Sloane Street in London, and roared off in an open-top sports Bentley for their honeymoon in Scotland.

* * *

After a gruelling twenty-four hours' driving at Brooklands, the chequered flag waved in the winning car – an MG Midget, driven by Freddie and his co-driver, Chris Staniland. They had covered 1,575 miles at an average speed of 65.6 m.p.h. in the famous 'Double-Twelve' race (a twenty-four-hour race run in two daytime legs), organised by the Junior Car Club. Not only was it a victory for Freddie but it was also a momentous occasion for MG Midgets; they swept the board taking first, second, third, fourth and fifth places. Dressed in white racing overalls, with a Gordon tartan silk scarf wrapped tightly around his neck, Freddie posed for the press with Staniland, perched on the back of their MG and holding an enormous silver cup. 'BABY CARS WIN BIG RACE', said the main headline in the *Daily Telegraph*, with the subtitle, 'Vain Challenge of Giants'.[31] It was a David-and-Goliath-style victory with the small MG cars trouncing the likes of Maserati, Lagonda and Bentley. 'This is my greatest effort,' said Freddie to the press, continuing, 'What pleases me perhaps most of all is that this is an achievement for British manufacturers. It shows what British light cars can do.'[32] As well as taking first place, Freddie also received the team prize and had the pleasure of seeing two other cars entered by him finish fourth and fifth.[33]

Freddie's win at Brooklands in May 1931 was the highlight of his racing career. Looking back, he admitted, 'I suppose I had one of the shortest motor-racing careers on record, that is if compared to the importance given to it by the press. But I must admit that it was by luck unbelievably successful.'[34] In May the previous year, Freddie had finished seventh in the Brooklands Double-Twelve driving a tiny Austin Seven with Arthur Waite, sales and competition director for Austin. Waite had talent-spotted Freddie when he had competed in a time trial at Brooklands in 1929.

Not long after the 1930 Double-Twelve race, Freddie had gone on to win the BRDC (British Racing Drivers Club) 500-Mile race, also at Brooklands, in a works Austin Seven 'Ulster'. His co-driver was Sammy Davis, a past winner of Le Mans. Freddie wrote up his account of the race for the *Daily Telegraph* under the headline 'BABY'S FEAT IN BROOKLANDS RACE', describing their victory over a huge 4½-litre Bentley. He ended his piece by modestly saying, 'To have shared a car with so great a master of the art as S. C. H. Davis is a privilege that I shall treasure as much as the thought of victory itself.'[35] It was around the same time that Freddie began writing a regular column for *The Light Car*, in his highly amusing and self-effacing style.

After his 1931 Brooklands win, Freddie became a team manager with equal success, winning the 1931 Irish Grand Prix and the Tourist Trophy. Alongside this, he set up his own car dealership with KD, known as Kevill-Davies & March. They took with them from Bentley their very capable secretary, Mrs Small, who became the 'mother-cum-corner-stone of the enterprise'. The business was very successful, netting them a profit of £4,000 in their first year.[36]

Freddie's career was unusual among those of his class. To be 'in trade' was frowned upon but that was certainly not going to stop Freddie. By blazing a path through tradition and prejudice, he was setting a precedent for succeeding generations, not only in his own family but also for others who would otherwise be stifled by their birth.

Never one to sit still, Freddie also began designing sports bodies for new cars. Almost every car had a separate chassis, so customers regularly ordered special bodies from the many coach-builders dotted around the country. Freddie was particularly well known for his 'traditional' English sports car look, and customers of Kevill-Davies & March could order a 'March' body for almost any chassis, including the 'March Special' for the Hillman Minx.[37] Dovetailing with this design work, Freddie also set up a model-making business, March Models, with intricate scale replicas and two-dimensional car reliefs on offer. Such was their renown that they were used on the Shell-BP stand at the 1934 London Motor Show in a diorama.[38]

Around this time, Freddie was bitten by the flying bug. Ever since he had witnessed the first ever detachment of military planes flying low over Molecomb during the Great War, he had been passionate about aviation. In 1917, the Royal Flying Corps had taken over a farm at Tangmere on the Goodwood estate and Freddie had asked the first commanding officer, Major William Strugnell – known as Struggie – whether he could come and watch the aeroplanes. From then on, until the war ended, he visited Tangmere nearly every day during his school holidays, learning as much about the planes as the pilots themselves. The climax of these visits was when he discovered a discarded joystick and rudder bar in a heap of rubbish. He carried them back home on his bicycle and installed them in his bedroom, using them to teach himself the rudiments of flying, aided by a book called *Aerobatics* – a present from Charlie just before he left for France.[39]

It was not until 1923 that Freddie enjoyed his first flight, when he and a friend paid five shillings to go up in an Avro biplane with an ex-RAF pilot who was touring the country. At the end of the Twenties, his Oxford friend Edmund Hordern borrowed an Avro Avian and flew with Freddie from Hendon, in Middlesex, to Goodwood for the day, gently landing on the cricket ground. From there, they taxied it to the grass circle in front of the house where they photographed each other, posing beside the plane before returning to Hendon. During the flight, Edmund handed over the controls periodically to Freddie, 'and realising that my flying was almost second sense after all those years of plane worship at Tangmere in my school days, I became sold, all over again, hook, line and sinker'.[40] For Freddie, the appeal lay not in the speed with which you could travel from one place to another, but the freedom it offered and 'the magic of it all, to say nothing of the beauty one beheld from those exquisite views and scenes of the world in which we live below'.[41]

Fired up with enthusiasm, Freddie took flying lessons at Hanworth under the auspices of the new National Flying Services. His instructor, a former fighter pilot, was amazed at his progress at the end of day one: 'You know you're going to be awful good,' he said to Freddie. Little did he realise Freddie had been practising with a joystick and rudder bar in his bedroom for years.[42]

Freddie and Edmund (whose father had been vicar of Singleton) went on to design a plane together – the Hordern-Richmond Autoplane. It was designed to be as easy to fly as driving a car, dispensing with the rudder bar and with folding wings so it could be stored in a barn. Freddie even had a thatched hangar built at Goodwood for the 'Autoplane'.

The Autoplane was to be short-lived. When a Dutch inventor told Freddie and Edmund about a resin-impregnated wood laminate called hydulignum, they changed tack and started producing aircraft propeller blades made out of the material, moving their factory from Denham Aerodrome to Haddenham airfield in Buckinghamshire.[43] Their hydulignum propellers would soon be in great demand.

*   *   *

Hilda was an indefatigable charity worker. During the dark days of the Great War, her upright figure was seen striding over the South Downs, clad in a long tweed skirt, tailored jacket and with a pheasant feather tucked into her hat. Breathing in the chilly November air and with a look of determination, Hilda was on her way to Charlton, to attend the first meeting of the Women's Institute in England. That was in 1915 and the meeting had taken place at the Fox Inn, hosted by the landlady, Mrs Laishley. The WI had started in Canada and was designed to encourage countrywomen to get involved in growing and preserving food during the war. It gained huge momentum during the war, so that by the end of 1919 there were over 1,400 branches in Britain.

Hilda was also a founder member of The Soldiers', Sailors' and Air Force Association, eventually becoming its vice-president, as well as a member of the West Sussex County Council. For all her faults, when Hilda set her mind to something, she was an extremely capable lady. After the seventh duke's death, Set and Hilda were faced with the Herculean task of paying off the death duties, amounting to some £180,000. This they tackled with grim determination and it was Hilda's immense energy that carried them through.

In February 1930, twelve lots of timber went under the auctioneer's hammer. 'SALE OF GOODWOOD BEECHES / 70,000 IN ONE LOT / TOLL OF DEATH DUTIES' read the headline in *The Times*. The 'special correspondent' reported how the auctioneer, Mr Stops, of Messrs Jackson Stops, had announced that 'the sale was due to special conditions with which taxpayers would sympathize'. Many of the trees (which included some oak and ash) were planted by the third duke, and the sale was said to be the largest of its kind that had ever taken place in the country. With buyers assembled from all over Europe, Mr Stops told the audience that he would offer all the timber – barring one small exception – in one lot amounting to nearly 2.4 million cubic feet, with the time to remove it extended to eight years. Bidding started at £25,000 and quickly reached £40,000.

Thereafter, it crept up in small increments to £45,000 when the hammer was finally brought down to a timber merchant from Chesterfield. *The Times* correspondent then went on to stress how the losses would have little effect on the beautiful views from the racecourse and added that none of the venerable trees in the park were being felled.[44]

In Scotland, Set – now the eighth Duke of Richmond – and Hilda sold the Inchrory and Kinrara estates and, over the course of a few years, managed to pay off nearly all of the death duties. They redecorated both Goodwood and Gordon Castle and generally put the estates into a sound position. In 1931, the Goodwood Estate Company was formed following an Act of 1929, which allowed estates to become limited companies, thereby alleviating the heavy tax burdens.

Set and Hilda brought with them to Goodwood some of their staff from Molecomb, including Marshall the butler and Tilbury the chauffeur. Set was able to get himself around the house using iron leg-supports and elbow crutches. For outdoors, he had a three-wheel chair in which he propelled himself by using hand levers. For the hills, he would call on someone – often a member of the family – to give him a push. His family would also be called upon to rescue him when he was trapped by bores at social events; as soon as they saw the 'hunted look' come over his face, they would rush over and 'save Pop'.[45]

While Hilda immersed herself in her charitable work, Set would spend time up in London staying at the Hyde Park Hotel. The level pathways in Hyde Park meant he could spend the morning there without needing someone to push him. Still good-looking and charming, he had many female friends, including Barbara Cartland and the actress Isabel Jeans. There was an artistic side to him (probably inherited from his mother) that meant he found the theatre world very attractive. However, he never gave full expression to this side of his character, being hemmed in as he was by his traditional military upbringing and the rules of upper-class behaviour. This was a great pity as his disability meant he could no longer participate in his former loves of hunting, shooting and fishing.[46]

One charity that did occupy Set was the Queen Alexandra Hospital Home which moved from Roehampton to Worthing in 1933. It cared for soldiers who had been permanently disabled in the Great War, pioneering medical and social care procedures. Set's involvement had been initially through the Royal Savoy Association, a charity that enabled paralysed men to have holidays, but when the two charities merged he became very involved and committed.[47]

Set's time as duke was far too brief. From about 1932, his health deteriorated and, on 7 May 1935, he died aged sixty-four. His funeral was held two days later in Boxgrove Priory. Unlike the previous seven Dukes of Richmond, Set was cremated. As the cortège made its way to Brighton crematorium, it diverted to Worthing to pass in front of the Queen Alexandra Hospital Home. There, the patients were lined up to say farewell to their 'true and loyal friend'. In accordance with Set's wishes, instead of flowers, friends were asked to send donations to the charity.[48]

*   *   *

'Fochabers Sale / Picture of Famous Gordon Fetches £460 / Attributed to Romney' was the title of a brief report in *The Scotsman*, following the second day of the auction of the contents of Gordon Castle. Over just five days, nearly five hundred years' worth of collecting was dispersed. Everything from arms and armour, books, family portraits, prints, furniture, clocks and china, right down to mattresses, curtains, fishing equipment and 'extra-long ladders' – all went under the auctioneer's hammer.[49] Although Jane, Duchess of Gordon's portrait fetched a large sum, generally the figures reached were small – a white marble bust of Jane's husband, Alexander, fetched only £16. Most of the books were scooped up by an Edinburgh bookseller with prices ranging from 10s to £3 10s.[50]

The sale, which took place at the end of August and beginning of September 1938, marked the end of the family's connection with Gordon Castle. The castle itself and almost the entire estate had already been sold by Freddie – now ninth Duke of Richmond – to pay off the death duties following his father's death. Realising he had taken a momentous step, he left for his descendants a detailed memorandum, succinctly giving his reasons for the sale.[51]

Freddie had been faced with death duties of about £170,000 and mortgages of £250,000. His first step had been to sell the Huntly estate for £80,000 in 1935, reducing his mortgages to £170,000. As the Scottish properties were only bringing in a net income of just under £5,000, there was no hope of ever paying off the debts out of income. Neither was it viable to sell off large chunks of the estate and the fishing on the Spey, as it would cut off the income needed to pay for the upkeep of Gordon Castle. Therefore, Freddie had decided to try and sell the Gordon Castle estate 'en bloc', while retaining Glenfiddich for sentimental and practical reasons (it was readily let-able).

After more than a year of discussions with the Crown Office, the estate had been sold to the Crown for £525,000, enabling Freddie to pay off all the death duties and mortgages and invest what was left over. Although it had been a tough decision to make, Freddie had realised how vulnerable the Gordon Castle estate was; if anything were to happen to the net fishing, four-fifths of the income would disappear overnight. Added to that were his own negative feelings about the sport at Gordon Castle: 'While we (my Father, Mother, Sisters and Brother) did our best with rod and gun, the fun of the sport was greatly marred by the ridiculous aspect put upon it all. The fishing was talked of with a reverence few display before the altar and the Spey looked upon as Buddha rather than a river.' Acknowledging his own feelings, he had purposely moved slowly in agreeing to the sale, so he could be sure he was being led by his head and not his heart. Less than a decade later, Glenfiddich was sold for just under £100,000. Against stiff competition from America (over fifty offers were received from New York alone), its purchaser was a Scotsman.[52]

*   *   *

As the storm clouds gathered over Europe in the summer of 1939, the weather in England was appropriately miserable. It was therefore a relief that the sun shone for raceweek. *Tatler* magazine proclaimed: 'Goodwood in Regulation Goodwood Weather – For Once!'[53] Freddie and Betty, still aged in their thirties, hosted a large house party at Goodwood that was made up of family and friends. Betty, who was an extrovert, came into her own on these occasions. Having been brought up in a large family, she loved the house being filled with people and was a natural hostess, making sure everyone was happy. Owing to the political situation in Europe, the king, George VI, was not at Goodwood, so the house party was more relaxed than usual.

Just one month later, on 3 September 1939, Britain declared war on Germany when the deadline for the withdrawal of German troops from Poland expired. Those who had lived through the horrors of the Great War could hardly believe it was happening all over again. This time, the country was more prepared. Country houses were soon requisitioned; some – like Blenheim Palace, Longleat and Chatsworth – played host to boarding schools, while others become hospitals, maternity units or command headquarters.[54] Freddie offered Goodwood House to the War Office as a hospital but heard nothing further.

Then, one day, when they were having tea on the library steps, a huge army convoy arrived without warning to set up a hospital and training establishment. All of the pictures were taken down and stored in the Tapestry Drawing Room, while the tapestries themselves were removed and stowed in the Ice House, below ground. Most of the furniture was piled high in the stables with some of the more valuable pieces going into storage in Taunton. [55] The books in the libraries were boarded up in their bookshelves and all the floors were covered in linoleum.[56] The state rooms were turned into hospital wards, with the Ballroom being made the central ward. Freddie and Betty were given the use of two rooms downstairs (the Small Library and adjoining private dining-room) and two bedrooms upstairs, one for them and one for their two sons, Charles and Nicholas. With the increasing threat of a German invasion along the south coast, the boys were evacuated to Canada in July 1940 accompanied by their aunt Molly. They remained there until 1943.[57]

As well as the house being requisitioned, a farm on the Goodwood estate at Westhampnett was taken over by the Air Ministry. In the 1930s, Freddie had built a thatched hangar there to house his planes. When the farm was taken over in 1938 – as an emergency landing ground for nearby RAF Tangmere – the hedges were flattened, and two grass runways were laid out. The idea was that any badly damaged aircraft that might block the runway at Tangmere could divert to Westhampnett. In the summer of 1940, just prior to the Battle of Britain, Westhampnett was upgraded to become a satellite station. It was soon home to 145 Squadron, who played an important role in the Battle of Britain, defending the south coast in their Hurricanes against the Luftwaffe. Within only twenty miles of Westhampnett there were four major bases placed to defend the Naval base at Portsmouth and Southampton docks.

After seeing heroic action, 145 Squadron was replaced by 602 (City of Glasgow) Squadron, who arrived on 13 August. Just three days later, 1,720 German planes attacked the south coast with Tangmere as a prime target. As Tangmere was attacked, support from Westhampnett proved to be vital. Casualties were rushed to hospital in Goodwood House as 602 Squadron's Spitfires screamed through the sky, bringing down eight German planes.[58] Among those who lost their lives that August was Billy Fiske, a double Olympic champion bobsled driver, who became the first American pilot to die in the war.

Over the winter of 1940-41, the airfield at Westhampnett became badly waterlogged. To ease operations, a perimeter track was built, and blister hangers erected. As the focus of the war turned from defending the south coast to going on the offensive, other squadrons came and went, including 610 (County of Chester) Squadron. The latter included the young Tony Gaze who would let off steam by racing his MG around the perimeter track against Dickie Stoop. In the spring of 1941, Wing Commander Douglas Bader arrived with 616 (South Yorkshire) Squadron. Bader was a famous flying ace who had lost both

his legs in a flying accident. This larger-than-life character always kept
his cool and inspired great loyalty. On one occasion, in the middle of
a dogfight, he radioed his colleague on the ground at Tangmere:
'Woody, old chap, Douglas here. I quite forgot to book a squash court
for 7 o'clock. Can you book one for me?'[59] He loved playing golf, so
made the most of the Goodwood golf course; if he was needed urgently,
a plane would fly low over the golf course and fire off a red flare. At
the signal, his driver would dash back to the Kennels, collect his car
and drive across the course to pick him up.[60]

In August of that year, Bader was shot down in France, losing one
of his false legs in the process. His captors offered to give free passage
to an RAF aircraft to drop off a replacement. The RAF refused on
principle and, a few days later, mounted a bombing operation during
which a new false leg was dropped by parachute.[61]

The summer of 1942 saw the arrival of an American Spitfire squadron at Westhampnett. These Americans were some of the first United
States Army Air Force (USAAF) pilots to see action in the European
theatre of war.[62] By then, RAF Westhampnett had grown considerably
with a mass of temporary and permanent buildings and eleven satellite
sites. Goodwood racecourse had become an accommodation site and
most of the local buildings had been taken over.

Freddie himself had joined the RAF in September 1941, leaving
Hordern-Richmond – which was now making propellers for Spitfires
– in the hands of Edmund Hordern. In 1943, Freddie was posted to
Washington on the staff of a friend, reuniting him and Betty with their
two sons. Back at home, Hawker Typhoons were operating out of
Westhampnett to devastating effect against the enemy. On D-Day
itself (6 June 1944), four sorties were carried out from the airfield.[63] On
22 June 1944, the family were hit by a personal tragedy when Evelyn,
Bernard's widow, was killed by a German flying bomb when it
destroyed the Guard's Chapel in London during morning worship.

As the fighting moved across the Channel towards the end of the
war, so the role of Westhampnett changed yet again to a care and
maintenance facility. When the airfield fell silent at the end of May

1946, it seemed like this chapter in the annals of Goodwood had come to an end; but it was to rise again phoenix-like from the ashes.

*   *   *

On 18 September 1948, Freddie started up the engine of his brand-new Bristol 400 and drove out of the paddock on to the new Goodwood Motor Circuit. Having completed a lap in this stylish post-war car, the circuit was officially declared open and Goodwood's very first motorsport meeting commenced. That afternoon, in front of 15,000 spectators, Stirling Moss won his first proper race in a little cream Cooper; it was the day after his nineteenth birthday.

RAF Westhampnett's conversion into a fully fledged motor circuit had come about quite quickly. With the loss of Donington Park, Crystal Palace and Brooklands, the country was lacking a proper circuit. The first post-war race meeting was held at Gransden Lodge aerodrome in Cambridgeshire in 1947 and it became apparent that using an aerodrome could work well. When Tony Gaze met Freddie, whom he had met during the war, he asked Freddie when they were going to have a car race at Westhampnett. Freddie replied, 'Bless my soul. What will the neighbours say?' Freddie then did a recce when he was next at Goodwood and, having looked over it in detail with experts, decided to stage a motor race. He was by then president of the Junior Car Club and had both the experience – from running raceweek – and the resources on the estate to pull it off. It was a daunting task as the airfield was covered with detritus from the RAF, the winter was unusually hard, and rationing was still in place. But with Freddie's enthusiasm and determination, the Goodwood Motor Circuit was born, and a new chapter in the estate's history began.[64]

Following the success of the first meeting, Freddie decided to run more and formed the Goodwood Road Racing Company. In January 1949, the Junior Car Club – which always sounded like an amateur affair for schoolboys – absorbed the rump of the Brooklands Automobile Racing Club (known as BARC) and became the British

Automobile Racing Club, thereby continuing the acronym BARC. As president, Freddie arranged for the club to run all of the meetings at Goodwood from then on; being run by Freddie and his racing chums gave Goodwood a unique atmosphere where everyone was made to feel welcome.[65]

Over the next eighteen years, Goodwood became the spiritual successor to Brooklands as the home of British motor racing. Local places and landmarks on the Goodwood estate were used for the names of the corners and straights of the 2.4-mile track: Lavant Corner and Lavant Straight after the nearby village and river; Woodcote Corner after a farm; Madgwick Corner after Madgwick Lane; Fordwater after the place where the River Lavant was forded in days gone by; and St Mary's after the church in Lavant. These names became legendary in the world of motorsport as some of the greatest drivers of the twentieth century competed for victory at Goodwood. It was a period when motor racing was possibly at its most glamorous and taking place on an aristocratic estate, famous for its sporting activities, only added to its allure.

Among the heroes who competed at Goodwood, Stirling Moss was the most successful. He particularly remembered 'the friendliness, the mix of all social classes sharing one over-riding passion, for motor racing. The overall mood had something of the feel of a polo match . . . But the friendly atmosphere in the paddock didn't mean the racing was any less competitive than anywhere else. Once we were on the track, there was absolutely no quarter given.'[66] Other famous drivers included Reg Parnell, Prince Bira of Siam (grandson of the king in *The King and I*), Mike Hawthorn, Tony Brooks, Juan Manuel Fangio, Roy Salvadori, John Surtees, Graham Hill and Bruce McLaren. The track record of 1 minute, 20.4 seconds (at an average speed of 107.4 mph) was set by two famous Scots: Jim Clark and Jackie Stewart, while the most famous quote came from Salvadori, who enthused, 'Give me Goodwood on a summer's day, and you can keep the rest of the world.'[67]

When Freddie looked back at the contribution of motor racing at Goodwood, he modestly admitted that 'Goodwood had played a major part in raising the prestige of British drivers and racing cars from the doldrums of the 1930s to the world supremacy that both had reached thirty years later.' [68]

*   *   *

When Goodwood House was returned to Freddie after the end of the war, it was filthy. Freddie was furious, so he rang up the War Office and gave them an earful. The man at the War Office replied, 'I am very, very sorry to hear that. I will send a company down to clean it up.' A huge army truck arrived shortly after as Freddie and Betty were having a gin and tonic in the Small Library. 'We heard it come right round to the old kitchens – crunch, crunch on the gravel. It stopped, tailgate crashed down, and we heard a lot of army "Wot we got 'ere?" talk. Then crunch as the first man jumped out, then second, then third, accompanied by tinkle tinkle – the third man's broom had broken a stable window. We choked with laughter – the Crazy Gang weren't in it.' [69]

Like many country houses, particularly after requisitioning, post-war life was very different. Funds were scarce and staff in short supply. At Goodwood, the Ballroom and Supper Room were split up with partitions to form offices for the different departments of the Goodwood Estate Company, and upstairs, many of the bedrooms were converted into staff flats. The house was opened to the public, and the guidebook stated, 'Today, Goodwood is wholly democratic and the section of the house for so many years occupied by royalty during raceweek has become a staff club.' [70] Together with his agent, Ralph Hubbard, 'a plan for survival' was formulated to enable Freddie 'to honour his obligations as a landlord and, by making the maximum use of the raw materials at his disposal and developing his farmlands, to transform the estate from a liability into an economic asset without interfering with the character of the place.' [71]

As well as the farms, agricultural properties and forestry, a market garden, commercial sawmill and turnery were created and another company, Goodwood Industries Ltd, was formed. Of the 7,000 acres of farmland, the Home Farm covered 1,200 acres, with the remainder tenanted. Flowers, fruit and vegetables were grown in the four-acre market garden, with 10,000 square feet under glass. As an article in *Country Life* said in 1952: 'The most skilful use seems to be made of all the estate's natural resources under the plan for modern Goodwood. As a result, 12,000 acres and a mansion – which, one might add, is regularly open to the public – have not only survived, but have been made to serve a useful purpose, providing employment for some and beauty and entertainment for many. That the idea has proved successful there is no doubt.'[72]

Freddie and Betty, who lived in London during the week, continued to hold annual house parties for raceweek, which had recommenced in 1948. In addition, house parties – with a very different guest list – were held for the meetings at the motor circuit, usually at Easter, Whitsun and in September.

In 1957, the aerodrome at the Goodwood Motor Circuit was reopened for civilian use for the first time since the Second World War. Once again, the sky above Goodwood was alive with aeronautical activity. Under Freddie's leadership, Goodwood was going at full throttle into the future, with cars racing, horses galloping, planes flying, guns shooting, golfers swinging and cricketers batting. Nowhere else in the world could motoring champions indulge in a game of cricket, as they did at Goodwood when the drivers' eleven took on the Duke of Richmond's eleven under the shade of its ancient cedars of Lebanon.

Epilogue

Freddie was ahead of his time in many ways. In 1964, he told his eldest son, Charles, that he planned to retire when he was sixty-five, and hoped that Charles would then return to Goodwood and become chairman of the Goodwood companies. In the meantime, Freddie made the reluctant decision to close the motor circuit in 1966. After eighteen very successful years, Freddie was tired, many of his friends were no longer around and the bureaucracy had become intolerable. Added to that was the danger of accidents to drivers and spectators alike; a very real threat that grew as the speeds increased.

Charles was enthusiastic about his father's intention to retire in 1969. The first thing he did was to sound out the National Trust to see if they were interested in taking on Goodwood House. 'Don't give us another of those places!' was the reply that came back. When he said that he was serious, the official told him that the Trust would want in return a considerable endowment, plus all of the contents. Charles replied, 'In that case, we'll have a go ourselves.'[1] He later wrote: 'And so on that afternoon, in the offices of the National Trust, the immediate future of Goodwood as part of our national heritage was settled. We would continue to retain the house and its contents in the ownership of the family company and trust; my family would move into part of the house; we would make maximum use of as much of the building as possible by continuing to open the major rooms to the public and by using most of the first floor for the Goodwood Companies' offices; we would knock down, if possible, those rooms in poor repair for which there seemed no sensible use; we would accept the challenge to make ends meet.'[2]

Work began in 1967 to consolidate Goodwood House for the future. Almost all of Wyatt's dilapidated north wing was demolished (leaving only the Tapestry Drawing Room remaining); new private and public entrances were created, alongside facilities for the public; the whole house was rewired and redecorated; and the Ballroom and Supper Room were restored to their former glory. There then began a new chapter with Charles at the helm.

Having trained as a chartered accountant, Charles – eventually the tenth Duke of Richmond – was well placed to steer Goodwood through the challenging economic period of the 1970s when taxation was so high, and many estates went under. He felt strongly that large landowners had 'a moral duty to make some of their land, as well as their historic houses, available for public use and enjoyment'.[3] That being said, he did all in his power to keep the estate – which by now had been reduced from 17,000 to 12,000 acres – and collection intact. He saw himself as a 'steward for the community' and believed that a family was far more likely to maintain a property like Goodwood 'as a living and continuing part of our national history' than the government or an organisation.[4]

Following in the footsteps of his ancestors, Charles introduced a new sport to Goodwood – dressage. Spearheaded by his wife, Susan, Goodwood hosted the international dressage championships for twenty-one years, including the Alternative Olympics in 1980.[5] One of the innovations that came out of this was dressage to music, now an Olympic discipline. These events raised the profile of the sport in the country, to the extent that the great dressage champion, Dr Reiner Klimke, said, 'Without Goodwood, you would not have dressage in England.'[6]

Much of Charles's energy was focused on the racecourse. Prior to him taking over, racing had been confined to raceweek, which only lasted four days. With Charles's influence, the season was extended to nineteen days, lasting from May to October, including evening meetings and the introduction of an extra day at raceweek. Three new grandstands were built (the March, Charlton and Sussex Stands) and Goodwood Racecourse was seen as an innovator, setting the fashions and standards, in much the same way it had done under the fifth duke.

Aside from his work at Goodwood, Charles was involved in a staggering array of charities. He had a gift for bringing out the best in people and for getting people to work together for the common good. In many ways, he was as radical as his ancestor, the third duke, unafraid to stand up for what he felt was right. Having trained at William Temple theological college, he held various posts in the Church of England and World Council of Churches, and with his wife became involved in the vision to make the developing world a better place, particularly in Africa. They demonstrated their commitment when they adopted two mixed-race baby girls, which was very controversial at the time.

Like his father before him, Charles saw the advantages of handing over the reins to the next generation when they are still young and energetic. His son, Charles – the eleventh and current duke – took over from his father in 1994, having given up a successful career as a photographer in London. He and his wife, Janet, moved into Goodwood House and oversaw its complete redecoration, including reinstating the Egyptian Dining-Room and rehanging the entire picture collection.

When Freddie had closed down the motor circuit in 1966, Charles – then an eleven-year-old boy – had vowed to reopen it one day. Although the circuit had been maintained for occasional use, such as Formula One testing, plans to reopen it were met with fierce opposition by some of the locals. Not to be thwarted, Charles staged a new event in the park at Goodwood – the Festival of Speed. This was a hill-climb event that saw drivers race down the drive in front of the house and then tear up the hill behind, just as they had done when Freddie had hosted (and won) a hill-climb for the Lancia Car Club in 1936. Expecting around 3,000 people to turn up, Charles and his team were amazed when a crowd of 25,000 descended upon Goodwood in June 1993. Since then, the event has grown to become the world's greatest annual celebration of motorsport with crowds of around 200,000 people.

After seven years of negotiation, on 18 September 1998 – exactly fifty years after Freddie had opened the motor circuit – his grandson, Charles, drove an identical Bristol 400 around the track and declared it reopened. The Goodwood Revival was born. The event was themed around the years the motor circuit was open (1948-66), with no cars made after 1966 taking part. It was an instant success, not only for the high-quality racing, but also for the meticulous set-dressing of the circuit itself. Inspired by the surroundings, the spectators ran with the theme and made every effort to dress up in period. Twenty years later, it attracts over 145,000 spectators annually and is the only major sporting event in the world to take place in a period theme.

With a focus on Goodwood's unique heritage, Charles, the eleventh Duke of Richmond, has built on the foundations laid by his forebears, to the extent that Goodwood now employs approximately 750 people full-time. The clubs, formed around the different sports, have a dedicated membership and events running all year round; the third duke's Kennels is now their club house. Inspired by his mother, who has been a member of the Soil Association since the 1950s, the Home Farm is now fully organic; it comprises mainly grazing for livestock, including award-winning Southdown sheep. Goodwood milk, cheese and meat can be found in top London restaurants and cafés, as well as enjoyed at the different restaurants on the estate and at the major events. On the outskirts of the estate, Rolls-Royce has a state-of-the-art factory from where it exports cars all around the globe.

In many ways, Goodwood is doing exactly what it did over three hundred years ago when it was home to the first Duke of Richmond – welcoming people to enjoy sport and the hospitality that comes with it. Each of the sports at Goodwood stems from one of the dukes' passions, quite often shared with the ladies of the family. What sets Goodwood apart from many other sporting estates is the generosity in sharing those passions with others – friends and strangers alike. Perhaps this stems from an inherited sense of *noblesse oblige*, often demonstrated in their social responsibilities. But in many ways, it is more than that. At Goodwood, the Dukes of Richmond have embraced change in a way that meets each generation in a new and fresh way, and it is that which has had such a positive response over the centuries. Each duke has done their duty in whichever way they thought fit, whether it be serving their country, monarch, church or local community. But it is for their sporting legacy that they are remembered chiefly.

When the current duke, Charles Richmond, staged the revival of the Charlton Hunt for one weekend in 2016, he was continuing in the spirit of his ancestors. Three hundred years ago, the dull crack of a willow cricket bat hitting a leather-covered ball could be heard reverberating through the park at Goodwood. The same sound can be heard today, intermingled with the distant whine of planes and the hum of motorcars. Goodwood's future as England's greatest sporting estate looks bright.

Acknowledgements

A book on Goodwood would not have been possible without the full support of the current Duke of Richmond, for whom I have worked for nearly a decade. I am particularly grateful for his constant support and encouragement throughout the whole process. I owe a huge debt of thanks to my predecessor, Rosemary Baird, Curator Emerita of the Goodwood Collection. Not only has her book on Goodwood blazed a trail for me to follow, but she read through the whole manuscript and gave me many helpful insights. The staff of the West Sussex Record Office, where the Goodwood archive is deposited, have been incredibly helpful, in particular Jennifer Mason, Wendy Walker and the late Frances Lansley. Tim McCann, formerly of the WSRO has been an endless source of information and help throughout, along with his wife, Alison. In tracking down obscure publications, I have been greatly aided by the staff at the Society of Antiquaries library, especially borrowing books on my behalf from the London Library. Others who have helped me in my researches include Roddy Balfour, Robert Balfour, Charlotte Brudenell, James Fennell, Anna Keay, the late David Legg-Willis, Mary Miers, David Miller,

Jeremy Musson, Richard Pailthorpe, John Martin Robinson, Rosalind Savill, Jacob Simon, Mark Carleton-Smith and Charlotte Townshend. I am grateful to Béraud de Vogüé for a wonderful stay at the Château de la Verrerie at Aubigny-sur-Nère and the late Anne McLaren for welcoming me and my family to Kinrara.

Various members of the Gordon Lennox family have been helpful in giving me information, including the Duchess of Richmond, Susan, Duchess of Richmond, Angus and Zara Gordon Lennox (Gordon Castle) and Sara Fergusson (daughter of Esmé Gordon Lennox). The late (tenth) Duke of Richmond was a fount of information on his family history and I am sad he did not live to see the book finished. Likewise, my friend Anthony Gordon Lennox who also died during its writing. At Goodwood, many people have helped me in various ways including Jo Ambrose, Alex Benwell, Lucinda Cresswell, Ann Dommett, Bridgid Dunn, Kate Palka, Catherine Peel, Luke Sargent and Lara Wilson.

My agent, Michael Alcock, has been enthusiastic from the start and I am delighted Andreas Campomar at Constable saw the potential (with a little nudge from John and Angie Walsh). Both Andreas and Claire Chesser at Constable have been supportive editors and the book is all the better for their input. Thanks to them and their team, including Jon Davies for his forensic copy-editing.

Both Robert Sackville and Sara Sheridan gave me helpful advice when the idea for a book was just a dream and other friends have helped 'birth' it along the way, including Harry and Pip Goring, Rick and Kirsty Goring, Michael and Mirabelle Galvin, and Toby and Katie Mason.

Family members have been very supportive, including Euan Anstruther-Gough-Calthorpe who lent us his home in Scotland for Scottish forays and Giles Lawson Johnston who by coincidence works at Gordon Castle.

My final and biggest thanks go to my wife, Saskia, who has both read and edited the text and supported me over the last five years as the book has come to fruition. It is dedicated to her and our four daughters, one of whom was born during its writing.

Bibliography

Anglesey, The Marquess of (ed.), *The Capel Letters, Being the Correspondence of Lady Caroline Capel and her daughters with the Dowager Countess of Uxbridge from Brussels and Switzerland, 1814-1817*, London, 1955.

Anon. ('WB'), *Under the Red Cross, Gordon Castle 1914-1919*, Banff and Turrif, 1921.

Anon. (ed.), 'Vertue Note Books Volume V', *Journal of the Walpole Society*, Oxford, 1938.

Anon., 'Goodwood House, The Sussex Seat of The Duke of Richmond & Gordon – Part II', *The Antique Collector*, December, 1939.

Anon., *A Brief History of RAF Tangmere and its Satellite Airfields Westhampnett and Merston*, published by The Tangmere Military Aviation Museum, Chichester, 2007.

Baird, Rosemary, *Mistress of the House, Great Ladies and Grand Houses, 1670-1830*, London, 2003.

Baird, Rosemary, 'Foxed by Fox Hall', *Sussex Archaeological Collections*, vol. 143, 2005.

Baird, Rosemary, *Goodwood, Art and Architecture, Sport and Family*, London, 2007.

Baird, Rosemary, 'Richmond House, Whitehall', *British Art Journal*, Autumn 2007, vol. VIII, no. 2 and Winter 2007/8, vol. VIII, no. 3.

Baker, John R., *Abraham Trembley of Geneva, Scientist and Philosopher 1710-1784*, London, 1952.

Barstow, Phyllida, *The English Country House Party*, Stroud, 1998.

Bateman, John, *The Great Landowners of Great Britain and Ireland*, London, 4th ed., 1883.

Bathurst, The Earl, *Letters from Three Duchesses of Richmond, 1721–1761*, privately printed, 1925.

Beckwith, Lady Muriel, *When I Remember*, London, 1936.

de la Bédoyère, Guy (ed.), *The Diary of John Evelyn*, Woodbridge, 2004.

Bevan, Bryan, *Charles the Second's French Mistress*, London, 1972.

Black, Jeremy, *France and the Grand Tour*, Basingstoke and New York, 2003.

Bliss, Philip (ed.), *Reliquiae Hearnianae: The Remains of Thomas Hearne, M.A. of Edmund Hall, Being Extracts from His MS. Diaries, Collected with a Few Notes by Philip Bliss*, Oxford, 1857.

Bowron, Edgar Peters and Peter Björn Kerber, *Pompeo Batoni, Prince of Painters in Eighteenth-Century Rome*, 2007.

Bracegirdle, Hilary, *A Concise History of British Horseracing*, Newmarket, 1999.

Bulloch, John Malcolm, *The Gordon Highlanders, The History of their Origin together with a Transcript of the First Official Muster*, Banff, 1913.

Cannadine, David, *The Decline and Fall of the British Aristocracy*, New Haven and London, 1990.

Cartwright, James Joel (ed.), *The Travels Through England of Dr Richard Pococke, Successively Bishop of Meath and of Ossory, during 1750, 1751, and Later Years*, London, 1889.

Cecil, Camilla, *et al.*, *Glorious Goodwood, 200 Years of the World's Most Beautiful Racecourse*, Westbourne, 2002.

Chichester, A Gentleman of, *A Full and Genuine History of the Inhuman and Unparalleled Murders of Mr. William Galley, a Custom-House Officer, and Mr. Daniel Chater, a Shoemaker, by fourteen Notorious Smugglers, with the Trial and Execution of seven of the bloody criminals at Chichester*, 1749.

Clayton, Tim, *Waterloo: Four Days that Changed Europe's Destiny*, London, 2014.

Cokayne, George Edward, *et al.*, *The Complete Peerage*, reprint of 1945 ed., Gloucester, 1987.

Coutu, Joan, *Then and Now, Collecting and Classicism in Eighteenth-Century England*, Montreal & Kingston, 2015.

Dalkeith, Earl of, *et al.*, *Boughton House, The English Versailles*, Derby, 2006.

Delpech, Jeanine, *The Life and Times of the Duchess of Portsmouth*, London, 1953.

Dennison, Matthew, *The First Iron Lady, A Life of Caroline of Ansbach*, London, 2017.

Dooley, Terence, *The Decline and Fall of the Dukes of Leinster, 1872-1948*, Dublin, 2014.

Eaton, Charlotte [An Englishwoman], *The Days of Battle: or, Quatre Bras and Waterloo*, London, 1853.

Farrant, David, *The Queen Alexandra Hospital Home For Disabled Ex-Servicemen, Worthing, A History*, Chichester, 2008.

Feluś, Kate, *The Secret Life of the Georgian Garden*, London and New York, 2016.

FitzGerald, Brian (ed.), *Correspondence of Emily, Duchess of Leinster (1731-1814)*, Dublin, 1949-57.

Forneron, H., *Louise de Kéroualle, Duchess of Portsmouth, 1649-1734: Society in the Court of Charles II*, London, 4th ed., 1891.

Foulkes, Nicholas, *Dancing into Battle, A Social History of the Battle of Waterloo*, London, 2006.

Foulkes, Nicholas, *Gentlemen and Blackguards or Gambling Mania and the Plot to Steal the Derby of 1844*, London, 2010.

Fraser, Antonia, *King Charles II*, London, 1979.

Gordon, George, *The Last Dukes of Gordon and their Consorts 1743-1864*, Aberdeen, 1980.

Gow, Ian, *Scotland's Lost Houses*, London, 2006.

Grant, Mrs. Colquhoun, *Brittany to Whitehall, Life of Louise Renée de Kéroualle, Duchess of Portsmouth*, London, 1909.

Grant of Rothiemurchus, Elizabeth, *Memoirs of a Highland Lady 1797-1827*, London, 3rd ed., 1967.

Granville, Castalia, Countess (ed.), *Lord Granville Leveson Gower (First Earl Granville), Private Correspondence 1781-1821*, London, 1916.

Green, Alan, *Priory Park, Chichester, Its Story in 100 Objects*, Gloucester, 2018.

Greville, Charles and Richard Henry Stoddard (ed.), *The Greville Memoirs: A Journal of the Reigns of King George IV and King William IV*, New York, 1875.

Guards, The Captain of a Company in One of the Regiments of, *A Short Review of the Recent Affair of Honor between His Royal Highness the Duke of York, and Lieutenant Colonel Lenox. With Free and Impartial Strictures and Comments upon the Circumstances Attending It*, London, 1789.

Hewitt, Rachel, *Map of a Nation, A Biography of the Ordnance Survey*, London, 2010.

Hillier, Mark, *A Fighter Command Station at War, A Photographic Record of RAF Westhampnett from The Battle of Britain to D-Day and Beyond*, Barnsley, 2015.

Hunn, David, *Goodwood*, London, 1975.

Ilchester, The Countess of, and Lord Stavordale (eds.), *The Life and Letters of Lady Sarah Lennox, 1745-1826, . . . also a Short Political Sketch of the Years 1760-1763 by Henry Fox, 1ˢᵗ Lord Holland*, London, 1901.

Ilchester, The Earl of (ed.), *Lord Hervey and His Friends, 1726-1738*, London, 1950.

Ingamels, John, *A Dictionary of British and Irish Travellers in Italy 1701-1800*, New Haven and London, 1997.

Jacques, D., *A Visit to Goodwood, the Seat of His Grace the Duke of Richmond, near Chichester*, Chichester, 1822.

Kent, John, *Racing Life of Lord George Cavendish Bentinck, M.P. and Other Reminiscences*, London, 1892.

Kent, John, *Records and Reminiscences of Goodwood and the Dukes of Richmond*, London, 1896.

Kidd, Jane, *Goodwood Dressage Champions*, Addington, 1994.

Laird, Mark, *A Natural History of English Gardening 1650-1800*, New Haven and London, 2015.

Lawrence, Mike, Simon Taylor and Doug Nye, *The Glory of Goodwood*, London, 1999.

Ledger, Allan P., *A Spencer Love Affair, Eighteenth-Century Theatricals at Blenheim Palace and Beyond*, Croydon, 2014.

Lee, Sidney (ed.), *Dictionary of National Biography*, London, 1891-1900.

Legg-Willis, David, *Some Goodwood Annals*, Cambridge, 2016.

Anon. [Lord William Pitt Lennox], *Memoir of Charles Gordon Lennox, Fifth Duke of Richmond, K.G., P.C.*, London, 1862.

Lennox, Lord William Pitt, *Fifty Years' Biographical Reminiscences*, London, 1863.

Lennox, Lord Nicholas Gordon, *The Tiddly Quid & After, A Memoir of Places and People Met Along the Way*, Brighton, 2006.

Lewis, W. S., *et al.* (ed.), *Horace Walpole's Correspondence*, New Haven and London, 1937-83.

Lincoln, Margarette (ed.), *Samuel Pepys: Plague, Fire, Revolution*, London, 2015.

Llewellyn, Timothy D., *Lettere artistiche del Settecento veneziano – 4, Owen McSwiny's Letters 1720-1744*, Verona, 2009.

Madan, Beatrice (ed.), *Spencer and Waterloo, The Letters of Spencer Madan, 1814-1816*, London, 1970.

Marshall, John, *The Duke who was Cricket*, London, 1961.

Martin, Meredith, 'Interiors and Interiority in the Ornamental Dairy Tradition', *Eighteenth-Century Fiction*, University of Toronto Press, vol. 20, no. 3, 2008.

Macky, Spring (ed.), *Memoirs of the Secret Services of John Macky, Esq. during the Reigns of King William, Queen Anne, and King George I*, London, 1733.

Mannings, David, *Sir Joshua Reynolds, A Complete Catalogue of His Paintings*, New Haven and London, 2000.

March, Earl of, *Records of the Old Charlton Hunt*, London, 1910.

March, Earl of, *A Duke and His Friends, The Life and Letters of the Second Duke of Richmond*, London, 1911.

Mason, William Hayley, *Goodwood, Its House, Park and Grounds with a Catalogue Raisonné of the Pictures in the Gallery of His Grace the Duke of Richmond, K.G.*, London, 1839.

McCann, Timothy J. (ed.), *Goodwood: Royal Letters, Mary Queen of Scots to Queen Elizabeth II*, 1977.

McCann, Timothy J. (ed.), *The Correspondence of the Dukes of Richmond and Newcastle, 1724-1750*, Sussex Record Society, vol. 73, Lewes, 1984.

McCann, Timothy J., '"Much troubled with very rude company . . .", The 2nd Duke of Richmond's Menagerie at Goodwood', *Sussex Archaeological Collections*, vol. 132, 1994.

McCann, Timothy J., 'The 4th Duke of Richmond and the Great Cricket Match at Goodwood in 1814', *West Sussex History*, no. 54, 1994.

McCann, Timothy J., 'The Temple of Neptune and Minerva at Goodwood', *Sussex Archaeological Collections*, vol. 155, 2017.

McCann, Timothy J., '"Two of the Stoutest Legs in England", The 2nd Duke of Richmond's Leg Break in 1732', *Sussex Archaeological Collections*, vol. 150, 2012.

Miers, Mary, *Highland Retreats, The Architecture and Interiors of Scotland's Romantic North*, New York, 2017.

Miller, David, *Lady De Lancey at Waterloo, A Story of Duty and Devotion*, Staplehurst, 2000.

Miller, David, *The Duchess of Richmond's Ball, 15 June 1815*, Staplehurst, 2005.

Mosley, Charles (ed.), *Burke's Peerage, Baronetage and Knightage*, Wilmington, Delaware, 107th ed., 2003.

Murland, Jerry, *Aristocrats Go To War, Uncovering the Zillebeke Churchyard Cemetery*, Barnsley, 2010.

Napier, Priscilla, *My Brother Richmond*, privately printed, 1994.

Nelson, E. Charles, and David J. Elliott (eds), *The Curious Mister Catesby*, Athens Georgia and London, 2015.

O'Neill, Raymond, 'Goodwood, The Gordon Lennox Dynasty and their Pekingese Dogs', *The Pekingese Club Year Book, 2007*.

Osborne, Edgar (ed., text by George Bonney), *Goodwood, An Illustrated Survey of the Historic Sussex Home of the Dukes of Richmond and Gordon*, Derby, 1950.

Plumb, Christopher, *The Georgian Menagerie, Exotic Animals in Eighteenth-Century London*, London and New York, 2015.

Portland, The Duke of, *Men, Women and Things, Memories of The Duke of Portland, K.G., G.C.V.O.*, London, 1937.

Rees, Simon, *The Charlton Hunt, A History*, Chichester, 1998.

Reese, Max M., *Goodwood's Oak, The Life and Times of the Third Duke of Richmond, Lennox and Aubigny*, London, 1987.

Reeve, Henry (ed.), *The Greville Memoirs, A Journal of the Reigns of King George IV and King William IV by the late Charles C. F. Greville, Esq., Clerk of the Council to those Sovereigns*, London, 4th ed., 1875.

Reid, Peter, *Gordon Chapel, A History and Guidebook*, Fochabers, 2017.

Ricardo, Sir Harry R., *Memories and Machines, The Pattern of My Life*, 1968.

Richardson, Ethel, *Long Forgotten Days (Leading to Waterloo)*, London, 1928.

Riding, Jacqueline, *Jacobites, A New History of the '45 Rebellion*, London, 2016.

Robinson, John Martin, *James Wyatt, Architect to George III*, New Haven and London, 2012.

Robinson, John Martin, *Requisitioned, The British Country House in the Second World War*, London, 2014.

Rolfe, W. D. Ian, 'William Hunter (1718-1783) on Irish "elk" and Stubbs's Moose', *Archives of Natural History*, 1983.

Russell, John (ed.), *Memorials and Correspondence of Charles James Fox*, London, 1853.

Saville, Richard (ed.), *The Letters of John Collier of Hastings, 1731-1746*, Sussex Record Society, vol. 96, 2013-2014.

Siborne, William, *History of the War in France and Belgium in 1815*, London, 1844.

Smith, Paul, *Disraelian Conservatism and Social Reform*, Michigan, 1967.

Monsieurs Soulié, Dussieux, de Chennevières, Mantz and de Montaiglon (eds.), *Journal du Marquis de Dangeau*, Paris, 1854-55.

Spencer, Charles, *To Catch a King, Charles II's Great Escape*, London, 2017.

Steer, Francis, 'The Funeral Account of the First Duke of Richmond and Lennox', *Sussex Archaeological Collections*, vol. 98, 1960.

Strong, Roy, Marcus Binney, John Harris *et al.*, *The Destruction of the Country House, 1875-1975*, London, 1974.

Sutherland, Douglas, *The Yellow Earl, The Life of Hugh Lowther, 5th Earl of Lonsdale, K.G., G.C.V.O., 1857-1944*, London, 1965.

Swinton, The Hon. Blanche (ed.), *A Sketch of the Life of Lady de Ros, with some reminiscences of her family and friends, including the Duke of Wellington*, London, 1893.

Taylor, David, *The Wild Black Region, Badenoch 1750-1800*, Edinburgh, 2016.

Tillyard, Stella, *Aristocrats, Caroline, Emily, Louisa and Sarah Lennox, 1740-1832*, London, 1994.

Tillyard, Stella, *Citizen Lord, Edward Fitzgerald 1763-1798*, London, 1997.

Tinniswood, Adrian, *The Long Weekend, Life in the English Country House Between the Wars*, London, 2016.

Torrance, David, *The Scottish Secretaries*, Edinburgh, 2006.

Trethewey, Rachel, *Mistress of the Arts*, London, 2002.

Verney, Peter, *The Micks: The Story of the Irish Guards*, London, 1970.

Queen Victoria, *More Leaves from the Journal of A Life in the Highlands, from 1862-1882*, London, 3rd ed., 1884.

Wake, Joan, *The Brudenells of Deene*, London, 1953.

Watson, J. N. P., *Marlborough's Shadow, The Life of the First Earl Cadogan*, Barnsley, 2003.

Webb, Richard, *Mrs. D, The Life of Anne Damer (1748-1828)*, Studley, 2013.

Williams, Brian and Brenda, *The Country House at War 1914-1918*, Pitkin Guide, Stroud, 2014.

Worman, John, *Under the Trundle, Goodwood Golf Club, 1892-1992*, Selsey, 1992.

Worsley, Lucy, *Courtiers, The Secret Life of the Georgian Court*, London 2010.

Wraxall, Sir Nathanial William, *Historical Memoirs of My Own Time*, London, 1904

Wulf, Andrea, *The Brother Gardeners, Botany, Empire and the Birth of an Obsession*, London, 2009.

Wymer, Norman, 'Preserving an Ancestral Estate', *Country Life*, 26 December 1952.

Yeowel, J., 'Replies. Charles Lennox, first Duke of Richmond', *Notes and Queries*, 2nd series, 1836.

PERIODICALS AND NEWSPAPERS

Aberdeen Press and Journal

The Autocar

Banffshire Journal, Aberdeenshire Mail, Moray, Nairn, and Inverness Review, and Northern Farmer

Daily Advertiser

The Daily Telegraph

The Edinburgh Evening Courant

The Evening Standard

The Gentleman's and London Magazine

Gentleman's Magazine

The Gentleman's Magazine and Historical Chronicle

The Graphic

The Illustrated London News

London Chronicle

The Manchester Courier

The Morning Post

Pearson's Magazine

Portsmouth Evening News

The Public Advertiser

The Scotsman

South of England Advertiser: Sussex, Surrey, Hampshire and Kent

The Sporting Life

The Sporting Times

The Standard

Sunday Pictorial

The Tatler

The Times

The Town and Country Magazine

West Sussex Gazette

Whitehall Evening Post

Endnotes

Chapter 1 – Royal Origins

1   Guy de la Bédoyère (ed.), *The Diary of John Evelyn*, Woodbridge, 2004, p. 186.

2   Quoted in Jeanine Delpech, *The Life and Times of the Duchess of Portsmouth*, London, 1953, p. 40.

3   Colbert to Louvois, 8 October 1671, quoted in H. Forneron, *Louise de Keroualle, Duchess of Portsmouth, 1649-1734: Society in the Court of Charles II*, London, 1891 (4th ed.), pp. 66-68.

4   *ibid.*, p. 67.

5   *ibid.*, p. 69.

6   de la Bédoyère (ed.), *op. cit.*, p. 186.

7   *ibid.*, p. 186.

8   *ibid.*, p. 186.

9   *ibid.*, p. 185.

10   Colbert to Louvois, 22 October 1671, quoted in Forneron, *op. cit.*, pp. 71-72.

11   Quoted in Forneron, *op. cit.*, p. 72.

12   Rosemary Baird, *Mistress of the House, Great Ladies and Grand Houses, 1670-1830*, London, 2003, p. 73.

13   de la Bédoyère (ed.), *op. cit.*, p. 264.

14   *ibid.*, p. 250.

15   Rosemary Baird, *op. cit.*, p. 69.

16   Delpech, *op. cit.*, p. 71.

17   Quoted in Forneron, *op. cit.*, pp. 150-151.

18   Delpech, *op. cit.*, p. 79.

19   Courtin, 24 September 1676. Quoted in Forneron, *op. cit.*, p. 156.

20   Courtin, 15 February 1677. Quoted in Forneron, *op. cit.*, p. 170.

21   Quoted in Forneron, *op. cit.*, p. 171.

22   Forneron, *op. cit.*, p. 189.

23   *ibid.*, p. 204.

24   Bryan Bevan, *Charles the Second's French Mistress*, London, 1972, p. 14.

25   Delpech, *op. cit.*, p. 84.

26   Sadly this ring was stolen from Goodwood in January 2016 and has not been
     recovered.

27   Baird, *op. cit.*, p. 70.

28   West Sussex Record Office (hereafter WRSO), GW MS 3 and Margarette
     Lincoln (ed.), *Samuel Pepys: Plague, Fire, Revolution*, London, 2015, p. 120,
     cat. 51.

29   Forneron, *op. cit.*, p. 187.

30   Delpech, *op. cit.*, p. 69.

31   Richmond and Settrington are both in Yorkshire (see *The Complete Peerage*,
     London, 1945, vol. X, p. 831).

32   Charles II to Sir Joseph Williamson, 31 July 1675, GW MS 1427. See also
     Timothy J. McCann (ed.), *Goodwood: Royal Letters, Mary Queen of Scots to
     Queen Elizabeth II*, 1977.

33   The title Lord Torboulton is variously spelt and sometimes referred to as
     Lord Methven of Torboltoun (*Complete Peerage, op. cit.*, p. 836, fn e). Lennox
     is often spelt Lenox, particularly with the first and second dukes.

34   See family tree in Bevan, *op. cit.* pp. 192-193.

35   *The Complete Peerage*, London, 1932, vol. VIII, p. 484, fn b, Forneron, *op. cit.*,
     p. 119 and Delpech, *op. cit.*, p. 85.

36   WSRO, GW MS 12. It is sometimes stated that he was given one shilling per
     cauldron of coal.

37   de la Bédoyère (ed.), *op. cit.*, pp. 269 & 271 (30 March & 23 October 1684).

38   Spring Macky (ed.), *Memoirs of the Secret Services of John Macky, Esq. during the
     Reigns of King William, Queen Anne, and King George I*, London, 1733, p. 48.

39   *The Complete Peerage*, London, 1945, vol. X, p. 837.

40   Delpech, *op. cit.*, p. 83 and Mrs. Colquhoun Grant, *Brittany to Whitehall, Life of Louise Renée de Keroualle, Duchess of Portsmouth*, London, 1909, p. 135.

41   Reported by Barrillon to Louis XIV, January, 1684. Forneron, *op. cit.*, p. 275.

42   Forneron, *op. cit.*, pp. 276-277.

43   Delpech, *op. cit.*, p. 150.

44   Hilary Bracegirdle, *A Concise History of British Horseracing*, Newmarket, 1999, pp. 2-3.

45   de la Bédoyère (ed.), *op. cit.*, p. 276.

46   Delpech, *op. cit.*, p. 179.

47   Forneron, *op. cit.*, p. 284.

48   Antonia Fraser, *King Charles II*, London, 1979, p. 448.

49   Delpech, *op. cit.*, p. 181.

50   Fraser, *op. cit.*, p. 456.

51   Quoted in Delpech, *op. cit.*, p. 183.

52   Forneron, *op. cit.*, pp. 286-290.

53   *ibid.*, p. 289 and Delpech, *op. cit.*, p. 189.

Chapter 2 – Exile

1   Earl of March, *A Duke and His Friends, The Life and Letters of the Second Duke of Richmond*, London, 1911, vol. I, p. 29.

2   Delpech, *op. cit.*, p. 191.

3   *ibid.*, p. 191.

4   *ibid.*, p. 191.

5   Sold at Christie's, 'Important Guns and Pistols and English and Oriental Weapons', 31 March 1958, lot 167 for 2,100 guineas (the property of the ninth Duke of Richmond).

6   Monsieurs Soulié, Dussieux, de Chennevières, Mantz and de Montaiglon (eds.), *Journal du Marquis de Dangeau*, Paris, 1854, vol. 2, pp. 122-123.

7   Delpech, *op. cit.*, p. 198.

8   Quoted in *ibid.*, p. 198.

9   Quoted in *ibid.*, p. 192.

10   Soulié *et al.*, *op. cit.*, vol. 2, p. 286.

11   de la Bédoyère (ed.), *op. cit.*, 329.

12   Soulié *et al.*, *op. cit.*, vol. 4, p. 18 and *Dictionary of National Biography* (entry for first Duke of Richmond).

13   Quoted in Delpech, *op. cit.*, p. 199.

14   J. Yeowel, 'Replies. Charles Lennox, first Duke of Richmond', *Notes and Queries,* 2nd series, 1836, v. 2, p. 51.

15   Soulié *et al.*, *op. cit.*, vol. 4, p. 235.

16   Joan Wake, *The Brudenells of Deene*, London, 1953, p. 200.

17   Quoted in March, *A Duke and His Friends*, vol. I, pp. 10-11.

18   Macky, *op. cit.*, p. 48.

19   Report by Dr. M. B. Roberts, UCL, *The establishment of the original park pale boundary of Goodwood Park*, April 2015.

20   Arundel Survey of 1570, Arundel Castle Archive, MD 535, f 29 (kindly supplied by Dr Caroline Adams and Richard Pailthorpe).

21   David Hunn, *Goodwood*, London, 1975, pp. 29-32.

22   WSRO, GW MSS 23 & 24.

23   WSRO, GW MS 23, ff 1/9, 1/3.

24   WSRO, GW MS 23, ff 1/84, 1/85.

25   WSRO, GW MS 23, ff 1/70, 1/74.

26   WSRO, GW MS 23, f 1/83.

27   WSRO, GW MS 23, ff 1/22, 1/94, 1/106.

28   WSRO, GW MS 23, f 1/58.

29   All WSRO, GW MS 23.

30   WSRO, GW MS 27.

31   WSRO, GW MS 23, f 1/92.

32   WSRO, GW MS 24, f 2/53.

33   WSRO, GW MS 24, f 2/93.

34   WSRO, GW MS 23, f 1/149.

35   WSRO, GW MS 23, f 1/148.

36   WSRO, GW MS 24, ff 2/18, 2/19, 2/72.

37   Richmond had been granted the Lennox estates in 1680 but Frances Stuart, Dowager Duchess of Richmond had a life interest. The main residence, Lethington Castle, East Lothian, was purchased by her trustees for the benefit of her kinsman, Walter Stuart, sixth Lord Blantyre. She had stipulated that the property be called 'Lennox's Love to Blantyre', which was subsequently shortened to Lennoxlove. In more recent times, it was the home of the seventh Duke of Richmond's granddaughter, Elizabeth, Duchess of Hamilton (1916-2008).

38   Quoted in March, *A Duke and His Friends*, vol. I, pp. 16-19.

39   WSRO, GW MS 28.

40 WSRO, GW MS 28. Betty Germain's brother, the third Earl of Berkeley, married Richmond's eldest daughter, Louisa in 1711.

41 Quoted in March, *A Duke and His Friends*, vol. I, pp. 14-16.

42 Soulié *et al.*, *op. cit.*, vol. 15, p. 189 and Jeremy Black, *France and the Grand Tour*, Basingstoke and New York, 2003, p. 109.

43 Quoted in March, *A Duke and His Friends*, vol. I, pp. 22-24 (letter from first Duke of Richmond to Louise de Keroualle (translated from the French), dated 9 January 1713).

44 WSRO, GW MS 6.

45 Quoted in March, *A Duke and His Friends*, vol. I, pp. 20-21 (letter from first Duke of Richmond to Louise de Keroualle (translated from the French), dated 5 August 1712).

46 Colquhoun Grant, *op. cit.*, pp. 254-155.

47 WSRO, GW MS 23, f 1/117. Receipt dated 14 August 1698 and finally paid 8 May 1703.

48 Baird, *op. cit.*, p. 79.

49 Forneron, *op. cit.*, p. 304.

50 Delpech, *op. cit.*, pp. 204-205.

51 Colquhoun Grant, *op. cit.*, p. 270.

52 Quoted in March, *A Duke and His Friends*, vol. I, pp. 24-25 (letter from first Duke of Richmond to Louise de Keroualle (translated from the French), dated 13 January 1714).

53 Colquhoun Grant, *op. cit.*, p. 237.

54 March, *A Duke and His Friends*, vol. I, pp. 34-35 and J. N. P. Watson, *Marlborough's Shadow, The Life of the First Earl Cadogan*, Barnsley, 2003, p. 216.

55 Rosemary Baird, *Goodwood, Art and Architecture, Sport and Family*, London, 2007, pp. 12-13.

56 Earl Bathurst, *Letters from Three Duchesses of Richmond, 1721–1761*, privately printed, 1925, p. 12.

57 March, *A Duke and His Friends*, vol. I, p. 56.

58 *ibid.*, vol. I, p. 57.

59 *ibid.*, vol. I, pp. 62-63

60 Louis de Rouvroy, duc de Saint-Simon, quoted in Delpech, *op. cit.*, p. 205.

61 March, *A Duke and His Friends*, vol. I, p. 71.

62 Francis Steer, 'The Funeral Account of the First Duke of Richmond and Lennox', *Sussex Archaeological Collections*, vol. 98, 1960, pp. 156-164.

63 Philip Bliss (ed.), *Reliquiae Hearnianae: The Remains of Thomas Hearne, M.A. of Edmund Hall, Being Extracts from His MS. Diaries, Collected with a Few Notes by Philip Bliss*, Oxford, 1857, vol. 2, pp. 494-495.

Chapter 3 – The Charlton Hunt

1 Charles Spencer, *To Catch a King, Charles II's Great Escape*, London, 2017, pp. 225-231.

2 WSRO, GW MS 151, *The Historicall Account of the Rise, and Progress of the Charleton Congress*, with a handwritten note at the beginning by the second Duke of Richmond: 'This was bought to me by a Porter in the beginning of February: 1737/8 R'; Simon Rees, *The Charlton Hunt, A History*, Chichester, 1998, p. 9; and Rosemary Baird, 'Foxed by Fox Hall', *Sussex Archaeological Collections*, vol. 143, 2005, p. 215.

3 Rees, *op. cit.*, p. 13.

4 Somerset was married to Lady Elizabeth Percy, the heiress whom Louise had hoped would marry her son, the first Duke of Richmond.

5 March, *A Duke and His Friends*, vol. I, pp. 64-66.

6 The Reverend Jeremiah Miller, *An Account of a Tour in Hampshire and Sussex to Kingscleer, Basingstoke, Alton, Midhurst, Petworth, Arundel, Chichester, Portsmouth, Southampton & Winchester, Begun on Thursday the 15th of September finished on Tuesday the 20th of September 1743*, British Library, Add MS 15776, ff. 221, 244 and 245.

7 Royal Institute of British Architects Drawings Collection (see Baird, *Goodwood*, p. 20).

8 The first hound list dates from November 1721 and lists fifteen couple (i.e. thirty) of old hounds in their joint ownership (WSRO, GW MS 2003).

9 Earl of March, *Records of the Old Charlton Hunt*, London, 1910, p. 25 quoting GW MS 151.

10 Baird, 'Foxed by Fox Hall', *Sussex Archaeological Collections*, vol. 143, 2005, pp. 227-229. Burlington went on to design the Council House in Chichester.

11 The exact location of the Great Room is discussed in Baird, *ibid.*, pp. 221-229.

12 WSRO, GW MS 99, f 9.

13 The purchase was financed by his marriage settlement in which the Earl Cadogan had agreed to buy him land to the value of £60,000 (see Baird, *op. cit.*, p. 220 and WSRO, GW MS 98).

14 WSRO, GW MS 149, A28.

15 WSRO, GW MS 149, A27.

16 WSRO, GW MS 149, A28.

17   Baird, *Goodwood*, pp. 50-51.

18   March, *A Duke and His Friends*, vol. I, p. 262.

19   WSRO, GW MS 99.

20   March, *A Duke and His Friends*, vol. I, p. 68 (Tom Hill to Richmond, 27 March 1723).

21   *ibid.*, p. 92.

22   *ibid.*, p. 195.

23   The Earl of Ilchester (ed.), *Lord Hervey and His Friends, 1726-1738*, London, 1950, p. 100.

24   The Rosalinde and Arthur Gilbert Collection, on loan to the Victoria and Albert Museum, London (GILBERT.1:1 to 3-2014).

25   March, *A Duke and His Friends*, vol. I, p. 303 (Richmond to Martin Ffolkes, 25 February 1735).

26   W. S. Lewis *et al.* (ed.), *Horace Walpole's Correspondence*, New Haven and London, 1937-1983, vol. 37, pp. 114-115 (Horace Walpole to Henry Conway, 31 October 1741).

27   *ibid.*, vol. 17, p. 184 (Horace Walpole to Horace Mann, 2 November 1741).

28   WSRO, GW MS 102, f 2.

29   WSRO, GW MS 102, f 5.

30   *Walpole's Correspondence*, vol. 30, p. 46 (Walpole to Lord Lincoln, 1733-1734).

31   *ibid.*, vol. 9, p. 57 (Horace Walpole to George Montagu, 26 May 1748).

32   *ibid.*, vol. ii, p. 114 (Horace Walpole to Horace Mann, 25 February 1750).

33   March, *A Duke and His Friends*, vol. II, p. 690.

34   March, *Old Charlton Hunt*, 1910, pp. 140-141.

35   WSRO, GW MS 152.

36   WSRO, GW, MS 2003, p. 79.

37   WSRO, GW, MS 152, p. 22.

38   WSRO, GW MS 2003, p. 23 (Richmond's transcript) and Rees, *op. cit.*, pp. 111-121.

39   March, *A Duke and His Friends*, vol. I, p. 194.

40   Bathurst, *op. cit.*, pp. 44-45.

41   March, *A Duke and His Friends*, vol. I, p. 304 and Richard Saville (ed.), *The Letters of John Collier of Hastings, 1731-1746*. Sussex Record Society, vol. 96 (issued to members of the Society for the years 2013 and 2014), p. 1737 (Collier to his wife, 19 May 1737).

42   March, *A Duke and His Friends*, vol. II, p. 614.

43   *ibid.*, vol. I, p. 212.

44   *ibid.*, vol. II, p. 650.

45   *ibid.*, vol. II, p. 504.

46   *ibid.*, vol. I, pp. 79-82.

47   March, *Old Charlton Hunt*, p. 90.

48   *ibid.*, p. 35.

49   Miller, *op. cit.*, f 244.

50   Baird, *Goodwood*, pp. 21-22.

51   *ibid.*, p. 98.

52   Bathurst, *op. cit.*, pp. 53-55.

Chapter 4 – Taming the Landscape

1   British Museum, Add. MS 28726, f 156.

2   WSRO, GW MS 23, f 1/51.

3   John Marshall, *The Duke who was Cricket*, London, 1961, p. 11.

4   Timothy J. McCann, 'The second Duke and his team' in commemorative programme to accompany the 250th Anniversary Cricket Match at Goodwood, 10 July 1977, pp. 4-5.

5   WSRO, GW MS 1884.

6   Timothy J. McCann, '"Two of the Stoutest Legs in England", The 2nd Duke of Richmond's Leg Break in 1732', *Sussex Archaeological Collections*, vol. 150, 2012, pp. 139-141.

7   WSRO, GW MS 110, f 78.

8   WSRO, GW MS 1885.

9   Christopher Plumb, *The Georgian Menagerie, Exotic Animals in Eighteenth-Century London*, London and New York, 2015, pp. 141-149 and Mark Laird, *A Natural History of English Gardening 1650-1800*, New Haven and London, 2015, p. 242.

10   March, *A Duke and His Friends*, vol. I, p. 163 and WSRO, GW MS 112, f 328.

11   Timothy J. McCann, '"Much troubled with very rude company …", The 2nd Duke of Richmond's Menagerie at Goodwood', *Sussex Archaeological Collections*, vol. 132, 1994, p. 145.

12   *ibid.*, p. 145.

13   *ibid.*, pp. 145-146.

14   *ibid.*, p. 147.

15   The Earl of Ilchester (ed.), *Lord Hervey and His Friends, 1726-1738*, London, 1950, p. 149.

16   Timothy J. McCann, 'The 2nd Duke of Richmond's Menagerie at Goodwood', p. 148.

17   Anon. (ed.), 'Vertue Note Books Volume V', *Journal of the Walpole Society*, Oxford, 1938, pp. 145-146.

18   *ibid.*, p. 146.

19   Laird, *op. cit.*, p. 241.

20   Andrea Wulf, *The Brother Gardeners, Botany, Empire and the Birth of an Obsession*, London, 2009, p. 90.

21   WSRO, GW MS 134.

22   WSRO, GW MS 134.

23   British Museum, Add. MS 28727, f 8.

24   British Museum, Add. MS 28726, f 127 (Richmond to Collinson, 28 December 1742).

25   Laird, *op. cit.*, p. 240 and James Joel Cartwright (ed.), *The Travels Through England of Dr Richard Pococke, Successively Bishop of Meath and of Ossory, during 1750, 1751, and Later Years*, London, 1889, p. 111.

26   British Museum, Add. MS 28726, f 108 (Richmond to Collinson, 22 November 1741).

27   British Museum, Add. MS 28726, f 124 (Richmond to Collinson, 17 December 1742).

28   E. Charles Nelson and David J. Elliott (eds), *The Curious Mister Catesby*, Athens, Georgia and London, 2015, pp. 245, 326, fig. 21-3.

29   Baird, *Goodwood*, pp. 70-71.

30   *ibid.*, p. 72.

31   Brian FitzGerald (ed.), *Correspondence of Emily, Duchess of Leinster (1731-1814)*, Dublin, 1949, vol. I, p. 164.

32   Kate Feluś, *The Secret Life of the Georgian Garden*, London and New York, 2016, pp. 55-56.

33   WSRO, GW MS 112, f 328.

34   March, *A Duke and His Friends*, vol. II, p. 721 (Knowles to John Russell, 4 April 1739).

35   British Museum, Add. MS 28727, f 12.

36   WSRO, GW MS 102 f 8 (Sarah to Richmond, 30 September 1740).

37   The Diary of Lady Newdigate's Tour of the South of England in July 1747 (Warwickshire County Record Office, CR 1841/7) quoted in Feluś, *op. cit.*, p. 118.

38   'Vertue Note Books', p. 145.

39   Timothy J. McCann, 'The Temple of Neptune and Minerva at Goodwood', *Sussex Archaeological Collections*, vol. 155, 2017, pp. 151-155.

40   'Vertue Note Books', p. 144.

41   *ibid.*, p. 143.

42   GW MS 2008 (Small Library, Goodwood House).

43   *Walpole's Correspondence*, vol. 21, p. 67 (Horace Walpole to Horace Mann, 17 March 1757).

44   WSRO, GW MS 224, f 5/1.

45   FitzGerald, *op. cit.*, vol, I, p. 38 (Countess of Kildare to Earl of Kildare, 22 May 1757).

46   *ibid.*, p. 43.

47   *ibid.*, p. 174 (Lady Caroline Fox to Countess of Kildare, 8 August 1758).

48   *ibid.*, pp. 178-79 (Lady Caroline Fox to Countess of Kildare, 26 August 1758).

49   *ibid.*, p. 240 (Lady Caroline Fox to Countess of Kildare, 5 July 1759).

50   *ibid.*, pp. 221-222 (Lady Caroline Fox to Countess of Kildare, May 1759).

51   *ibid.*, pp. 226 and 229 (Lady Caroline Fox to Countess of Kildare, 15 and 17 June 1759).

52   *ibid.*, pp. 229-230 (Lady Caroline Fox to Countess of Kildare, 17 June 1759).

53   *ibid.*, pp. 226 and 230 (Lady Caroline Fox to Countess of Kildare, 15 and 17 June 1759).

54   *ibid.*, p. 226 (Lady Caroline Fox to Countess of Kildare, 15 June 1759).

55   *ibid.*, p. 271 (Lady Caroline Fox to Countess of Kildare, 31 January 1760).

56   *ibid.*, p. 276 (Lady Caroline Fox to Countess of Kildare, 1 March 1760).

57   *ibid.*, 1953, vol. II, p. 173 (Lady Sarah Bunbury to the Duchess of Leinster, 21 April 1776).

58   D. Jacques, *A Visit to Goodwood, the Seat of His Grace the Duke of Richmond, near Chichester*, Chichester, 1822, pp. 80-81 and William Hayley Mason, *Goodwood, Its House, Park and Grounds with a Catalogue Raisonné of the Pictures in the Gallery of His Grace the Duke of Richmond, K.G.*, London, 1839, p. 159.

59   Meredith Martin, 'Interiors and Interiority in the Ornamental Dairy Tradition', *Eighteenth-Century Fiction*, University of Toronto Press, vol. 20, no. 3 (Spring, 2008), pp. 368-370.

60   Jacques, *op. cit.*, p. 76.

61   Quoted in Laird, *op. cit.*, p. 164 (Peter Collinson to Cadwallader Colden, 1764).

62   British Museum, Add. MS 28727, f 62 (Richmond to Collinson, 11 March 1756).

63   British Museum, Add. MS 28727, f 77 (Richmond to Collinson, 14 September 1760).

64   British Museum, Add. MS 28727, f 88 (Richmond to Collinson, 26 September 1762).

65   *Walpole's Correspondence*, vol. 11, p. 118 (Horace Walpole to Mary Berry, 16 October 1790).

66   *ibid.*, pp. 118-119, fn 7.

67   Max M. Reese, *Goodwood's Oak, The Life and Times of the Third Duke of Richmond, Lennox and Aubigny*, London, 1987, p. 250.

68   W. D. Ian Rolfe, 'William Hunter (1718-1783) on Irish "elk" and Stubbs's Moose', *Archives of Natural History*, 1983, volume 11, part 2, pp. 263-290.

69   Baird, *Goodwood*, pp. 105-106.

70   Jacques, *op. cit.*, pp. 87-88.

Chapter 5 – The Renaissance Duke

1   Timothy J. McCann (ed.), *The Correspondence of the Dukes of Richmond and Newcastle, 1724-1750*, Sussex Record Society, vol. 73, Lewes, 1984, p. 101.

2   March, *A Duke and His Friends*, vol. I, pp. 35-36 (March to the Duchess of Richmond, 17 July 1720).

3   John Ingamels, *A Dictionary of British and Irish Travellers in Italy 1701-1800*, New Haven and London, 1997, p. 203.

4   March, *A Duke and His Friends*, vol. I, pp. 38-39.

5   Timothy D. Llewellyn, *Lettere artistiche del Settecento veneziano – 4, Owen McSwiny's Letters 1720-1744*, Verona, 2009, pp. 291-292, 297.

6   *ibid.*, pp. 145-146.

7   WSRO, GW MS 103, f 145 (Angela Polli to Earl of March, 28 February 1722).

8   March, *A Duke and His Friends*, vol. I, p. 255 (Richmond to Martin Folkes, 12 August 1733).

9   *ibid.*, vol, I, p. 51 (Earl Cadogan to Earl of March, 28 October 1721).

10   Llewellyn, *op. cit.*, pp. 79-136.

11   'Vertue Note Books', pp. 149-150.

12   Llewellyn, *op. cit.*, p. 295 quoting McSwiny to Richmond, 28 November 1727.

13   WSRO, GW MS 99.

14   'Vertue Note Books', p. 145.

15   WSRO, GW MS 56, ff M4 & M5.

16   WSRO, GW MS 56, f M5.

17   Ilchester (ed.), *op. cit.*, pp. 166-167 (Hervey to Richmond, 18 July 1733).

18   McCann, *Correspondence*, p. 92 (Richmond to Newcastle, 28 November 1742).

19   WSRO, GW MS 99, ff 77-80.

20   March, *A Duke and His Friends*, vol. I, pp. 104-106.

21   *ibid.*, p. 107.

22   *ibid.*, p. 112.

23   WSRO, GW MS 120 ff 76 and 90.

24   March, *A Duke and His Friends*, pp. 141-142.

25   Ilchester (ed.), *op. cit.*, p. 216.

26   Baird, *Goodwood, Art and Architecture, Sport and Family*, London, 2007, pp. 30-31 and Matthew Dennison, *The First Iron Lady, A Life of Caroline of Ansbach*, London, 2017, p. 257.

27   Baird, *Goodwood*, p. 31.

28   Ilchester (ed.), *op. cit.*, p. 142 (Hervey to Stephen Fox, 7 October 1732).

29   For the rebuilding of Richmond House, see Rosemary Baird, 'Richmond House, Whitehall', *British Art Journal*, Autumn 2007, vol. VIII, no. 2, pp. 3-15 and Winter 2007/8, vol. VIII, no. 3, pp. 3-14.

30   WSRO, GW MS 103, f 244 (Hill to Richmond, 20 May 1746).

31   March, *A Duke and His Friends*, vol. II, pp. 415-416.

32   *ibid.*, vol. II, p, 468.

33   *ibid.*, vol. II, pp. 471-472.

34   *ibid.*, vol. II, pp. 481-482.

35   *ibid.*, vol. II, p. 485.

36   Jacqueline Riding, *Jacobites, A New History of the '45 Rebellion*, London, 2016, pp. 481-482.

37   March, *A Duke and His Friends*, vol. I, pp. 266-267.

38   *ibid.*, vol. I, pp. 269-70.

39   *ibid.*, vol. I, p. 270.

40   See A Gentleman of Chichester, *A Full and Genuine History of the Inhuman and Unparalleled Murders of Mr. William Galley, a Custom-House Officer, and Mr. Daniel Chater, a Shoemaker, by fourteen Notorious Smugglers, with the Trial and Execution of seven of the bloody criminals at Chichester*, 1749 and March, *A Duke and His Friends*, vol. II, pp. 573-589.

41   McCann, *Correspondence*, pp. 276-277 (Pelham to Richmond, 12 November 1748).

42   *ibid.*, p. 281 (Pelham to Richmond, 21 February 1749).

43   *ibid.*, pp. xxx-xxxi.

44   Stella Tillyard, *Aristocrats, Caroline, Emily, Louisa and Sarah Lennox, 1740-1832*, London, 1994, p. 30.

45   *Walpole's Correspondence*, vol. 18, p. 450 (Horace Walpole to Horace Mann, 29 May 1744).

46   March, *A Duke and His Friends*, vol. II, p. 640 (Richmond to Princess Trivulci, translated from the French).

47   *ibid.*, p. 436 and Tillyard, *op. cit.*, p. 77.

48   *Walpole's Correspondence*, vol. 9, p. 80 (Horace Walpole to George Montagu, 18 May 1749).

49   British Library, Add. MS 51,424, f. 93 (Richmond to Henry Fox, 8 June 1750).

50   McCann, *Correspondence*, p. 304 (Richmond to Newcastle, 18 July 1750).

51   *Whitehall Evening Post*, 31 July 1750.

52   Information about the circumstances of the second Duke of Richmond's death and its cause is taken from an unpublished essay by Timothy McCann, *The Death of the 2nd Duke of Richmond in 1750, A Case of Misadventure*.

53   Steer, *op. cit.*, vol. 98, pp. 163-164.

Chapter 6 – The Radical Duke

1   Quoted in Reese, *op. cit.*, p. 13.

2   John R. Baker, *Abraham Trembley of Geneva, Scientist and Philosopher 1710-1784*, London, 1952, p. 137.

3   *ibid.*, pp. 188-204.

4   Edgar Peters Bowron and Peter Björn Kerber, *Pompeo Batoni, Prince of Painters in Eighteenth-Century Rome*, Exhibition Catalogue, 2007, pp. 37-38, fig. 37.

5   Reese, *op. cit.*, p. 51.

6   Quoted in *ibid.*, p. 53.

7   Joan Coutu, *Then and Now, Collecting and Classicism in Eighteenth-Century England*, Montreal & Kingston, 2015, p. 4.

8   For a fuller discussion of the Sculpture Gallery, see Coutu, *ibid.*, pp. 93-126.

9   *Walpole's Correspondence*, vol. 21, p. 173 (Horace Walpole to Horace Mann, 9 February 1758).

10   *London Chronicle*, 25 February 1758; *Daily Advertiser*, 28 February 1758, *Gentleman's Magazine*, March 1758, p. 141 (quoted in Coutu, *op. cit.*, p. 93).

11   Baird, *Goodwood*, p. 98.

12   *Walpole's Correspondence*, vol. 9, pp. 386-388 (Horace Walpole to George Montagu, 24 September 1761).

13   Bathurst, *op. cit.*, pp. 83-86.

14   FitzGerald (ed.), *op. cit.*, vol. I, pp. 303-304.

15   GW MS 2008 (Small Library, Goodwood House).

16   Baird, *Goodwood*, p. 100.

17   David Mannings, *Sir Joshua Reynolds, A Complete Catalogue of His Paintings*, New Haven and London, 2000, text vol., pp. 304-05, plates vol., pl. 25, figs. 388, 469.

18   Mannings, *ibid.*, p. 304.

19   Information from Dame Rosalind Savill.

20   See Baird, *Goodwood*, pp. 110-112.

21   FitzGerald (ed.), *op. cit.*, vol. I, pp. 461-462 (Lady Holland to Marchioness of Kildare, 25 August 1766).

22   Five drawings in the Sir John Soane's Museum, London (SM Adam volumes 10/73, 28/58, 28/57, 22/147, 22/148).

23   WSRO, GW MS E5140.

24   John Martin Robinson, *James Wyatt, Architect to George III*, New Haven and London, 2012, p. 28.

25   D. Jacques, *op. cit.*, pp. 70-71.

26   The carpet can be seen in 'Goodwood House, The Sussex Seat of The Duke of Richmond & Gordon – Part II', *The Antique Collector*, December, 1939, p. 265.

27   Viscount Palmerston, from the *Tour of Sussex* section of his unpublished *Travel Diary* (Hampshire Record Office, 27M60/1924), copy at WSRO (MP 854). Quoted in Baird, *Goodwood*, p. 136.

28   *ibid.*, p. 153.

29   Charles Greville and Richard Henry Stoddard (ed.), *The Greville Memoirs: A Journal of the Reigns of King George IV and King William IV*, New York, 1875, p. 286.

30   Quoted in Reese, *op. cit.*, p. 161.

31   *Walpole's Correspondence*, vol. 24, p. 371 (Horace Walpole to Horace Mann, 9 April 1778). An important manuscript copy of the American Declaration of Independence in the WSRO, dated to the 1780s, is very likely to have once belonged to the third Duke of Richmond (see Danielle Allen and Emily Sneff, *Summary of Findings, Declaration Resources Project Research Trip to West Sussex Record Office, August 4, 2017*, 28 June 2018, unpublished MS in WSRO (MS MP 8482)).

32   Sidney Lee (ed.), *Dictionary of National Biography*, London, 1893, vol. XXXIII, p. 45.

33   *Walpole's Correspondence*, vol. 29, pp. 51-55 (Horace Walpole to Rev. William Mason, 4 June 1780).

34   Priscilla Napier, *My Brother Richmond*, privately printed, 1994, pp. 217-218.

35   FitzGerald, *op. cit.*, vol. III, pp. 59-60 (Lady Louisa Conolly to the Duchess of Leinster, 10 April 1772).

36   *The Town and Country Magazine*, May, 1787, p. 226.

37   Allan P. Ledger, *A Spencer Love Affair, Eighteenth-Century Theatricals at Blenheim Palace and Beyond*, Croydon, 2014, pp. 25-27.

38   *Walpole's Correspondence*, vol. 33, p. 588 (Horace Walpole to the Countess of Upper Ossory, 15 December 1787).

39   ibid., vol. 34, p. 5 (Horace Walpole to the Countess of Upper Ossory, 14 February 1788).

40   *The Town and Country Magazine*, May, 1788, p. 210.

41   Richard Webb, *Mrs. D, The Life of Anne Damer (1748-1828)*, Studley, 2013, p. 102.

42   ibid., p. 104.

43   For reports of the fire see *The Public Advertiser*, 22 and 23 December 1791.

44   Jacques, *op. cit.*, p. 18.

45   Reese, *op. cit.*, p. 233.

46   Sir Nathanial William Wraxall, Bart., *Historical Memoirs of My Own Time*, London, 1904, pp. 453-454.

47   Baird, *Goodwood*, p. 140.

48   Rachel Hewitt, *Map of a Nation, A Biography of the Ordnance Survey*, London, 2010, pp. 102-103.

49   ibid., p. 305.

50   *Dictionary of National Biography*, *op. cit.*, p. 46 quoting Russell (ed.), *Memorials and Correspondence of Charles James Fox*, London, 1853, vol. 1, p. 455.

51   Quoted in Baird, *Goodwood*, p. 143.

52   *Walpole's Correspondence*, vol. 34, pp. 221-222 (Horace Walpole to Countess of Cork & Ossory, 13 November 1796).

53   FitzGerald, *op. cit.*, vol. III, p. 216 (Lady Louisa Conolly to Duchess of Leinster, 23 August 1776).

54   Napier, *op. cit.*, p. 427.

55   Stella Tillyard, *Citizen Lord, Edward Fitzgerald 1763-1798*, London, 1997, pp. 296-297.

56   For the early history see David Hunn, *Goodwood*, London, 1975, pp. 72-75 and Camilla Cecil *et al.*, *Glorious Goodwood, 200 Years of the World's Most Beautiful Racecourse*, Westbourne, 2002, pp. 17-22.

57   WSRO, GW MS E5140. The East Dean estate cost £17,000.

Chapter 7 – Brussels Interlude

1   The Captain of a Company in One of the Regiments of Guards, *A Short Review of the Recent Affair of Honor between His Royal Highness the Duke of York, and Lieutenant Colonel Lenox. With Free and Impartial Strictures and Comments upon the Circumstances Attending It*, London, 1789, p. 26.

2   *ibid.*, pp. 26-27.

3   For example, *The Town and Country Magazine or Universal Repository of Knowledge, Instruction, and Entertainment*, vol. XXI, 1789, pp. 258-260.

4   *The Gentleman's Magazine and Historical Chronicle*, vol. LIX, pp. 565-566.

5   *The Gentleman's and London Magazine*, July, 1789, p. 387.

6   WSRO, GW MS 224 ff 5/8-5/11 (Richmond to Lennox, 5 June 1806).

7   WSRO, GW MS 352 f 11.

8   Castalia, Countess Granville (ed.), *Lord Granville Leveson Gower (First Earl Granville), Private Correspondence 1781-1821*, London, 1916, vol. II, pp. 333-334.

9   *The Gentleman's Magazine*, vol. 84, part 1, June 1814, pp. 612-619 and 684-691 and Jacques, *op. cit.*, pp. 21-23.

10 Timothy J. McCann, 'The 4th Duke of Richmond and the Great Cricket Match at Goodwood in 1814', *West Sussex History*, no. 54, 1994.

11 WSRO, GW MS 1887.

12 The Marquess of Anglesey (ed.), *The Capel Letters, Being the Correspondence of Lady Caroline Capel and her daughters with the Dowager Countess of Uxbridge from Brussels and Switzerland, 1814-1817*, London, 1955, p. 57.

13 Beatrice Madan (ed.), *Spencer and Waterloo, The Letters of Spencer Madan, 1814-1816*, London, 1970, pp. 30-43.

14 *ibid.*, pp. 23 and 82.

15 *ibid.*, p. 62.

16 Anglesey, *op. cit.*, p. 69.

17 Madan, *op. cit.*, p. 12.

18 *ibid.*, p. 53.

19 *ibid.*, p. 49.

20 *ibid.*, p. 102.

21 *ibid.*, p. 101.

22 Anglesey, *op. cit.*, pp. 82-83.

23 *ibid.*, p. 102.

24 *ibid.*, p. 102.

25 *ibid.*, p. 107.

26 Ethel Richardson, *Long Forgotten Days (Leading to Waterloo)*, London, 1928, p. 373. Quoted in David Miller, *The Duchess of Richmond's Ball, 15 June 1815*, Staplehurst, 2005, p. 52 and Nick Foulkes, *Dancing into Battle, A Social History of the Battle of Waterloo*, London, 2006, pp. 133-134.

27 Eaton, Charlotte [An Englishwoman], *The Days of Battle: or, Quatre Bras and Waterloo*, London, 1853, p. 13 quoted in Foulkes, *op. cit.*, p. 136.

28 See Miller, *op. cit.*, pp. 55-126 for an analysis of the guest list.

29 The Hon. Blanche Swinton (ed.), *A Sketch of the Life of Lady de Ros, with some reminiscences of her family and friends, including the Duke of Wellington*, London, 1893, p. 123.

30 Miller, *op. cit.*, p. 139.

31 Anglesey, *op. cit.*, p. 70.

32 Madan, *op. cit.*, p. 104.

33 Swinton, *op. cit.*, pp. 132-133.

34 Captain Digby Mackworth's *Journal* quoted in Miller, *op. cit.*, p. 140.

35 Swinton, *op. cit.*, p. 133 and Miller, *op. cit.*, p. 141.

36 David Miller, *Lady De Lancey at Waterloo, A Story of Duty and Devotion*, Staplehurst, 2000, p. 170.

37 Foulkes, *op. cit.*, pp. 160-161.

38 Madan, *op. cit.*, pp. 105-106.

39 *ibid.*, pp. 106-107.

40 William Siborne, *History of the War in France and Belgium in 1815*, London, 1844, vol. 2, pp. 35-36 fn.

41 Swinton, *op. cit.*, p. 135.

42 Madan, *op. cit.*, p. 107.

43 Tim Clayton, *Waterloo: Four Days that Changed Europe's Destiny*, London, 2014, p. 560.

44 Miller, *op. cit.*, p. 170-172.

45 Swinton, *op. cit.*, p. 137.

46 John Kent, *Records and Reminiscences of Goodwood and the Dukes of Richmond*, London, 1896, p. 50.

47 Lord William Pitt Lennox, *Fifty Years' Biographical Reminiscences*, London, 1863, vol. 1, p. 265.

48 Anglesey, *op. cit.*, p. 135.

49 For Richmond's final days see the accounts by Colonel Francis Cockburn and Major George Bowles, of which a manuscript copy is in the Goodwood Library (Large Library, H7). Major Bowles' report was published in *The Edinburgh Evening Courant*, 8 November 1819, p. 4. It is discussed in more detail in Baird,

Goodwood, pp. 170-171. See also WSRO, GW MS 364, four letters written by Louisa, Charlotte and Sophia to their mother from Canada, one tragically dated the day after Richmond's death of which they were as yet unaware.

Chapter 8 – Glorious Goodwood

1   Anon. [Lord William Pitt Lennox], *Memoir of Charles Gordon Lennox, Fifth Duke of Richmond, K.G., P.C.*, London, 1862, pp. 304-305.

2   *ibid.*, pp. 70-72; William Hayley Mason, *Goodwood, Its House, Park and Grounds with a Catalogue Raisonné of the Pictures in the Gallery of His Grace the Duke of Richmond, K.G.*, London, 1839, pp. 126-128; and Kent, *Records and Reminiscences*, pp. 207-209.

3   Mason, *op. cit.*, pp. 39-41.

4   Anon. [WPL], *op. cit.*, p. 9.

5   Mason, *op. cit.*, pp. 121-124 and WSRO, GW MS 1604, ff 1250, 1252, 1261, 1266, 1276, 1279-1281, 1284.

6   Anon. [WPL], *op. cit.*, p. 69.

7   *ibid.*, pp. 76-78.

8   John Kent, *Racing Life of Lord George Cavendish Bentinck, M.P. and Other Reminiscences*, London, 1892, pp. 61-75.

9   Hilary Bracegirdle, *A Concise History of British Horseracing*, Newmarket, 1999, p. 52.

10   Hunn, *op. cit.*, p. 117.

11   Kent, *Bentinck*, p. 112.

12   Nicholas Foulkes, *Gentlemen and Blackguards or Gambling Mania and the Plot to Steal the Derby of 1844*, London, 2010, pp. 63-64.

13   Kent, *Bentinck*, p. 226 and Foulkes, *Gentlemen and Blackguards*, pp. xiii-xiv.

14   Hunn, *op. cit.*, pp. 119-120 and Baird, *Goodwood*, p. 188, fn 22.

15   Anon. [WPL], *op. cit.*, pp. 288-291.

16   Kent, *Bentinck*, pp. 241-247.

17   Henry Reeve (ed.), *The Greville Memoirs, A Journal of the Reigns of King George IV and King William IV by the late Charles C. F. Greville, Esq., Clerk of the Council to those Sovereigns*, London, 4th ed., 1875, vol. I, pp. 199-200.

18   *ibid.*, vol. III, p. 15.

19   Kent, *Records and Reminiscences*, pp. 76-77.

20   Timothy J. McCann, *The Correspondence of the 5th Duke of Richmond*, October 2012 (private document).

21   Hunn, *op. cit.*, p. 121.

22   *The Illustrated London News*, 4th August 1866, no. 1383, vol. XLIX, p. 106.

23   Hunn, *op. cit.*, p. 111.

24   *ibid.*, p. 133.

25   Anon. [WPL], *op. cit.*, pp. 330-331.

26   WSRO, GW MS 747.

27   Cecil *et al.*, *op. cit.*, p. 111.

28   Raymond O'Neill, 'Goodwood, The Gordon Lennox Dynasty and their Pekingese Dogs', *The Pekingese Club Year Book 2007*, pp. 54-63.

29   *West Sussex Gazette*, 5 November 1883.

30   *The Standard*, 'The Duke of Richmond on Agriculture', 11 June 1894.

31   Quoted in Hunn, *op. cit.*, p. 149.

Chapter 9 – Scottish Interlude

1   WSRO, GW MS 1171, f 77 quoted in Rachel Trethewey, *Mistress of the Arts*, London, 2002, p. 24.

2   John Malcolm Bulloch, *The Gordon Highlanders, The History of their Origin together with a Transcript of the First Official Muster*, Banff, 1913, p. 11; George Gordon, *The Last Dukes of Gordon and their Consorts 1743-1864*, Aberdeen, 1980, pp. 86-87; and Baird, *Mistress of the House*, pp. 224-225.

3   Baird, *Mistress of the House*, p. 213.

4   Mary Miers, *Highland Retreats, The Architecture and Interiors of Scotland's Romantic North*, New York, 2017, p. 82

5   Elizabeth Grant of Rothiemurchus, *Memoirs of a Highland Lady 1797-1827*, London, 1967, 3rd ed., p. 204.

6   Baird, *Mistress of the House*, p. 220.

7   Wraxall, *op. cit.*, p. 459.

8   Miers, *op. cit.*, pp. 14-17.

9   Quoted in Trethewey, *op. cit.*, p. 24.

10   Grant, *op. cit.*, pp. 32-33.

11   David Taylor, *The Wild Black Region, Badenoch 1750-1800*, Edinburgh, 2016, p. 219.

12   *ibid.*, p. 220.

13   Queen Victoria, *More Leaves from the Journal of A Life in the Highlands, from 1862 to 1882*, London, 3rd ed. 1884, pp. 89-102.

14   *ibid.*, p. 94.

15 *ibid.*, p. 95.

16 *ibid.*, p. 100.

17 *ibid.*, p. 97.

18 *ibid.*, p. 97.

19 *ibid.*, p. 99.

20 *ibid.*, p. 100.

21 WSRO, GW MS 860, f E3 (Sir Thomas Biddulph to sixth Duke of Richmond, 22 November 1867).

22 Lady Muriel Beckwith, *When I Remember*, London, 1936, p. 42.

23 WSRO, GW MS 1418.

24 WSRO, GW MSS 1119 and 1120.

25 Paul Smith, *Disraelian Conservatism and Social Reform*, Michigan, 1967, p. 244 quoted in *Oxford Dictionary of National Biography* under 'Charles Gordon-Lennox, 6th Duke of Richmond'.

26 *Oxford Dictionary of National Biography*.

27 David Torrance, *The Scottish Secretaries*, Edinburgh, 2006, pp. 5-12.

28 Letter from Victoria to Disraeli quoted in *Oxford Dictionary of National Biography*.

29 *The Standard*, 'The Duke of Richmond on Agriculture', 11 June 1894 and David Cannadine, *The Decline and Fall of the British Aristocracy*, New Haven and London, 1990, pp. 710-711.

30 John Bateman, *The Great Landowners of Great Britain and Ireland*, London, 4th ed., 1883, p. 380 and *The Standard*, 'The Duke of Richmond on Agriculture', 11 June 1894.

31 WSRO, GW MS 819, f 106 quoted in McCann, *Goodwood: Royal Letters*, pp. 20-21.

32 WSRO, GW MS 819, f. 107.

33 Beckwith, *op. cit.*, p. 229.

34 *ibid.*, pp. 29-30.

35 Miers, *op. cit.*, p. 14.

36 *ibid.*, p. 19.

37 Ian Gow, *Scotland's Lost Houses*, London, 2006, pp. 91-99.

38 Trethewey, *op. cit.*, p. 205.

39 Beckwith, *op. cit.*, p. 300.

40 WSRO, GW MS 820, f 229 quoted in McCann, *Goodwood: Royal Letters*, p. 28.

41 Beckwith, *op. cit.*, pp. 47-48.

42   Gordon Castle weighing book, 23 September 1899.

43   Beckwith, *op. cit.*, pp. 60-61.

44   Professor Peter Reid, *Gordon Chapel, A History and Guidebook*, Fochabers, 2017, p. 9.

45   Beckwith, *op. cit.*, pp. 203-204.

46   *Banffshire Journal, Aberdeenshire Mail, Moray, Nairn, and Inverness Review, and Northern Farmer*, Tuesday, 29 September 1903, p. 5.

47   *ibid.*, p. 5.

Chapter 10 – Widowerhood

1   Beckwith, *op. cit.*, p. 35.

2   *The Evening Standard*, Wednesday, 11 November 1868, 'Marriage in High Life'.

3   Sir Harry R. Ricardo, *Memories and Machines, The Pattern of My Life*, 1968, p. 28.

4   Rosemary Baird, 'The Duchesses' exhibition at Goodwood House, 2001.

5   WSRO, GW MS 1035.

6   Professor Peter Reid, *Gordon Chapel, A History and Guidebook*, Fochabers, 2017, p. 8.

7   The first Duke of Richmond's great-granddaughter, Lady Elizabeth Berkeley, had married the 6th Baron Craven, Isobel's great-great-grandfather.

8   WSRO, GW MS 2116, Frederick, ninth Duke of Richmond, unpublished MS, 1973 (hereafter referred to as Richmond, *Memoir*), pp. 15-16.

9   *ibid.*, pp. 17-18.

10   WSRO, GW MS 1042, f A3.

11   WSRO, GW MS 1042, f A8.

12   WSRO, GW MS 1042, f A5.

13   WSRO, GW MS 1042, f A9.

14   Information kindly supplied by General Sir Mark Carleton-Smith.

15   Peter Verney, *The Micks: The Story of the Irish Guards*, London, 1970, p. 4.

16   Newspaper article entitled 'The Sussex Militia. Arrival Home Yesterday' (undated) in the seventh Duke of Richmond's photograph album.

17   Beckwith, *op. cit.*, pp. 235-237.

18   Reid, *op. cit.*, p. 10.

19   Beckwith, *op. cit.*, pp. 100, 225 and 226.

20   WSRO, GW MS E5494 (accounts of George Trollope & Sons, West Halkin Street, Belgrave Square, London).

21   'Kings Before the Camera', *Pearson's Magazine*, 1909, pp. 347-355.

22   Phyllida Barstow, *The English Country House Party*, 1998, Stroud, pp. 50-52.

23   Cecil *et al.*, *op. cit.*, p. 111

24   Hunn, *op. cit.*, pp. 154-155.

25   *The Morning Post*, Saturday, 4 August 1906, p. 3.

26   *The Sporting Life*, Friday, 3 August 1906, p. 2.

27   *The Sporting Times*, Saturday, 4 August 1906, p. 2.

28   Beckwith, *op. cit.*, p. 150.

29   *ibid.*, p. 232.

30   Cecil *et al.*, *op. cit.*, p. 124 (diary entry for 2 August 1906).

31   Beckwith, *op. cit.*, p. 72.

32   *ibid.*, p. 79.

33   *ibid.*, pp. 73-74.

34   *ibid.*, p. 76.

35   *ibid.*, p. 90.

36   *South of England Advertiser: Sussex, Surrey, Hampshire and Kent*, 4 June 1914, p. 11.

37   *The Manchester Courier*, 1 June 1914, p. 7.

38   John Worman, *Under the Trundle, Goodwood Golf Club, 1892-1992*, Selsey, 1992, pp. 13-25.

39   *The Manchester Courier*, 1 June 1914, p. 7.

Chapter 11 – The Great War

1   Elisalex de Baillet Latour, '1897-1937' in The Duke of Portland, *Men, Women and Things, Memories of The Duke of Portland, K.G., G.C.V.O.*, London, 1937, p. 333.

2   WSRO, GW MS 1026.

3   Diary extracts and quotes from letters taken from *Lord Bernard*, a booklet compiled by his descendants in 2014. See also Jerry Murland, *Aristocrats Go To War, Uncovering the Zillebeke Churchyard Cemetery*, Barnsley, 2010.

4   John Worman, *op. cit.*, p. 25.

5   WSRO, GW MS 1026.

6   WSRO, GW MS 1035, dated 4 December 1913.

7   Beckwith, *op. cit.*, pp. 240-241.

8   'WB', *Under the Red Cross, Gordon Castle 1914-1919*, Banff and Turrif, 1921.

9   Information taken from *ibid*.

10   Murland, *op. cit.*, p. 166.

11   WSRO, GW MS 1199.

12   Information kindly supplied by his daughter, Lady Fergusson and the RHQ Scots Guards.

13   Brian and Brenda Williams, *The Country House at War 1914-1918*, Pitkin Guide, Stroud, 2014, p. 18.

14   Biographical information about Hilda, Duchess of Richmond and the Brasseys is taken from Richmond, *Memoir*, pp. 3-8 and 19-20.

15   WSRO, GW MS 1226.

16   Richmond, *Memoir*, pp. 135-136.

17   *ibid*. p. 136.

18   *ibid*., p. 100.

19   *ibid*., p. 110.

20   *ibid*., pp. 139-140.

21   *ibid*., pp. 143-144.

22   *ibid*., pp. 150-151.

23   *ibid*., p. 153.

24   *ibid*., p. 154

25   WSRO, GW MS 2103 (Lord Settrington to the Earl of March, 26 July 1919).

26   WSRO, GW MS 2105 (Statement by Albert Pearce-Davies sent to the ninth Duke of Richmond, 1 August 1977).

27   Richmond, *Memoir*, p. 160.

28   Presentation album embossed '26TH AUGUST 1919', given to the seventh Duke of Richmond with press cuttings from the occasion, p. 3.

29   *ibid*., p. 3.

30   *ibid*., p. 4.

31   Cannadine, *op. cit.*, p. 109.

32   *ibid*., pp. 88-89.

Chapter 12 – Horse Power

1   Mike Lawrence, Simon Taylor and Doug Nye, *The Glory of Goodwood*, London, 1999, p. 8.

2   WSRO, GW MS 1212 (Harold Drewitt to the seventh Duke of Richmond, 7 February 1921).

3   *Portsmouth Evening News*, 14 March 1921, p. 2.

4   Alan Green, *Priory Park, Chichester, Its Story in 100 Objects*, Gloucester, 2018, pp. 53-58.

5   *ibid.*, p. 59.

6   Terence Dooley, *The Decline and Fall of the Dukes of Leinster, 1872-1948*, Dublin, 2014, p. 211.

7   *The Daily Telegraph*, 18 May 1922.

8   Cannadine, *op. cit.*, p. 89.

9   *The Graphic*, 2 August 1919, p. 147.

10 Douglas Sutherland, *The Yellow Earl, The Life of Hugh Lowther, 5th Earl of Lonsdale, K.G., G.C.V.O., 1857-1944*, London, 1965, p. 64.

11 Beckwith, *op. cit.*, pp. 138, 139 and 142.

12 Richmond, *Memoir*, pp. 88-91.

13 *ibid.*, p. 210.

14 *ibid.*, p. 258.

15 *ibid.*, p. 273.

16 *Aberdeen Press and Journal*, Monday, 23 January 1928, p. 4.

17 Frederick, ninth Duke of Richmond, *The Bentley Story*, handwritten MS, pp. 6-12.

18 Richmond, *Memoir*, pp. 164-169.

19 *ibid.*, pp. 178-190.

20 *ibid.*, pp. 198-200.

21 *ibid.*, p. 216.

22 *ibid.*, pp. 213-215.

23 *ibid.*, p. 217.

24 *ibid.*, pp. 218-219.

25 *ibid.*, p. 220.

26 *ibid.*, p. 222.

27 *ibid.*, pp. 223-227.

28 *ibid.*, pp. 243-248.

29 *ibid.*, pp. 253-254.

30 *ibid.*, pp. 255-256.

31 *The Daily Telegraph*, undated press cutting in photograph album of the ninth Duke of Richmond.

32 *Sunday Pictorial*, undated press cutting in photograph album of the ninth Duke of Richmond.

33 *The Autocar*, 15 May 1931, pp. 894-903.

34 Richmond, *Memoir*, p. 282.

35   *The Daily Telegraph*, undated press cutting in photograph album of the ninth Duke of Richmond.

36   Richmond, *Memoir*, pp. 288-289.

37   Lawrence *et al.*, *op. cit.*, p. 26 and Richmond, *Memoir*, p. 289.

38   Lawrence *et al.*, *op. cit.*, p. 26.

39   Richmond, *Memoir*, pp. 144-145.

40   *ibid.*, p. 276.

41   *ibid.*, p. 277.

42   *ibid.*, p. 284.

43   Lawrence *et al.*, *op. cit.*, pp. 28-29.

44   *The Times*, 7 February 1930 (printed extract framed at Goodwood).

45   Richmond, *Memoir*, pp. 290-291.

46   *ibid.*, pp. 291-292.

47   David Farrant, *The Queen Alexandra Hospital Home For Disabled Ex-Servicemen, Worthing, A History*, Chichester, 2008, pp. 72-73, and 83.

48   *ibid.*, p. 93.

49   Anderson & England, Elgin, auction catalogue of the contents of Gordon Castle, 29 August – 3 September 1938.

50   *The Scotsman*, Wednesday, 31 August 1938, p. 8.

51   Memorandum of Frederick, ninth Duke of Richmond, dated November 1937 (and signed November 1939).

52   *[Aberdeen] Press and Journal*, 16 May 1946, p. 4. and Messrs. Jackson Stops & Staff, auction sale particulars of 'The Historic Lands and Renowned Sporting Estates of Glenfiddich', 28 May 1946.

53   *The Tatler*, 2 August 1939, p. 191.

54   Adrian Tinniswood, *The Long Weekend, Life in the English Country House Between the Wars*, London, 2016, pp. 368-369 and John Martin Robinson, *Requisitioned, The British Country House in the Second World War*, London, 2014, pp. 9, 46-55 and 72-81.

55   David Legg-Willis, *Some Goodwood Annals*, Cambridge, 2016, p. 19.

56   Lord Nicholas Gordon Lennox, *The Tiddly Quid & After, A Memoir of Places and People Met Along the Way*, Brighton, 2006, pp. 3 and 29.

57   *ibid.*, pp. 4 and 26-27.

58   Lawrence *et al.*, *op. cit.*, pp. 33-39.

59   Mark Hillier, *A Fighter Command Station at War, A Photographic Record of RAF Westhampnett from The Battle of Britain to D-Day and Beyond*, Barnsley, 2015, p. 74.

60   *ibid.*, p. 72.

61   *ibid.*, pp. 76-77.

62   *ibid.*, p. 104.

63   *A Brief History of RAF Tangmere and its Satellite Airfields Westhampnett and
      Merston*, published by The Tangmere Military Aviation Museum,
      Chichester, 2007, p. 14.

64   Lawrence *et al.*, *op. cit.*, pp. 47-53.

65   *ibid.*, pp. 66-67.

66   *ibid.*, pp. 8 and 10.

67   *ibid.*, p. 74.

68   Quoted in *ibid.*, p. 212.

69   David Legg-Willis, 'Notes from His Grace', 31 October 1983, file note in
      Curatorial archive.

70   Edgar Osborne (ed., text by George Bonney), *Goodwood, An Illustrated
      Survey of the Historic Sussex Home of the Dukes of Richmond and Gordon*,
      Derby, 1950, p. 15.

71   Norman Wymer, 'Preserving an Ancestral Estate', *Country Life*,
      26 December 1952, p. 2094.

72   *ibid.*, p. 2095.

Epilogue

1   Roy Strong, Marcus Binney, John Harris *et al.*, *The Destruction of the
     Country House, 1875-1975*, London, 1974, pp. 169-170.

2   *ibid.*, p. 170.

3   *ibid.*, p. 171.

4   *ibid.*, p. 171.

5   Jane Kidd, *Goodwood Dressage Champions*, Addington, 1994, p. 153.

6   *ibid.*, p. 65.

Index